DON'T THINK TWICE
IT'S ALL RIGHT

Bob Dylan, the early years

this is a carlton book

Published in the United States by
Thunder's Mouth Press
841 Broadway, Fourth Floor, New York, NY 10003

ISBN 1 56025 185 9

Library of Congress Catalog Card Number
98-60115

Distributed by Publishers Group West,
1700 Fourth Street, Berkeley, CA 94710

Printed and bound in Italy

Project Editor: Lucian Randall
Copy Editor: Mike Flynn
Senior Art Editor: Zöe Maggs
Design: Mary Ryan
Picture Research: Jane Lambert
Production: Sarah Schuman

For Linda

DON'T THINK TWICE
IT'S ALL RIGHT

Bob Dylan, the early years

Andy Gill

THUNDER'S
MOUTH
PRESS

Contents

Foreword   6

1   Bob Dylan   8

2   The Freewheelin'
Bob Dylan   18

3   The Times They
Are A-Changin'   36

4   Another Side Of
Bob Dylan   52

5   Bringing It All
Back Home   64

6   Highway 61
Revisited   78

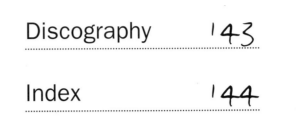

Discography   143

Index   144

7 Blonde On
     Blonde   92

8 The Basement
     Tapes   108

9 John Wesley
     Harding   124

10 Nashville
     Skyline   136

Foreword

Of all the stars thrown up by the pop explosion of the Sixties, none has exerted as deep or lasting an influence on our culture as Bob Dylan. Others may have been prettier, or sold more records, or made a smoother transition into today's gossip-column celebrocracy, but none has so irreversibly altered our conception of what is possible within a popular song, and particularly within its lyrics. He was pop's great emancipator: from Hendrix to the Beatles, Clapton to Cohen, Beach Boys to Beck, virtually all of rock music has been inspired or influenced in some way by Dylan's creative ambition. It's testament to that ambition that, almost four decades on from his recording debut, Bob Dylan remains a restless, quixotic figure, heedless of musical trends, exasperatingly uneven, but still capable of stunning work like 1997's *Time Out Of Mind*.

But whatever the merits (or otherwise) of his subsequent work, and notwithstanding in particular the greatness of *Blood On The Tracks*, it's upon his sixties songs that Bob Dylan's reputation ultimately rests: that extraordinary sequence of records which unerringly tracked the tenor of the times as he moved through his various incarnations as raw young folkie, prince of protest, folk-rock innovator, symbolist rocker and country-rock pioneer.

Dylan's progress through that decade is a trail which constituted the primary motor for my own development, as it did for so many others; yet to a younger generation his position grows progressively less clear, more vague and blurred—possibly because of his constant creative flux, but also, I think, simply as a result of the accelerating erosion of knowledge which seems to accompany our supposed "information society." A case in point: in a weekly British music paper recently, the guitarist with a highly successful American post-grunge rock band—we'll call him James—cited Dylan's 'The Lonesome Death Of Hattie Carroll' as one of his favorite songs. Fine, except that he erroneously claimed it was a fictional story—and one which, furthermore, was apparently issued on an album called *Don't Look Back*. Which doesn't exist.

This book is basically to help people like James. In it, I've tried to give some idea of the forces—musical, political, historical, literary, philosophical and personal—at play in each of Dylan's songs through this period of his greatest achievement, along with brief accounts of their recording, where appropriate. For research material, I consulted much of the available trove of Dylan literature, of which the most useful were the three classic biographies—Anthony Scaduto's no-nonsense *Bob Dylan*, Bob Spitz's iconoclastic *Dylan—A Biography*, and Robert Shelton's exhaustively detailed *No Direction Home*—all of which proved fascinating funds of information.

Dylan's own *Lyrics 1962–1985* sparked as many questions as it provided answers, and Craig McGregor's excellent compilation *Bob Dylan—A Retrospective* contained a wealth of contemporary essays and interviews. Two other compilations, *All Across The Telegraph* (ed. Michael Gray and John Bauldie) and *The Dylan Companion* (ed. Elizabeth Thomson and David Gutman), offered stimulating blends of opinion and explication. Other books consulted include Levon Helm's autobiography *This Wheel's On Fire*; Greil Marcus's examination of *The Basement Tapes*, *Invisible Republic*; Clinton Heylin's account of Dylan's recording sessions, *Dylan Behind Closed Doors*; and Tim Riley's *Hard Rain: A Dylan Commentary*. On more general social and political matters, the following were helpful: Hugh Brogan's *Kennedy*; Morison, Commager and Leuchtenburg's *The Growth Of The American Republic*, and David Steigerwald's *The Sixties And The End Of Modern America*.

I've also drawn on interviews I conducted at various times with Joan Baez, Don Pennebaker, Sam Lay, Robbie Robertson and Al Kooper; I am particularly indebted to Robbie and Al for their time

and generosity. I'd also like to thank my editors at *The Independent*, *Q*, *Mojo* and the *NME*—in whose pages various of the opinions contained herein were originally ventilated in one form or another— particularly Neil Spencer, Mark Ellen, Giles Smith, Nick Coleman and Mat Snow.

Other friends, colleagues and musicians who have directly contributed to my greater understanding of Dylan throughout the years, or who have helped this project in some other way, include—first and foremost—the late John Bauldie, who helped re-ignite my dormant interest; and also Phil Barnes, Pete Bennion, Jackson Browne, Paul Du Noyer, Barry Everard, Patrick Humphries, Daniel Lanois, Jared Levine, Roger Longmore, Phil Manzanera, Gavin Martin, Rainer Ptacek, Leon Russell, Patrick Smith, Paul Trynka, Don & David Was, Lucian Randall at Carlton Books, and most of all, the lovely Linda, who kept me sane enough to finish it. My love goes out to all of them, and to each and every underdog in the whole wide Universe.

ANDY GILL, JUNE 1998

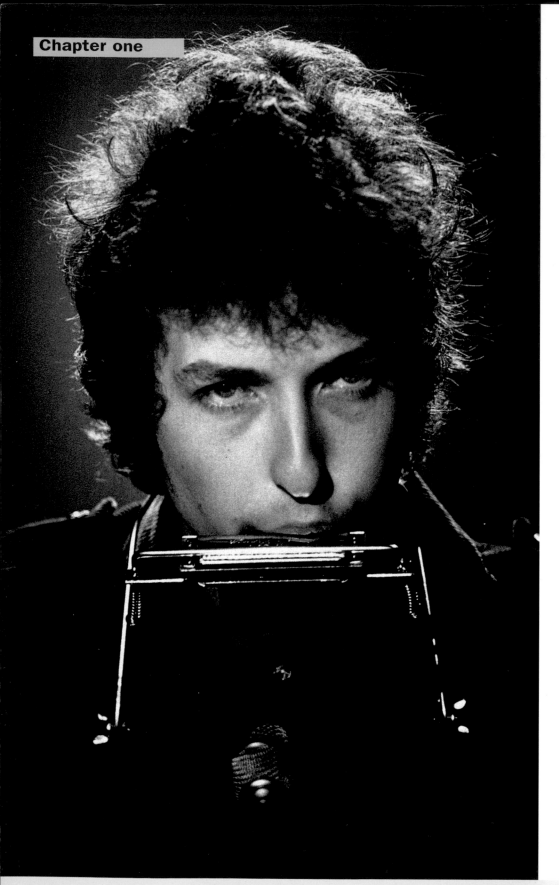

YOU'RE NO GOOD
(JESSE FULLER)

TALKIN' NEW YORK

IN MY TIME OF DYIN'
(TRAD. ARR. DYLAN)

MAN OF CONSTANT SORROW
(TRAD. ARR. DYLAN)

FIXIN' TO DIE
(BUKKA WHITE)

PRETTY PEGGY-O
(TRAD. ARR. DYLAN)

HIGHWAY 51 BLUES
(CURTIS JONES)

GOSPEL PLOW
(TRAD. ARR. DYLAN)

BABY, LET ME FOLLOW
YOU DOWN
(REVEREND GARY DAVIS)

HOUSE OF THE RISIN' SUN
(TRAD. ARR. VAN RONK)

FREIGHT TRAIN BLUES
(ROY ACUFF)

SONG TO WOODY

SEE THAT MY GRAVE IS
KEPT CLEAN
(BLIND LEMON JEFFERSON)

Bob Dylan

When Bob Dylan recorded his first album in late November of 1961, he had been in New York less than a year, most of it spent scuffling for low-paying gigs on the coffee-house folk music circuit based in Greenwich Village. Folk music had joined jazz as the hip musical choice of bohemian beatniks and students through the late Fifties, as a more "authentic" response to what was increasingly perceived as the gaudy insincerity of rock 'n' roll: the raw power of originators like Chuck Berry, Bo Diddley and Little Richard was being supplanted by tame corporate copyists like Pat Boone and Fabian, and the music industry was riven by payola scandals which left a strong stench of materialist corruption around rock 'n' roll.

For the more serious-minded young adult, American folk music offered a comparatively clean breath of righteous fresh air, having served as the rallying cry of liberals, lefties and outsiders through the conservative Eisenhower era. Just as importantly, the older, pre-war songs which were the bread and butter of any folk performer's act came from a time before America had assumed imperial dominance over the world, and were considered unsullied by the plastic desires of the Fifties. Their themes and mythographies bore the authenticating stamp of a timeless oral tradition, and though collectors like Alan Lomax, Paul Oliver and Harry Smith may have recorded or compiled the classic folk and blues performances in the early decades of the century, there was no telling how old the songs themselves actually were, or how many generations further back they stretched. For a country which had effectively wiped out its native Indian culture during its brutal colonizing years, these songs provided a badly-needed sense of cultural heritage.

The folk movement received its biggest boost in 1958, when The Kingston Trio, a San Francisco-based folk group, had a huge, chart-topping hit with 'Tom Dooley', a song traceable back at least as far as 1866. Suddenly saleable, folk music started to be regarded with something approaching mild interest by the big record companies, who joined specialist labels like Folkways, Elektra and Vanguard in signing up the genre's leading lights. Columbia had Pete Seeger and The Clancy Brothers & Tommy Makem, and Vanguard itself scored a coup when the young Joan Baez became the toast of the scene after her appearance at the 1959 Newport Folk Festival.

By 1961, folk music was still largely the preserve of die-hard traditionalists, who considered these old songs to be texts just as sacred as any fundamentalist's Bible; their performance should be as close to the original version as possible, any deviation being deemed a bowdlerization or corruption of the song's integrity. But there were signs of a split in the folkie ranks, between these older, "High Folk" types and a new breed of "Low Folk" performers like Ramblin' Jack Elliott and Dave Van Ronk, who sought pleasure in the music, rather than being concerned to be intellectually truthful in their interpretations. The young Dylan was very much in the latter camp, drawn by Elliott's and Van Ronk's unashamedly "black" inflections applied to "white" material, and he quickly developed a distinctive singing style of his own, part-Woody Guthrie, part-blues moan, which some found quite comical. Nevertheless, it was unmistakably his own. Along with the piercing blasts of harmonica (which he played in a wire brace similar to the one he had seen bluesman Jesse Fuller using during a three-week stay in Denver) and a stage style that incorporated little Chaplinesque moments of physical comedy with an engaging line of patter, Bob Dylan soon became an accomplished performer with an easily discernible, inimitable character.

The campus town of Cambridge, Massachusetts, had evolved a folk scene of its own. Its leading lights were Joan Baez, Tom Rush, Jim Kweskin and Eric Von Schmidt—the latter became Dylan's host on his visits there. On one such trip, he introduced Bob to Texan folk singer Carolyn Hester and her husband Richard Fariña, who instantly took a shine to him. Hester was about to record her third album—her first on a major label—with the legendary John Hammond Sr. Always a man with an eye for the main chance, Dylan played her a couple of his own tunes, and Hester decided to use one, a blues called 'Come Back Baby', on her new album. Doubly fortunate, from Bob's point of view, was the fact that the song featured an extended harmonica break, which Bob himself would play. He was, after all, a professional blues-harpist, his only recording session to

◀

DYLAN BLOWS UP A STORM IN 1965.

▲

CAROLYN HESTER
AT THE NEWPORT
FOLK FESTIVAL.
BOB'S BIG BREAK
WOULD COME THROUGH
PLAYING HARMONICA
ON HER ALBUM.

date having been as a sideman, playing harmonica on an album by Harry Belafonte. (He would also play harmonica at sessions for Victoria Spivey and Big Joe Williams before Hester's album was recorded.) Hester and Dylan agreed to meet for rehearsals at the apartment of poet Ned O'Gorman in New York, which is where John Hammond first encountered the young man who would become the crowning glory of his career in A&R.

It was already an illustrious career, to say the least. Hammond had discovered and launched the career of Billie Holiday, and had been instrumental in the successes of Benny Goodman, Count Basie, Lionel Hampton, Benny Carter and the celebrated boogie-woogie pianists Albert Ammons, Pete Johnson and Meade "Lux" Lewis. A devoted fan of jazz and blues, his ground-breaking promotion of the *Spirituals To Swing* concerts at Carnegie Hall in 1938/9 was the single greatest factor in the dissemination of the various forms of black music to a wider—and whiter—audience. He was, in short, a giant of 20th century music, with a proven ear for original talent.

At the rehearsal, Hammond was immediately intrigued by the young Dylan. "I saw this kid in the

peaked hat playing not terribly good harmonica, but I was taken with him," Hammond later recalled. "I asked him, 'Can you sing? Do you write? I'd like to do a demo session with you, just to see how it is.' It was just one of those flashes. I thought, 'I gotta talk contract right away.' " Checking that Dylan would be available for the session, he set a recording date for the afternoon of September 29, 1961. In the interim, fate played an auspicious part in Dylan's life.

The New York Times chose that very day to run a glowing review, which their music critic Robert Shelton had written, of Bob's performance at Gerdes Folk City on September 26, where he was supporting The Greenbriar Boys, a well-liked bluegrass group. Under a photo of Bob in his trademark cap, and the headline "Bob Dylan: A Distinctive Stylist," the perspicacious Shelton raved about the "bright new face" that was "bursting at the seams with talent," offering a detailed account of Dylan's performing style and material, and concluding, with remarkable foresight, that "...it matters less where he has been than where he is going, and that would seem to be straight up."

All the Village folkies were knocked out by Shelton's piece—except for The Greenbriar Boys, who were relegated to the final four paragraphs of the review, a virtual afterthought. Dylan, unsurprisingly, was elated. He arrived at the Hester recording session clutching the review, which he showed to Hammond. "I could tell Hammond was hooked from the very start," Hester later recalled. "The longer we worked, the more I could see Hammond's interest in Bob developing, until the two of them were thick as thieves." He played harmonica on three tracks of her album, including his own 'Come Back Baby', and secured an invitation to come in later to cut some demos of his own with Hammond. Dylan's studio technique, the producer discovered, was undisciplined—"he popped every P, hissed every S, and habitually wandered off mike"—but Hammond heard enough in his performance to convince him that here was a major talent in the raw, who should be snapped up quickly. Dylan, of course, was exhilarated when he left the studio. "I couldn't believe it," he said later. "I remember walking out of the studio. I was, like, on a cloud. It was up on 7th Avenue, and when I left I happened to walk by a record store. It was one of the most thrilling moments in my life. I couldn't believe that I was staring at all the records in the window—Frankie Laine, Frank Sinatra, Patti Page, Mitch Miller, Tony Bennett and so on—and soon I myself would be among them in the window. I guess I was pretty naive, you know."

Hammond was fortunate in that the new Director of A&R at Columbia, David Kapralik, had been appointed a few weeks before with the brief to strengthen the company's youth roster. "Dylan's an extraordinary young man," Hammond told his boss. "I don't know if he's going to sell, but he has something profound to say." Such was Kapralik's faith in Hammond's ears that he allowed the young folkie to be signed without even hearing him. There were initial problems in signing the contract—which was for one year, with four subsequent yearly options—when Dylan, still a minor, claimed he had no parents who could sign for him; but Hammond decided to let him sign anyway, a judgment call that would cause a few problems a year or two later. At the age of 20, Bob Dylan became a Columbia recording artist.

It wasn't that great a gamble on Columbia's part. The album was recorded in a couple of late November afternoons, with Dylan accompanied by just his own guitar and harmonicas (which he kept moist in a glass of water), and it cost a piffling $402 to make. Hammond, who believed in catching the spontaneous flow of inspiration, rarely pushed Bob beyond two or three takes of any song, and encouraged him to vent his hostility through his performances. "There was a violent, angry emotion running through me then," Dylan explained in his first teen magazine interview, with *Seventeen* magazine. "I just played guitar and harmonica and sang those songs, and that was it. Mr Hammond asked me if I wanted to sing any of them over again but I said no. I can't see myself singing the same song twice in a row. That's terrible." At one point, he borrowed his girlfriend Suze Rotolo's lipstick holder to use as a slide for his guitar on the bleak spiritual 'In My Time Of Dyin' ', a song he never performed live. He was pleased when, during his recording of Bukka White's 'Fixin' To Die', an old black janitor stopped working and stepped into the studio to listen.

The material on Dylan's debut album—"some stuff I've written, some stuff I've discovered, some stuff I stole"—offers a rough cross-section of the kind of songs that could be heard any night at any coffeehouse folk club in Greenwich Village in 1961. Suze Rotolo's sister Carla worked for the musicologist Alan Lomax, and through her and other notable collectors such as Bob and Sidsel Gleason, Dylan gained access to a treasure-trove of folk classics, on albums such as Harry Smith's celebrated six-LP *Anthology Of American Folk Music* and Lomax's own *Folk Songs Of North America* compilation.

The songs he chose were picked to provide as comprehensive a demonstration of his styles as possible, though he wisely chose to downplay his interest in Woody Guthrie, apart from his own 'Song To Woody'. Besides this and his 'Talkin' New York', there was the resigned 'Man Of Constant Sorrow', which he had heard Judy Collins singing (as 'Maid Of Constant Sorrow') on his brief sojourn in Denver; 'You're No Good', a song by another Denver acquaintance, the one-man blues band Jesse Fuller; revved-up versions of the old spiritual 'Gospel Plow' and the traveling songs 'Highway 51' and 'Freight Train Blues'; 'Fixin' To Die', 'In My Time Of Dyin' ' and Blind Lemon Jefferson's 'See That My Grave Is Kept Clean'; a satirical romp through the traditional 'Pretty Peggy-O', which poked fun at more precious interpretations; a beguiling arrangement of 'Baby Let Me Follow You Down' which, as he explained in a spoken introduction, had been taught him by Ric Von Schmidt "in

> *"Dylan's an extraordinary man. I don't know if he's going to sell, but he has something profound to say"* **JOHN HAMMOND**

the green pastures of Harvard University," and which would, with minor revisions, provide The Animals with their first hit as 'Baby Let Me Walk You Home'; and another song which heavily influenced the British R&B band, the brothel lament 'House Of The Rising Sun'.

This last inclusion would cause a bitter split in Dylan's friendship with Dave Van Ronk, who had originally developed the dark, haunting arrangement he used, and could thus be presumed to have first option on the song in that form. Shortly after the sessions, Dylan bumped into Van Ronk and asked him if he could record the song. "I'd rather you didn't," replied Van Ronk, "because I'm going into the studio soon and I'd like to record it for my album." Embarrassed, Dylan had to admit that he'd already recorded it, and couldn't pull it from the album because Columbia wanted it included. Furious, Van Ronk stormed off, and didn't speak to Dylan for the next two months. Bob never really regained his former friend's full trust.

One notable aspect of the material chosen for his debut is the pervasive presence of death in many of the songs,

▼

DYLAN IN LONDON, 1966: A SYMPHONY IN SUEDE.

particularly for such a young man. Bob Dylan had been preoccupied by death—obsessed, some say—since his youth in Hibbing, Minnesota, where he was involved in several car and motorcycle accidents. In New York, several friends, including Suze Rotolo, perceived an undertow of pessimistic despair beneath Dylan's comic exterior, and it is entirely possible that this dichotomy was what attracted people to him. Years later he admitted to Robert Shelton that, during this time, he was terrified of dying before he had said all that he had to say, but that, ironically, he was partly dependent on this fear for creative inspiration. "I don't write when I'm feeling groovy," he explained. "I play when I'm feeling groovy. I write when I'm sick." Of death itself, he seemed remarkably cynical: "All this talk about equality—the only thing people really have in common is that they are all going to die."

There was a five-month wait between the recording of the album and its release, due to David Kapralik's cold feet about his newest artist. There was no obvious single with which to promote the LP, and its cheapness meant that there was an obvious temptation to cut losses by not releasing it. Some company operatives had even tagged Dylan "Hammond's Folly," so low was their enthusiasm. Hammond, though, would have none of it. "It was the same way the first time I played Billie Holiday's record," he recalled, "so to me, this negative reaction was almost a recommendation, and I was more determined than ever to get Bobby's album released."

Going over Kapralik's head to his friend, CBS president Goddard Lieberson, Hammond secured a release date of March 19, 1962, when *Bob Dylan* duly appeared with a front cover photo of Bob wearing his trademark cap and a suede sheepskin-style jacket he had chosen after seeing how cool Ian Tyson, of folk duo Ian & Sylvia, looked wearing a similar jacket on their album cover. A glance at the stringing of Bob's guitar, however, indicates that the photograph was actually printed the wrong way round. On the back cover, Robert Shelton contributed scholarly annotations of the songs under the pseudonym Stacey Williams. Minimal promotion ensured the LP sold less than 5,000 copies in its first year, but by the time it was released, Dylan had already far outgrown the record anyway.

Talkin' New York

Asly commentary on his early days in the New York folk scene done in the talking blues style popularized by his hero Woody Guthrie, 'Talkin' New York' is the earliest of Bob Dylan's own songs to be recorded. He had previously written several other comic monologues in the same style, including 'Talkin' Hava Negilah Blues', which satirized the "ethnic" folksong fashion of performers such as Harry Belafonte and Theodor Bikel, and 'Talkin' Bear Mountain Picnic Massacre Blues', a humorous riff about a disastrous boat trip which derived from a newspaper clipping shown to him by Noel Stookey (later Paul of Peter, Paul & Mary).

The talking blues is an easy mode to write in, and a devastatingly effective one to perform, involving as it does a simple, steady guitar vamp around three or four chords underneath the spoken lyrics, each verse usually capped by a sardonic, throwaway punch-line followed, in Dylan's case, by a brief, double-time rush of harmonica which stands in for the absent chorus. In many ways, the talking blues was a direct precursor of rap music, enabling the performer to serve as a kind of journalist, reporting on current events with an immediacy and vitality denied to the more portentous, long-winded ballad form. As such, it served Woody Guthrie well during his decades as a labor activist and troubadour, and Dylan was to make good use of it through most of the Sixties, with comic riffs like 'I Shall Be Free' and 'Bob Dylan's 115th Dream'. Even flat-out rock tracks like 'Tombstone Blues' and 'Highway 61 Revisited', and surreal nightmares like 'On The Road Again' and 'Stuck Inside Of Mobile With The Memphis Blues Again' are ultimately just customized versions of the talking blues.

'Talkin' New York' wittily presents the young Bob Dylan as a country naïf cast adrift amid the chilly winds of the big city, eventually throwing up in "Green-witch Village," where callous coffee-house proprietors initially turn him away for sounding too much like a hillbilly, before he gets a job playing harmonica for a dollar a day. The song oozes cynical disillusion, with Dylan even borrowing Woody Guthrie's famous image from 'Pretty Boy Floyd' about people who can "rob you with a fountain pen." But despite the narrator's clear dislike of the harsh realities of the New York folkie's life, he's ultimately unable to break away completely: though he heads off for "western skies" in the final verse, he gets only as far as neighboring East Orange, New Jersey—where Guthrie resided in Greystone Hospital. The suggestion is, perhaps, that Dylan's many visits to his ailing hero served to strengthen his ambition, to turn his steps back towards New York whenever his resolve was weakening.

Certainly, the song reflects Woody's hold on Dylan's imagination at the time, both in its style and in its borrowings from Guthrie songs like

"I don't write when I'm feeling groovy; I play when I'm feeling groovy. I write when I'm sick" **BOB DYLAN**

'Pretty Boy Floyd' and 'Talkin' Subway', the latter of which likewise talks of the singer's bemusement at the way people go "down into the ground" in subway and traffic tunnels. Dylan did, however, claim to have written 'Talkin' New York' at a truck stop while hitch-hiking westwards in May 1961, a trip that took him only as far as his old stamping-ground of Minneapolis.

The disenchantment which underscores 'Talkin' New York' does, however, seem rather unfair. No other folk singer working in Greenwich Village at the time experienced as meteoric a rise as Dylan, who made his big-time debut at Gerde's Folk City within months of his arrival, and recorded an album—for a major label—well before his first year in the city was up. Indeed, virtually from the moment of his arrival, he was the golden boy of the folk scene, loved and mothered by a succession of benevolent friends, such as Bob and Sid Gleason, Mikki Isaacson, Dave and Terri Van Ronk, Eve and Mac Mackenzie, and Mel and Lillian Bailey, on whose couches he appears to have crashed in rotation for several months, before acquiring his first apartment on 4th Street.

"I bummed around," Dylan later claimed of his early days in New York. "I dug it all—the streets and the snows and the starving and the five-flight walk-ups and sleeping in rooms with ten people. I dug the trains and the shadows, the way I dug ore mines and coal mines. I just jumped right to the bottom of New York." But though Dylan showed little compunction in using others ruthlessly—as in his appropriation of Dave Van Ronk's arrangement of 'House Of The Rising Sun', against his friend's express wishes—he seems to have believed that there was some sort of conspiracy operating against him in the folk scene, that people were going out of their way to retard his progress.

This perception probably originated in his frustration at trying to get coverage in folk magazines like *Sing Out!*, and attempting to score a record deal with the specialist folk-music labels like Elektra, Vanguard and Folkways mere months after his arrival in New York. "I went up to Folkways," Dylan said bitterly. "I said, 'Howdy. I've written some songs, will you publish them?' They wouldn't even look at them. I'd heard that Folkways was good. Irwin Silber didn't even talk to me, and I never got to see Moe Asch. They just about said 'Go!' And I had heard that *Sing Out!* was supposed to be helpful and friendly, big-hearted, charitable. Must have been in the wrong place—but *Sing Out!* was written on the door. Whoever told me they had a big heart was wrong."

▼

DYLAN'S MENTOR WOODY GUTHRIE, WHO WAS ALREADY SUFFERING FROM HUNTINGTON'S CHOREA WHEN BOB FIRST MET HIM IN 1961.

Song to Woody

Of all the influences which the young Bob Dylan soaked up in his late teens, the folk singer Woody Guthrie had by far the greatest impact. Indeed, so closely associated did Dylan become with the legendary troubadour that he was twice offered the lead role in a film of Guthrie's life based on his autobiography *Bound For Glory*; he turned it down both times, and David Carradine eventually took the part.

The composer of more than a thousand songs, including such standards as 'So Long, It's Been Good To Know You', 'Pastures Of Plenty' and 'This Land Is Your Land', Guthrie was the prototype hobo minstrel, thumbing rides and jumping freight-trains to criss-cross the USA through the Thirties and Forties, supporting leftist causes and singing of the tribulations and essential dignity of the common working man. "I hate a song that makes you think that you are just born to lose," he said. "Songs that run you down or songs that poke fun at you on account of your bad luck or your hard traveling...no matter what color, what size you are, how you are built. I am out to sing the songs that make you take pride in yourself and in your work." Throughout his life, he considered himself simply a mouthpiece for the people, a journalist noting down the way things really were.

His empathy with the downtrodden was well-founded in his own experience, which was tough at the beginning, tough at its conclusion, and unremittingly hard in between. Born in Oklahoma in 1912, named Woodrow Wilson Guthrie after the American President who founded the League of Nations, Guthrie had a childhood scarred by family tragedy, with both his sister and father killed in fires and his mother dying from the degenerative nerve disease Huntington's Chorea. This ailment would be passed on to her son, who would spend the last years of his life, from 1954 to his death in October 1967, in hospitals, slowly wasting away—a cruelly tragic conclusion to a life so full of movement.

By the age of 17, the orphaned Guthrie had begun the rootless drifting which would characterize most of his life, joining the disenfranchised migra-

tory workers from the ruined Dust Bowl farmlands of Oklahoma, Texas and Arkansas on their journey to the fruit farms of California—the social disaster dramatized by John Steinbeck in *The Grapes Of Wrath*. Taking his cue from his cousin, country singer Jack Guthrie, Woody began writing songs, adapting traditional folk tunes with his own lyrics, and quickly became the folk-poet of the underdog. Working solo, with his traveling companion Cisco Houston, or as part of The Almanac Singers with Pete Seeger, Lee Hays and Millard Lampell, Guthrie offered an alternative viewpoint to the prevailing mean-spiritedness

"I am out to sing the songs that make you take pride in yourself" **WOODY GUTHRIE**

of the times which would eventually result in the Communist witch-hunts of Senator Joe McCarthy's notorious House Un-American Activities Committee.

Seeger, who was condemned by that committee, persuaded Guthrie to write about his own extraordinary life, and the result, *Bound For Glory*, caused a sensation when it was published during the Second World War. It was this autobiography which captured the interest of the young Bob Dylan in Minneapolis, where he could be found avidly devouring the book in the coffeeshops of the "Dinkytown" campus/bohemian district, memorising passages and drawing inspiration from Guthrie's tales of hard traveling and social injustice. Though he was by that time familiar with some of Guthrie's material, he subsequently spent more and more of his time unearthing and learning Guthrie's songs—a close friend from Minneapolis, David Whittaker, recalls him listening over and over again to a record of Guthrie's half-hour epic ballad 'Tom Joad', day after day. Another college acquaintance, Ellen Baker, gave Dylan access to her parents' huge collection of folk magazines, such as *Sing Out!*, and records by Guthrie: her parents were impressed with his interest, though like many who encountered Dylan at this period, they felt he was drawing on Guthrie's life in a more than merely musical sense, trying to build himself a more interesting identity to replace the relatively ordinary one he had grown up with. His slim repertoire of folk songs soon bulged with Guthrie material, and his vocal inflection changed from a rather sweet voice to an imitation of the Okie's brusque nasal twang.

Dylan's obsession with Guthrie grew into a standing joke among Dinkytown friends, particularly his ambition to meet his hero; some would play jokes on him when he was drunk, telling him Guthrie was outside or on the phone. But he did try and contact the singer one snowy night in December 1960, Whittaker affirms, phoning Greystone Hospital in New Jersey, where Guthrie

"That boy's got a voice. Maybe he won't make it in his writing, but he can really sing it" **WOODY GUTHRIE**

was dying of Huntington's Chorea. The ward doctor told Dylan that Woody was too sick to come to the phone. That seemed to settle matters once and for all. "I'm going to see him," Dylan told Whittaker, "I'm going to New York right now." And he was off, hitch-hiking East through a blizzard.

Dylan got to meet his idol in late January or early February 1961, at the home of Bob and Sid (Sidsel) Gleason, a folk-enthusiast couple with whom Guthrie spent weekends at their place in East Orange, New Jersey, where Sundays were a kind of open-house hootenanny session for such noted luminaries of the folk scene as Pete Seeger and Cisco Houston, along with lesser lights such as Peter LaFarge, Logan English, Lionel Kilburg and Guthrie disciple Ramblin' Jack Elliott. Dylan had apparently hitched out to Greystone Hospital a few days earlier, and had visited Guthrie's family home in Howard Beach, Queens, where he gave Woody's young son Arlo an impromptu harmonica lesson, but the Sunday session at the Gleasons' was probably the first time Guthrie —or any of the folkie crowd, for that matter—was made aware of his existence. Having heard of the Gleasons in his first few weeks as a coffeehouse folkie in Greenwich Village, Dylan had called on them and secured an invite to the following Sunday's session, where he sat quietly on the floor by the couch where Guthrie lay, frail and palsied, while Houston chatted to Guthrie

▶

DYLAN CONTEMPLATES ONE MORE CUP OF COFFEE IN NEW YORK'S CENTRAL PARK, 1963.

about his own illness (which claimed his life later that year), and Elliott tried vainly to cheer proceedings up. It was, by all accounts, a somewhat dismal afternoon. When Dylan finally sang a few songs, the old master was impressed. "He's a talented boy," one of those present recalls Guthrie saying, "Gonna go far."

Shortly after this first meeting, Dylan wrote 'Song To Woody', basing the melody on Guthrie's own '1913 Massacre'. A sincere, if sentimental, tribute from an acolyte to an icon done in a gentle waltz-time, it acknowledges the pupil's debt to the master, reflects with longing upon the master's earlier, rambling days and concludes with an assurance that the pupil, too, will seek out experiences with the same diligence and integrity. Over the following weeks, Dylan visited Guthrie several times in hospital and frequently attended the Gleasons' weekend soirees where, much to the envious chagrin of Kilburg and English, he became a firm favorite of Woody's. The first question Guthrie would ask when the Gleasons arrived at the hospital to pick him up was "Is the boy gonna be there?"; and when, one Sunday, the boy played 'Song To Woody' for him, Guthrie beamed with pleasure and assured him, "That's damned good, Bob!" After Dylan had left, Woody told the Gleasons, "That boy's got a voice. Maybe he won't make it by his writing, but he can really sing it."

The boy was growing up, however, and he grew to realize that Woody was far from the idealized hero of his imagination, that, though touched with genius, he was just as petty, irresponsible and egotistical as the next man. This undoubtedly had a significant effect on Dylan's songwriting and performing styles and his attitude to life. A few years later, he told Nat Hentoff of *The New Yorker* magazine, "After I'd gotten to know him, I was going through some very bad changes, and I went to see Woody, like I'd go to somebody to confess to. But I couldn't confess to him. It was silly. I did go and talk with him—as much as he could talk—and the talking helped. But, basically, he wasn't able to help me at all. I finally realized that. So Woody was my last idol."

The original song manuscript—a sheet of yellow legal paper—ended up with the Gleasons. On it is the song and Dylan's note, "Written by Bob Dylan in Mills Bar on Bleecker Street in New York City on the 14th day of February, for Woody Guthrie."

BLOWIN' IN THE WIND

GIRL FROM THE NORTH COUNTRY

MASTERS OF WAR

DOWN THE HIGHWAY

BOB DYLAN'S BLUES

A HARD RAIN'S A-GONNA FALL

DON'T THINK TWICE, IT'S ALL RIGHT

BOB DYLAN'S DREAM

OXFORD TOWN

TALKING WORLD WAR III BLUES

CORRINA, CORRINA

HONEY, JUST ALLOW ME ONE MORE CHANCE

I SHALL BE FREE

SINGLE:
MIXED UP CONFUSION

The Freewheelin' Bob Dylan

After the poor sales of his debut album, there was talk at Columbia of Dylan's contract being dropped before he could make a second record. John Hammond, however, would have none of it, and blocked David Kapralik's move to offload "Hammond's Folly" by appealing over his head to Columbia president Goddard Lieberson, an old friend whom he had been responsible for bringing into the company years before. Helped by the support of Johnny Cash, one of the label's leading country stars, who made no secret of his admiration for the youngster, Hammond was able to secure an extension of Dylan's contract, for which Columbia was presumably eternally grateful. A giant leap beyond his raw debut, *The Freewheelin' Bob Dylan* was the first of a string of Dylan masterpieces that changed the face of first folk, then rock music.

There are two basic driving forces behind the *Freewheelin'* album: Dylan's involvement in the civil rights movement; and his girlfriend Suze Rotolo's absence in Italy, which spurred him into a prolific fever of songwriting. Since Suze was the person who drew Dylan into the civil rights arena in the first place, her position alongside the singer on the album cover was more than justified. Bob and Suze had bumped into each other a few times before through her sister Carla—who worked for folk archivist Alan Lomax and was an early supporter of Dylan—but the two became an "item" following a benefit concert he played on July 29, 1961, for the Riverside Church's radio station WRVR-FM. The youngest daughter of politically-active Italian immigrant parents, Suze was already involved in desegregation and anti-nuclear campaigns, working as a secretary for the Congress On Racial Equality. She helped Bob bring his general concern for the underdog and dislike of injustice into sharper, more specific focus.

The pair began an intense, but problematic, two-year affair. At first, Suze had the effect of smoothing out Bob's spikier side, sweetening his demeanor and encouraging him to smarten up a little. But after they took a tiny apartment at 161 West 4th Street, the demands of his ego began to encroach upon her own ego-space, and she started to feel smothered by his attention. She was an intelligent young woman with interests of her own in the theater and visual arts—she intro-duced Bob to the work of Bertolt Brecht, who would be a big influence on his work—but Dylan seemed to require nothing more of her than that she be "Bob's girl." As early as November 1961, before Dylan had released any records, she confided in a letter to a friend, Sue Zuckerman, "I don't want to get sucked under by Bob Dylan and his fame. I really don't. It sort of scares me... It really changes a person when they become well known by all and sundry. They develop this uncontrollable egomania... Something snaps somewhere, and suddenly the person can't see anything at all except himself... I can see it happening to Bobby..."

Besides which, Dylan was, even then, not the most forthcoming of people. "It's so hard to talk to him," Suze told another friend. "Sometimes he doesn't talk. He has to be drinking to open up." She sensed a pervasive air of despair about Dylan, a pessimism about people which bordered on paranoia and made him reluctant to leave the flat. Suze's mother, Mary, disapproved of her relationship with this scruffy 19-year-old kid who had dubious personal hygiene and a cavalier way with the truth, particularly concerning his own past. She persuaded her daughter to travel with her in the summer of 1962 to Italy, where Suze took a course at the University of Perugia. The trip, which was meant to be for a few months, was ultimately extended to a total of six months, during which time Dylan pined terribly for her.

Like many an artist before him, however, Dylan learned how to transmute his pain into creative energy: the period of Suze's absence marks the first full flowering of his poetic talent, with songs of high quality pouring out of him at a phenomenal rate. A friend, Mikki Isaacson, recalls going on a car trip with him at the time, and being amazed at his industry: "He had a small spiral notebook, and must have had four different songs going at once. He would write a line in one and flip a couple of pages back and write a line in another one. A word here and a line there, just writing away." Another friend, the singer Tom Paxton, recalled strolling late at night through Greenwich Village with Dylan as he scribbled away on scraps of paper. "His mind was on fire. Between the club and wherever he was heading, he'd start as many as five songs—and finish them!"

The most frequently used word to describe Dylan at the time was "sponge"—he would listen

◄

BOB LAYS DOWN TRACKS FOR HIS SECOND ALBUM AT COLUMBIA'S NEW YORK STUDIOS.

quietly to friends' conversations, making notes, and later on they would find phrases, stories and nuggets of information from their conversation appearing in his songs. He was omnivorously open to influences, but unlike most of his contemporaries, he had the drive and application to build something of his own out of the accumulated fragments. During a radio interview with Pete Seeger, Dylan explained his working methods. "I don't even consider it writing songs," he claimed. "When I've written [a song] I don't even consider that I wrote it when I got done... I just figure that I made it up or I got it some place. The song was there before I came along, I just sort of took it down with a pencil..."

Having written a song effectively as a poem, he would then try and find a melody for it, often borrowing or adapting an old folk tune, some of which he learned from English folk singers on a trip he made to Europe in December 1962 through January 1963. Ironically, just as he rushed over to Italy to see Suze, she was sailing back to New York, where she managed to settle in before Bob returned a few weeks later, hoping to pick up their relationship where it had left off six months before. Suze was reluctant—she had matured considerably in her time away, and did not want to become just "Bob's girl" again—but Dylan was persuasive, and after a short time staying with her sister, she moved back into the 4th Street apartment.

Things had changed radically, however. Bob's fame had grown rapidly while she was away, and it seemed that everyone was trying to get to him

"The song was there before I came along, I just sort of took it down with a pencil" **BOB DYLAN**

through her, that nobody was interested in her for her own sake and that the process of objectification was even stronger than it had been before—particularly since songs like "Don't Think Twice, It's All Right" had effectively made their relationship public. And Bob himself, encouraged by his new manager Albert Grossman, was becoming reclusive, aloof, all the more paranoid, and she found it more difficult than before to communicate with him. Before long, the old stresses and strains

began to pull them apart all over again.

Besides several songs, such as 'Boots Of Spanish Leather' and 'Tomorrow Is A Long Time', which were written specifically about Suze during her absence, Dylan also continued maturing as a protest songwriter, with songs like 'Oxford Town' and particularly 'A Hard Rain's A-Gonna Fall', whose strings of imagery reflected the influence of the French Symbolist poet Arthur Rimbaud, a favorite of Bob and Suze's. With John Hammond again at the helm, recording for the new album began with a couple of sessions in April 1962, but it was not until July that Dylan started laying down the more distinctive material that would set this new album firmly apart from his debut and establish him as a songwriter of great power and individuality.

Several of the protest songs that would appear on *Freewheelin'*, such as 'Blowin' In The Wind' and 'Masters Of War', were originally published in the folk/protest magazine *Broadside*, a small but influential disseminator of new views for whom Dylan served as a contributing editor. (Later on, in 1963, he would also contribute to an album of *Broadside Ballads* using the pseudonym Blind Boy Grunt so as not to infringe his contract with Columbia Records.) The first issue of *Broadside* included the lyrics to one of his earliest songs, an amusing talking blues called 'Talkin' John Birch Paranoid Blues', which took a broad satiric swipe at the right-wing anti-communist organization: in the song, the narrator searches for communists so avidly he finds them everywhere, eventually spotting one in his mirror.

The song, which was slated for inclusion on *Freewheelin'*, caused a problem when Dylan tried to perform it on *The Ed Sullivan Show*, the country's premier television variety showcase. He had been booked on the May 12 show by Sullivan's son-in-law, Bob Precht, a folk fan who had managed to smooth over the obvious absurdity of having Dylan share a bill with Teresa Brewer, Irving Berlin, Al Hirt and the mouse puppet Topo Gigio. But when Stowe Phillips, the network censor, heard the song in rehearsal, he had cold feet and refused to let Dylan perform it on the show, fearing that it might libel members of the John Birch Society. Would Bob, he wondered, care to sing something else instead?

He would not. "If I can't play my song, I'd rather not appear on the show," he said, and walked out, hours before curtain time. In one way, it was a fortuitous refusal: Dylan had already come in for criticism from some of the Greenwich Village folkies for selling out when he told them he was due to appear, and his walk-out stopped that flak and generated some more favorable publicity besides. But there were further repercussions: *The Ed Sullivan Show* was on the CBS network, Columbia Records' parent company, and the same fears of libel brought pressure to remove the song from *Freewheelin'* as well, on the eve of its release. Since his contract gave them the right to censor such material, Dylan had no option but to comply, particularly since his first album had been a commercial failure.

Though he was angry at first, Dylan quickly got over his frustration, and took the opportunity to replace several of the songs which were scheduled to be on the album, which he felt were too old-fashioned, with more contemporary, "finger-pointing" songs. Out went 'Talkin' John Birch Paranoid Blues', 'Rocks And Gravel', 'Rambling Gambling Willie' and 'Let Me Die In My Footsteps', and in came 'Bob Dylan's Dream', 'Masters Of War', 'Talkin' World War III Blues' and 'Girl From The North Country'—but not before a few hundred copies of the album with the original running-order had been pressed up and released. (The rarest items in Dylan's back catalog, they now command thousands of dollars on the infrequent occasions they appear for sale.)

These four substitute tracks had been recorded at a late session in April 1963, four months after the rest of the album had been completed. They marked the debut of Dylan's new producer, a young black man called Tom Wilson, who had previously worked on jazz recordings by performers such as Sun Ra's Arkestra, and who would later go on to produce early efforts by such seminal Sixties groups as The Velvet Underground and Frank Zappa's Mothers Of Invention. Wilson had taken over production duties from John Hammond when Albert Grossman, alarmed at Hammond's casual approach to recording, threatened to walk away from the Columbia contract on the grounds that Dylan had been a minor when he signed it, thus rendering it null and void.

Since Dylan had recorded several times since turning 21, however, Grossman could not extricate

him from the contract, although he could still cause enough of a fuss to get Hammond replaced. But Columbia had a policy which dictated that Columbia artists must only use Columbia's in-house producers, and there were no exceptions to the rule—certainly not unproven talents like Dylan. "We don't want anything to do with any producer at Columbia," Grossman told David Kapralik, "because you don't have a producer that under-stands Bob Dylan." Realizing that because Wilson was black, Dylan and Grossman would not dismiss him out of hand, Kapralik suggested Dylan chat with Wilson awhile. His ploy worked: the next day, Wilson was accepted as Bob's new producer and, shortly after, they recorded the songs which completed *Freewheelin'*.

The album was released on May 27, 1963, with a cover photo of Bob and Suze strolling happily down a slush-covered 4th Street. As *Freewheelin'* picked up airplay, acclaim and sales of around 10,000 a month (particularly when Peter, Paul & Mary scored a huge hit with 'Blowin' In The Wind' that July), Suze was the envy of every folk singer's girlfriend and female college student. But even as the record was being released, Dylan was on the far side of the country, following his May 18 appearance at the Monterey Folk Festival by spending a fortnight—unknown to Suze—at the Carmel pad of his new friend, Joan Baez.

▲

BOB ENTERTAINS
AT THE SINGERS CLUB
CHRISTMAS PARTY
ON HIS FIRST TRIP
TO BRITAIN,
DECEMBER 22, 1962.

Mixed Up Confusion

The second official Bob Dylan record released by Columbia, the single of 'Mixed Up Confusion' sold even more poorly than his debut album. A rollicking rockabilly rave-up, it's a complete anomaly set against what preceded and succeeded it.

Shortly after the November 1962 sessions at which it was recorded, Dylan told folk historian Israel Young that he'd written the song in the taxi *en route* to the studio, and it sounds like it. An impromptu burst of disaffection, the song perhaps reflects the pressures that Dylan's growing reputation was bringing to bear upon him, with "too many

A MIXED UP, CONFUSED DYLAN PONDERS HIS FUTURE.

▼

" I finally got to the point where I said to myself: 'Jesus, Dylan, you ain't written no songs about you' " **BOB DYLAN**

people" wanting a piece of him, either to do some promotional work, or give them advice on songwriting (as his old Greenwich Village colleague Mark Spoelstra had requested, embarrassingly for all concerned), or to make an appearance in support of some cause or other. "They're all too hard to please," fumes Dylan, desperately.

In one of his trips back West to Minneapolis that August, his chum Tony Glover had taped Dylan singing some songs and moaning about the demands made upon his time by people like the activists from the Congress Of Racial Equality. "CORE is a white organization for Negro people," he sneered. "I am sick of writing songs for everybody." He went on to sing a satiric talking blues which asked, "What kind of hippo is a hypocrite?" before returning to his theme of self-sacrifice. "I figure I've been writing too many songs for other people," he said. "I finally got to the point where I said to myself: 'Jesus, Dylan, you ain't written no songs about you. You've got to get somebody to write a song about you.' Then I said to myself, 'I can write songs about me as well as anybody else can.' " With 'Mixed Up Confusion', he certainly expresses one side of himself clearly, blurting out a cathartic torrent of frustration.

Even the recording of the song, as it happens, left him angry and frustrated, probably due to the interference of his managers Albert Grossman and John Court at the sessions. Perturbed at what he saw as John Hammond's lackadaisical approach to recording, Grossman had begun to stick his oar in, and while his eye for business was without peer, his ear for music was less reliable. "Albert had the brilliant idea that Bobby ought to be recorded with a Dixieland band on 'Mixed Up Confusion'," recalled Hammond. "It was a disaster."

Whether the version released on the single is what Hammond (or Grossman) considered "Dixieland," it's not really that great a disaster. Indeed, as a historical document, it marks the very first folk-rock recording, a good three years before *Bringing It All Back Home*. Herbie Lovelle's rattling-train snare-drum licks and Gene Ramey's bass drive along an arrangement that leans heavily on Dick Wellstood's Jerry Lee Lewis-style rock-a-boogie piano, with the guitars of Bruce Langhorne and George Barnes dancing around the riff. Something of a throwback to the teenage Robert

Zimmerman's Little Richard-influenced high-school bands, it was released as a single in December 1962, with 'Corrina, Corrina' on the B-side, but was felt to be at variance with Dylan's emergent reputation as a serious young commentator, and was swiftly withdrawn.

Three years later, it was reissued by the Dutch arm of CBS in a sleeve featuring one of the Daniel Kramcr photographs of Dylan seated at an upright piano, taken at the *Bringing It All Back Home* sessions. Some copies were imported into the UK, where it was widely believed to be a recent recording, so congruent was it with Dylan's contemporary folk-rock material. It was never included on an album until the 1985 retrospective collection *Biograph*—but even then, with typical Dylanesque inscrutability, a different version of the song was chosen. That wasn't Dixieland, either.

Blowin' In The Wind

'**B**lowin' In The Wind' marked a huge jump in Bob Dylan's songwriting. Prior to this, efforts like 'The Ballad Of Donald White' and 'The Death Of Emmett Till' had been fairly simplistic bouts of reportage songwriting, taking news stories—in these cases, about the disparity of the American legal system's treatment of, respectively, a Negro murderer and a Negro murder victim—and turning them into narrative dramas of social conscience.

'Blowin' In The Wind' was different: for the first time, Dylan discovered the effectiveness of moving from the particular to the general. Whereas 'The Ballad Of Donald White' would become completely redundant as soon as the eponymous criminal was executed, a song as vague and all-encompassing as 'Blowin' In The Wind' could be applied to just about any freedom issue, at any time. It remains the song with which Dylan's name is most inextricably linked, and safeguarded his reputation as civil libertarian through any number of subsequent changes in style and attitude.

Sometimes derided for its lack of substance, the song features a particularly clever piece of poetic sleight-of-hand, hiding its string of unanswerable, rhetorical queries behind a strong, specific opening image (of a man walking down a road) which connects to both the Woody Guthrie road-song tradition of Dylan's immediate past and to the civil rights marchers who were then altering the course of their country's history. From there, the song offers less specific questions couched in more abstruse images, repeatedly dissolving into the wistful uncertainty of the chorus in a way that struck a strong chord with the youthful protest movement, validating their concern while absolving them from the obligation to come up with absolute answers to the problems about which they protested. There are no hard and fast answers, the song says, the only obligation is to care. "The first way to answer these questions," said Dylan, "is by asking them. But lots of people have to first find the wind."

The inspiration for the song came to him one afternoon in April 1962, during a long political discussion with friends in the Commons, a Greenwich Village coffeehouse across MacDougal Street from the Gaslight Club. As the conversation petered out into silence, an idea struck him. "The idea came to me that you were betrayed by your silence," he told friends, "that all of us in America who didn't speak out were betrayed by our silence, betrayed by the silence of the people in power. They refuse to look at what's happening. And the others, they ride the subways and read the *Times*, but they don't understand. They don't know. They don't even care, that's the worst of it." With his friend David Cohen (who became the folk singer David Blue) strumming the chords for him, Dylan quickly wrote down the words, and then the pair dashed over to Gerde's Folk City to play the new song for the club's singing MC, Gil Turner. Deeply impressed, Turner got Dylan to teach him the song and that very night he gave 'Blowin' In The Wind'

▲
DYLAN'S PRODUCER JOHN HAMMOND, WHOSE PREVIOUS SUCCESSES INCLUDED BENNY GOODMAN AND BILLIE HOLIDAY.

► THE GASLIGHT CAFE ON MACDOUGAL STREET IN NEW YORK'S GREENWICH VILLAGE, ACROSS THE ROAD FROM WHERE DYLAN WROTE "BLOWIN' IN THE WIND".

its first public recital, to great acclaim.

After the song was featured that May on the cover of the sixth issue of *Broadside* magazine—a small, mimeographed bulletin set up by Pete Seeger, Sis Cunningham and Gordon Friesen for the dissemination of new topical songs and analysis, and largely run by Gil Turner—it became part of every folkie's repertoire, the new *lingua franca* of folk protest. Pete Seeger was especially impressed, and became one of Dylan's most fervent supporters, convinced the kid was a genius, even if he had borrowed the tune from the old folk song 'No More Auction Block' for 'Blowin' In The Wind'. If anything, that just authenticated it for him, anchoring the new song in the grand old folk tradition of adaptation and interpretation. Not that it prevented Dylan copyrighting the tune as his own, of course. (More sinister, however, was the later rumor, reported in *Newsweek*, that the lyrics had been written by a student in New Jersey, Lorre Wyatt, from whom Dylan had purchased them. Wyatt himself first tried to explain away the situation by saying "some kids" had confused Dylan's

song with another which he himself had written, called 'Freedom Is Blowing In The Wind', and that only the titles were similar, before finally admitting, in a 1974 magazine article, that it was all bullshit and that there was no truth in the rumor. "The coat of fakelore I stitched years ago is threadbare now —it never fit me very well," he wrote. "I'm just sorry it's taken me 11 years to say 'I'm sorry.' ")

Dylan's friend Dave Van Ronk, still rankling from the way Bob appropriated his arrangement of 'House Of The Rising Sun', was less complimentary than Turner and Seeger when the song was played for him the day after Turner had debuted it at Gerde's. "What an incredibly dumb song!" he spluttered with typical bluffness. "I mean, what the hell is blowing in the wind?" But a few weeks later, after hearing someone parodying the song in Washington Square Park, he realized that Dylan had come up with an enduring cliché. So did Dylan's manager, Albert Grossman, who also knew the commercial value of such a cliché. In a masterstroke of managerial synthesis, he earmarked the song for his other main act, Peter, Paul & Mary, the folk group he had created the previous year, who were establishing themselves as the commercial folk heirs to The Kingston Trio with hit versions of folk standards like 'Lemon Tree' and 'If I Had A Hammer'. The following summer, a few months after the release of *The Freewheelin' Bob Dylan*, their version of 'Blowin' In The Wind' went to number two on the American pop charts, becoming Warner Brothers' fastest-selling single ever and cementing Dylan's position as the crown prince of folk-protest.

Belatedly realizing their artist's true potential, Columbia rushed out a single of Dylan's version in August 1963, a month after Peter, Paul & Mary's. It failed to chart, leaving Dylan tagged for some time primarily as a songwriter, rather than a performer. The song was, however, used as the theme for *Madhouse On Castle Street*, a BBC television play in which Dylan played his first dramatic role, appearing as an American protest singer—hardly a stretch, one would have thought.

Girl From The North Country

Though some commentators, most notably Dylan biographer Robert Shelton, claim that the girl from the North Country is actually Bonnie Beecher—a bohemian actress Bob fell in love with during his time in Minneapolis, and at whose apartment Tony Glover recorded several of the early Dylan tapes—most agree it is more likely to be Echo Helstrom, his first serious girlfriend from his schooldays back in Hibbing.

Bob met Echo in October 1957, when he was just 17, and she 16. At the time, Bob Zimmerman was a nice enough middle-class boy, clean-cut and round-faced, while Echo was from a poorer working-class family, definitely from the wrong side of the tracks. They discovered a shared interest in R&B music, which both would listen to late at night on the radio, on the DJ Gatemouth Page's program, or on stations in Chicago and Little Rock, Arkansas,

which had particularly powerful transmitters. Nobody else in Hibbing, it seemed, was interested in this music, but they were obsessed with it: the first time they met, Bob used his pocket-knife to break into the Moose Lodge where he had earlier been practicing with his band, in order to play her his Little Richard piano licks.

Already, Bob knew what he was going to do with his life. "By the time I met him," recalled Echo later, "it was just understood that music was his future. All along we knew there was no other way for him to get out of there, to leave Hibbing." His ambition sometimes led him to playful fantasy pranks, as when he played Bobby Freeman's 'Do You Want To Dance?' down the phone to Echo, claiming it was him and his band; but she and her mother recognized, even at this early stage, Bob's intrinsic empathy with the underdog. His later interest in country music may have stemmed from his association with Echo, too: he and his friend John Buckland would trawl through Echo's mother's large collection of Country & Western 78s, trying out the songs on their guitars, particularly the sad songs about prison fires, dying children and similar depressing subjects.

For a while, Bob and Echo were sweethearts, swapping identity bracelets and even attending the prom together, albeit as outsiders somewhat cut off from the school mainstream. The 1958 Hibbing High yearbook records Bob's feelings for Echo: "Let me tell you that your beauty is second to none, but I think I told you that before... Love to the most beautiful girl in school." But, by that summer, they were growing apart. Increasingly restless and pinched by the confines of Hibbing, Bob's boot heels had taken to wandering, and his weekends would be spent out of town, in Duluth or Minneapolis, while Echo pined away miserably at home. She realized he was probably seeing other girls and so, one Monday morning, she handed his ID bracelet back in the school corridor. "Don't do this in the hall," pleaded Bob, "let's talk about it later." But it was already too late.

Bob Dylan finished writing the song on his brief trip to Italy in the first week of 1963, where he had hoped to meet up with Suze Rotolo again. Alas, she had left to return to New York mere days before. He had, he later claimed, been carrying the song around in his head for a year, and it seems as though the manic swing from anticipation to disappointment caused it to burst out of him. Equally important in its eventual appearance was his sojourn in England on the same European trip, where Dylan went to appear in the BBC play *Madhouse On Castle Street*. In the company of old chums Richard Fariña and Ric Von Schmidt—over there to record an album on which Dylan, credited as "Blind Boy Grunt," would play impromptu harmonica—he did the rounds of the London folk clubs, where he picked up some old English folk songs from traditional singers such as Martin Carthy. Like another expatriate American folkie, Paul Simon, Dylan seems to have been particularly attracted to the old English folk song 'Scarborough Fair', and adapted it to fit his own ends.

Masters Of War

This diatribe against the arms industry is the bluntest condemnation in Dylan's songbook, a torrent of plain-speaking pitched at a level that even the objects of its bile might understand, with no poetic touches to obscure its message. Despite its directness, however, it has had scant effect: even today, armaments manufacturers are virtually the only companies that governments are prepared to prop up and subsidize, whatever the cost, despite the often flagrant incompetence and fraudulent misuse of public funds exhibited by these companies in cahoots with the military establishment.

President Dwight D. Eisenhower's final advice to the incoming President John F. Kennedy in January 1961 was to beware of this military-industrial complex, which he belatedly realized had effectively dictated much of American foreign and economic policy in the postwar years, encouraging the Cold War arms race and reckless military adventurism in order to serve their own vested interests, rather than the interests of the country as a whole. Their influence spread into other areas, particularly science and education, which became heavily dependent on Defense Department funding, and which in turn became more tightly focused on military research, at the expense of

other areas. By 1960, the Federal Government was subsidizing research in universities to the tune of over a billion dollars a year; thanks to Federal funds, a single institution like the Massachusetts Institute Of Technology (M.I.T.) could spend more money on scientific research than all the universities of the British Isles combined.

Kennedy either ignored Eisenhower's advice or found himself over a Cold War barrel rolled under him by his hawkish Chiefs Of Staff. He had been in office a few months when he authorized a massive arms procurement program worth an $3 billion on top of the already substantial arms budget, with an additional $207 million earmarked for civil defense. The money pouring into the arms companies' coffers has grown even greater since, as armaments have become more technologically complex, like Stealth bombers and Cruise missiles, or more fanciful, like Reagan's comic-book "Star Wars" Strategic Defense Initiative.

First debuted by Dylan at Gerdes Folk City on January 21, 1963, 'Masters Of War' remains as pertinent almost four decades later. Its lyrics were published in the 20th issue of *Broadside* magazine in February 1963, accompanied by a couple of drawings by Suze Rotolo—one of a man carving up the world with a knife and fork while a family watches forlornly, and another of a baby-carriage kitted out with a gun and tank-tracks. The tune is an adaptation of the traditional melody to the English folk song "Nottamun Town", probably learnt from Martin Carthy on one of Dylan's English trips.

Down The Highway

'Down The Highway' is the closest Dylan comes on *Freewheelin'* to the dark soul of country blues as practiced by performers such as Robert Johnson or Son House. It's a bare, basic blues format, worked around a 12-bar scheme in which a single strummed guitar chord teeters through the verses, collapsing into a flat-picked resolution at the end of each couplet, the evocative musical equivalent of the piteous sinking of shoulders after an impassioned *cri du coeur*. The subject matter, a girlfriend who has

abandoned him for some "far-off land" which proves, in the penultimate verse, to be a desolate "Italy, Italy...," is clearly about the pain caused by the absence of Suze Rotolo, who was pursuing her own life on an extended trip to that country.

The narrator is stranded, lovelorn, on some endless highway, lugging his suitcase to nowhere special: wherever he goes, she won't be there, so what does it matter? It's possible that Dylan came up with the song as he was returning to see old friends in Minnesota: the same day, June 8, that he saw Suze's ship off at the docks in New York, he himself set off for Minneapolis. Shortly after, back in New York, Dave and Terri Van Ronk were surprised to receive a phone call at four in the morning from Bob, who was standing in a Minneapolis phone box in sub-zero temperatures, crying for Suze. Upon his return to Greenwich Village, all his friends were surprised at how list-less and melancholy he had become, and how he had changed physically as well as emotionally—the puppy-fat apparent on his first album cover had disappeared, leaving him looking gaunt and weary, like Woody Guthrie. "He was falling apart at the seams," said Mikki Isaacson, a Village friend. "He was so depressed we were afraid he was going to

do something to himself." Time did little to ease his pain. On a tape made by his old friend Tony Glover on another trip back to the twin cities a couple of months later, Dylan can be heard pining for Suze: "My girl, she's in Europe right now. She sailed on a boat over there. She'll be back September 1, and till she's back, I'll never go home. It gets kind of bad sometimes."

The mention of gambling in the third verse could be a reference to the Greenwich Village folkies' back-room poker games, but in the context of Dylan's life is far more likely to refer to his perilous hand-to-mouth existence in his time in New York. Since dropping out of college in Minneapolis a year before, he had bummed around a bit, to nearby Madison and Chicago, and as far afield as Colorado and New Mexico, before heading East to eke out a virtual hobo existence on peoples' floors in New York, heavily reliant on the compassion of strangers while he tried to develop a career in music. It had all been a huge gamble, and just as it seemed he might be set for the big jackpot pay-off, with a beautiful girlfriend, a record deal, burgeoning acclaim and the imminent prospect of both fame and fortune, his girl had gone and left him "without much more to lose."

▲

IN HIS EARLY PUBLICITY PHOTOS, DYLAN (LEFT) SELF-CONSCIOUSLY COPIED THE ARRESTING STYLE OF HIS HERO WOODY GUTHRIE (RIGHT).

Bob Dylan's Blues

Despite providing the original working title for *Freewheelin'*, the trifling 'Bob Dylan's Blues' is probably more important for its position in the album's running-order than for any intrinsic merit. Coming after the intensely emotional opening sequence of four songs, it offers a moment of light relief before the testing blizzard of imagery in 'A Hard Rain's A-Gonna Fall', the LP's centerpiece. At the recording session on July 9, it perhaps served a similar purpose, immediately preceding the taping of 'Blowin' In The Wind'. An example of how blues expression can lighten the spirit, its attitude of cheeky irrelevance punctures the self-pity at its heart. Nevertheless, it's interesting for a couple of reasons: the line "Go away from my door and my window too" is a premonitory echo of the shorter, snappier opening line of 'It Ain't Me Babe'; and the presence of the Lone Ranger and Tonto in its opening line marks the first appearance in Dylan's recorded work of the gallery of pop-culture icons that would populate much of his later work.

A Hard Rain's A-Gonna Fall

'Blowin' In The Wind' may have established Bob Dylan as the principal anthemist of the Civil Rights movement, but it was 'A Hard Rain's A-Gonna Fall', written later that same year, which established him as the folk-poet of a new generation. Its strings of surreal, apocalyptic imagery were unlike anything that had been sung before, and the song's rejection of narrative progression in favor of accumulative power lent a chilling depth to its warning. It was the closest folk music had come to the Revelation of St. John, and every bit as scary.

The root inspiration for the song came from the Cuban Missile Crisis—the moment at which, it's commonly agreed, the Cold War came closest to boiling over into all-out nuclear catastrophe. The crisis came about in the wake of Fidel Castro's revolutionary 1959 transformation of Cuba into a communist state. In 1961, the young new American President, John F. Kennedy, revealed his inexperience and immaturity by supporting a CIA plot to overthrow Castro, to which end many of the anti-Castro Cuban refugees pouring into America were enlisted in an insurrectionary force of 1,500 men, who were trained in Guatemala for a counter-revolutionary invasion of Cuba.

Despite widespread antipathy towards the plot from the British government—who warned that the invasion would breach international law—and such weighty American political advisors as Dean Acheson, Arthur Schlesinger and Senator J. William Fulbright, who counseled that "the Castro regime is a thorn in the flesh, but it is not yet a dagger in our heart," Kennedy proceeded with the plan. It was a disaster: when the invasion force attempted to establish a beach-head at the Bay Of Pigs on April 17, 1961, it was summarily wiped out by Castro's waiting defenders.

Kennedy's reputation was badly damaged by the abortive mission, which led his Soviet opposite number, the bombastic, bullying Nikita Khruschev, to adopt a fiercely aggressive stance at the Vienna summit negotiations that June over the future of Berlin. The summit went badly, ending with Khruschev asserting, "I want peace—but if you want war, that is your problem." The outcome of the failed negotiations was the building of the Berlin Wall in August 1961, and the deepening of mistrust on both sides.

Meanwhile, stung by the Bay Of Pigs fiasco, President Kennedy had authorized further covert measures against the Castro regime, under the code name "Operation Mongoose," ranging from the absurd (slipping El Presidente a poisoned cigar) to the effective, most notably the crippling of the Cuban economy through fifth-columnist saboteurs. So when, in the summer of 1962, the US Navy held intimidatory military maneuvers just outside Cuban territorial waters, Castro sought an alliance with the Soviet Union, who in return for economic subsidies were secretly granted permission to install nuclear missile bases on the island, on the justifiable pretext of defending Cuba's independence against any further invasion. To the Soviets, forced to tolerate American nuclear missiles in Turkey, right on its own southern border, this was simply a tit-for-tat retaliation in the USA's backyard—"Nothing more," Khruschev claimed in his memoirs, "than giving them a little taste of their own medicine." But to an America emotionally sore from years of red-baiting paranoia, it was as if the country had, for the first time, suffered an invasion of its own.

By mid-October, the world was at the brink of nuclear war, while Kennedy and Khruschev walked a perilous tightrope of political brinkmanship. Rejecting the foolish suggestions of his bellicose military chiefs that he should bomb or invade Cuba (or both), which would surely have caused an escalation of hostilities leading to all-out war, Kennedy decided to call Khruschev's bluff by opting for a policy of "quarantining," or blockading, the island, to prevent it receiving any further Soviet supplies. On Monday October 22, the seventh day of the crisis, he appeared on television to announce his decision. "The path we have chosen for the present is full of hazards," he explained, "as all paths are...[but] one path we shall never choose...is the path of surrender or submission."

Two fraught, nervous days later, the policy bore fruit: Soviet vessels delivering further arms supplies turned back. "We are eyeball to eyeball," said Kennedy advisor Dean Rusk, "and the other fellow just blinked." But this still left some missiles already installed on the island, which the Soviets were rushing toward preparedness. The situation was apparently not helped when an American U2 spy-plane was shot down over Cuba the following Saturday, October 27, though in retrospect this seems to have decided both leaders to settle the issue quickly, before it got out of hand. Khruschev had been hoping to secure the removal of the US missiles in Turkey in exchange for dismantling the Cuban missiles, but all he received publicly was a promise that the USA would not invade Cuba; secretly, however, Kennedy agreed to remove the Jupiter missiles in Turkey, which were obsolete anyway. The crisis was over, though the proximity to imminent catastrophe left lingering ripples in the American consciousness, poetically addressed in Dylan's song.

"It's just a hard rain, not the fallout rain, it isn't that at all. The hard rain that's gonna fall is in the last verse, where I say 'the pellets of poison are flooding us all'" **BOB**

"I wrote that," said Dylan, in his most famous commentary on any of his songs, "when I didn't figure I'd have enough time left in life, didn't know how many other songs I could write, during the Cuban thing. I wanted to get the most down that I knew about into one song, the most that I possibly could, and I wrote it like that. Every line in that is actually a complete song, could be used as a whole song. It's worth a song, every single line."

The "hard rain" of the song is not, however, nuclear fallout. "It's not atomic rain," explained Dylan. "It's just a hard rain, not the fallout rain, it isn't that at all. The hard rain that's gonna fall is in the last verse, where I say 'the pellets of poison

▲

DYLAN'S FOLK SINGER COLLEAGUE TOM PAXTON, ONE OF THE FIRST TO HEAR "A HARD RAIN'S A-GONNA FALL".

are flooding us all'—I mean all the lies that are told on the radio and in the newspapers, trying to take peoples' brains away, all the lies I consider poison."

The song, which Dylan wrote in late September in his friend Chip Monck's apartment below the Gaslight club, began as a long, free verse poem, a French Symbolist-style extension of the opening lines of the epic ballad *Lord Randal*. That night, he showed it to the folk singer Tom Paxton at the club. "It was a wild, wacky thing, the likes of which I'd never seen before," recalled Paxton. "As a poem it totally eluded me, so I suggested he put a melody to it. A few days later I heard him perform it as 'A Hard Rain's A-Gonna Fall'." Within days, the song was being acclaimed by friends as Dylan's greatest work. "We all thought it was the greatest thing since sliced bread," said Dave Van Ronk. "I was acutely aware that it represented the beginning of an artistic revolution."

Don't Think Twice It's All Right

The most explicit of the songs reflecting Dylan's feelings toward the absent Suze Rotolo, 'Don't Think Twice, It's All Right' was one of the most popular of his earlier compositions, being widely recorded, though usually more blithely than in Dylan's original version, which has an understated air of resigned rancor quite unlike any other love songs of the period. Noel "Paul" Stookey, who would sing the song with Peter, Paul & Mary, recognized its magical quality as soon as he heard it: "I thought it was beautiful, a masterful statement... It was obvious that Dylan was stretching the folk idiom, [that] a new spirit had come." He was right. For a folk song, it was unusually modern in attitude, with a daring balance struck between affection and bitterness. Later on in his career, Dylan would become an expert at all-out vindictiveness, so much so that friends became wary of approaching him, for fear of being subjected to his acid tongue or poison pen; but here, his obvious disappointment is tinged more with simmering regret, only boiling over into mild spite in the penultimate line of each verse, where Suze is variously castigated for being immature, uncommunicative, wanting his soul when he offered his heart and, in the most dismissive of put-downs, wasting his "precious" time. Ironically, though it was Suze who had actually left Bob, the song salvages his pride by claiming it is he who is "trav'lin' on."

Some of his friends were embarrassed by the song. "Bobby was rolling it out like a soap opera," said Dave Van Ronk. "It was pathetic. The song was so damn self-pitying—but brilliant." Upon her return from Italy, Suze at first found it strange, if flattering, to hear others singing this song written about her, but it eventually contributed to her split from Bob when, at the 1963 Newport Folk Festival that July, Joan Baez introduced the song as being "...about a love affair that has lasted too long." For Suze, this confirmed the rumors she had heard about Bobby and Joanie, the new "King and Queen of Folk," and she stormed away from the festival.

While the song's lyric was revolutionary in form, the melody was again purloined from a traditional source, an Appalachian tune called 'Who's Gonna Buy Your Chickens When I'm Gone', which Dylan's friend, the folk singer Paul Clayton, had discovered and adapted for his own song 'Who's Gonna Buy Your Ribbon Saw'. Many of their friends were angered by the way Dylan brazenly neglected to credit either the traditional source or (especially) Clayton, who was notoriously short of cash due to his drug problems. "The honorable thing would have been for Bobby to cut him in on the copyright," believed Dave Van Ronk, "but that wasn't Bobby's way." Instead, after a mild legal tussle, Dylan ensured that his publishers gave Clayton "a substantial sum," and the two remained friends, Clayton accompanying Bob on his cross-country drive in February 1964.

The liner-notes to *Freewheelin'* mistakenly claim that the song was recorded with the band that played on 'Corrina, Corrina' and 'Mixed Up Confusion', but while it was certainly recorded at the same session, it is clearly a solo performance. Some commentators have speculated that it may have originally been recorded with a band accompaniment that was subsequently wiped, but the limitations of early-Sixties recording technology mean that it would have been virtually impossible to have erased the extra guitar, drums, bass and piano completely without leaving a certain amount of "spillage," which would have been captured on Dylan's own microphone. It's feasible that the band backing may have been added later on another track, and then erased, but the actual song as heard on the album is by Dylan alone.

Bob Dylan's Dream

The last song recorded for the *Freewheelin'* album, 'Bob Dylan's Dream' offers the most telling indication of just how fast Bob Dylan was maturing as a person, and of how rapidly his attitudes were changing. A wistful reverie of lost youth, the song finds Dylan, not yet 22, looking back on the innocent idealism of his teenage years with the world-weary sadness of one apparently much older.

Like Dickens in *A Christmas Carol*, Dylan uses a dream to observe his former self and his friends "talkin' and a-jokin'," having fun, chewing the fat and putting the world to rights with the blithe certitude of youth. His loss, he realizes, is twofold: not only has the easy-going innocence of those days passed, but the convictions once held so firmly— "It was all that easy to tell wrong from right"—as issues of simple black and white clarity have blurred into infinite shades of gray complexity.

Dylan claims, in the liner-notes, that the inspiration for the song came from a conversation he had with the singer Oscar Brown Jr. one night in Greenwich Village, though he carried the idea around in his head for some while before it took on a more concrete form. Dylan's several return journeys to Minnesota, both before and after the release of his first album, undoubtedly helped crystallize the theme of the song, as he realized the disparate paths taken by himself and his old friends from Hibbing and the Dinkytown campus neighborhood of Minneapolis.

"It was obvious he'd grown," recalled his country-blues chum Spider John Koerner after one such visit. "He was friendly and all that, but it was obvious he was into something stronger than we got into. You could see it, something forceful, something coming off." By summer of 1962, old folkie friends like Tony Glover, Paul Nelson and Jon

"...he was into something stronger than we got into. You could see it, something forceful, something coming off' **SPIDER JOHN KOERNER**

Pankake, who published the Minneapolis folk magazine *Little Sandy Review*, were chiding Dylan about his new protest-song direction, suggesting he should try and strike a balance between his new style and his older, traditional style, and though he was already feeling used by certain civil rights organizations, Dylan clearly felt his Minnesota friends were being left behind.

A year later, the gap was growing wider, as he made clear in a promotional appearance for his forthcoming album on April 26 on Chicago's WFMT radio station, where he was interviewed by Studs Terkel about his life and work. Asked about childhood friends, Dylan replied: "They still seem to be the same old way... I can just tell by conversation that they still have a feeling that isn't really free... They still have a feeling that's...tied up in the town, with their parents, in the newspapers that they read which go out to maybe 5,000 people. They don't have to go out of town. Their world's really small."

Dylan's world, by contrast, was growing larger all the time, as demonstrated by the melody he appropriated for 'Bob Dylan's Dream' from the traditional British folk ballad 'The Franklin', which Dylan had heard performed by the English folk singer Martin Carthy while visiting London in December 1962.

Oxford Town

After the serious, sometimes angry tone taken on social matters earlier on the album, 'Oxford Town' is shorter and sweeter in style, if not in subject matter, offering a jaunty, hootenanny-singalong treatment of a specific civil rights issue: the violent struggle for the registration of the first black person at the University Of Mississippi ("Ole Miss") in September 1962.

After winning a Federal court ruling allowing him to register at the university, James Meredith was denied entry to the university registrar's building by demagogic state governor Ross Barnett, who was attempting to ride the tide of resentment rolling through the South at the imposition of what Southerners saw as Yankee directives aimed at breaking their spirit. Attorney General Robert Kennedy inquired whether Barnett would make a deal to allow Meredith to register, and was informed, "I would rather spend the rest of my life in a penitentiary than do that." Mississippi, Kennedy pointed out, had to obey, being part of the United States, to which Barnett responded, "We have been a part of the United States, but I don't know whether we are or not." "Oh," asked Kennedy, "are you getting out of the Union?"

He wasn't, but the idea clearly appealed to Barnett, who made a strident speech in defense of the principle of segregation on the pitch at half-time of the Ole Miss–Kentucky football game on September 29, announcing to roars of appreciation that he loved Mississippi, her people and her "customs"—a veiled reference to racism. At the same time, he was indeed cutting a deal with the Kennedys, who had threatened to make the negotiations public on national Television. Meredith, he suggested, could be registered late on Sunday night, September 30; and so, while 300 federal marshals acted as decoys, surrounding the administration building, that evening the black would-be student was smuggled into a campus dormitory. The double-crossing Barnett then announced that the defenders of the Southern way of life had been over-powered, triggering the build-up of an angry mob.

That night, President John F. Kennedy made a televised speech urging the students to comply with the law: "The honor of your university and state are in the balance," he said. "Let us preserve both the law and the peace and then, healing those wounds that are within, we can turn to the greater crises that are without, and stand united as one people in our pledge to man's freedom." Stirring words, but they made little impression on the white students who were, even as he spoke, pelting stones at the federal marshals, who responded with tear-gas. Reluctantly, Kennedy called out the National Guard, but not before the racist students had been joined by older rioters who brought guns, with which they shot 30 marshals and bystanders, killing two people. In all, 300 people were wounded. The battle raged all night but by dawn it was, literally, academic: James Meredith had been registered as a student at Ole Miss. Not, of course, that deeply ingrained racist attitudes were changed overnight: the troops remained in Oxford until Meredith graduated in the summer of 1963.

The stand-off became one of the emblematic events of the civil rights struggle, and Dylan's rapid response to it—the song was first published in the November 1962 issue of *Broadside* magazine—illustrates the journalistic efficacy of the topical protest song. As he was recording it in early December, John Hammond was trying to persuade Don Law, head of Columbia's Nashville operation, that Dylan ought to be recording with the hot musicians down in Nashville. "You have to come up and hear this Dylan kid," he told Law, who dropped by the studio just as Dylan was doing 'Oxford Town'. After listening a while, Law turned to Hammond and said, "My God, John, you can never do this kind of thing in Nashville. You're crazy!"

▼
RACIST WHITE STUDENTS PROTEST AT THE ENROLMENT OF NEGRO JAMES MEREDITH AT 'OLE MISS', THE UNIVERSITY OF MISSISSIPPI IN OXFORD.

Talkin' World War III Blues

One of the last songs to be recorded for *Freewheelin'*, it seems likely that this talking blues was written to replace the 'Talkin' John Birch Paranoid Blues' which so frightened the Columbia executives. If so, the result is a net gain: partly improvised in the studio, this is a far superior piece to its bigot-baiting predecessor, whose narrow-focus concerns lay more in the past of the McCarthyite communist witch-hunts than with the more pressing problems of the Sixties. 'Talkin' World War III Blues', by comparison, zeroed in on a couple of more pertinent contemporary issues: the growing American fascination with psychoanalysis that had enabled Alfred Hitchcock to have a hit movie (*Psycho*) based on a specious psychoanalytic theme; and the looming specter of nuclear annihilation, which was coming to a head with the Cuban Missile Crisis. There was also room in the song for a few offhand side-swipes at things like the gratuitous materialism of automobile adverts ("Cadillac...good car to drive after a war"), and the pitiful state of Tin Pan Alley pop, which was rapidly approaching its nadir at the time (between January and April 1963, when this track was recorded, such giants as Steve Lawrence, Paul & Paula, The Rooftop Singers and Little Peggy March had topped the American charts). The communist witch-hunt theme of 'Talkin' John Birch Paranoid Blues' was telescoped into a one-line aside, which is just about what it deserved.

▶

COMMIE-SEEKING SENATOR JOSEPH MCCARTHY (RIGHT) UP TO HIS USUAL WITCH-HUNTING TRICKS IN THE FIFTIES.

"My God, John, you can never do this kind of thing in Nashville. You're crazy!"

DON LAW

Corrina, Corrina

First registered as 'Corrine Corrina' by Bo Chatman, Mitchell Parish and J.M.Williams in 1932, this lilting blues had been recorded several times by such artists as Blind Lemon Jefferson and most notably on several occasions by Big Joe Turner, before its revival in the early Sixties.

Dylan's version is of a completely different stripe from Turner's good-natured R&B swing, not least through the addition of a verse about having "a bird that whistles...a bird that sings," adapted from Robert Johnson's 'Stones In My Passway'. Dylan was at the time clearly fascinated by the mercurial Johnson—an earlier, unreleased solo take of the same song also featured fragments from the legendary bluesman's 'Me And The Devil Blues' and 'Hellhound On My Trail', too. Subsequently, he attributed the song's style to

Honey, Just Allow Me One More Chance

C oming toward the end of a largely down-beat album of protest songs and lovelorn blues, this jaunty adaptation of a song originally written by the Texan country bluesman Henry Thomas offers a more light-hearted, breezy expression of Dylan's pain over the absent Suze. It's a swaggering performance, which best exemplifies Dylan's understanding of the blues as a means of cathartic healing, as explained in the sleevenote to *Freewheelin'*: "What made the real blues singers so great is that they were able to state all the problems they had; but at the same time, they were standing outside of them and could look at them. And in that way, they had them beat."

another, more mellifluous blues legend, Lonnie Johnson (no relation to Robert), who shares with T-Bone Walker the pioneer status of "inventor of the electric blues."

"I was lucky to meet Lonnie Johnson at the same club I was working and I must say he greatly influenced me," Bob admitted later. "You can hear it in 'Corrina, Corrina'—that's pretty much Lonnie Johnson. I used to watch him and sometimes he'd let me play with him."

The song features one of Dylan's more beguiling vocal performances, a wistful lamentation in which the depths of his heartbreak are signaled by the gentle falsetto catch in the throat that recurs in the last line of each verse. The inspiration is obviously Suze's absence. The album version is all that resulted from three otherwise largely unproductive sessions with a full backing band, although another take, marked by a wheeze of harmonica on the intro and a more strident harmonica solo in the break, was released prior to the album, as the B-side of 'Mixed Up Confusion'.

I Shall Be Free

F irst recorded for the November 1962 issue of *Broadside* magazine, this comic talking blues trifle closes the album almost as an afterthought, as if the stage performer in Dylan realizes how intense the album is as a whole, and wants to "leave 'em laughing." He wouldn't be so concerned to do this on later records, but here he goofs around with a cast that includes Yul Brynner, Charles De Gaulle, President Kennedy and several of the world's most beautiful women, to no particular end.

Undeniably politically incorrect by today's standards, this light-hearted account of Dylan's womanizing does, however, prefigure some of his later work in its tone of blithe nonsense: for one who was being increasingly painted as the serious young spokesman of a generation, Dylan seems determined in this song to keep open his options on different modes of meaning. Or in this case, meaninglessness.

THE TIMES THEY ARE
A-CHANGIN'

BALLAD OF HOLLIS BROWN

WITH GOD ON OUR SIDE

ONE TOO MANY MORNINGS

NORTH COUNTRY BLUES

ONLY A PAWN IN THEIR GAME

BOOTS OF SPANISH LEATHER

WHEN THE SHIP COMES IN

THE LONESOME DEATH OF
HATTIE CARROLL

RESTLESS FAREWELL

The Times They Are A-Changin'

In the few short months between the release of *The Freewheelin' Bob Dylan* in May 1963 and *The Times They Are A-Changin'* in January of 1964, Bob Dylan became the hottest property in American music, stretching the boundaries of what had previously been viewed as a largely collegiate folk-music audience. His third album would establish him as the undisputed king of protest music, though even as he was being crowned, he was experiencing grave misgivings about both that type of song, fame in general and his own position as reluctant leader of a movement—misgivings which grew when, as he was recording *The Times They Are A-Changin'* that November, President John F. Kennedy was assassinated. From that point on, he would be harder to pin down, both in his songs and in person. "Being noticed can be a burden," he explained later. "Jesus got himself crucified because he got himself noticed. So I disappear a lot."

There would be significant changes on the personal front, too. Following his first liaison with Joan Baez following the Monterey Folk Festival, rumors quickly spread about the nature of their relationship, placing further stress on his already strained relations with Suze, though she initially doubted that his ego would cope with Baez's fame. "Bobby couldn't love Joan Baez," she told friends. "He couldn't love *anybody* that big!"

For both parties, this new affiliation was probably motivated as much by career considerations as anything more romantic, blossoming later into a more emotional or sexual connection. For Dylan, the advantages of teaming up with the Queen of Folk were obvious, given that her reputation and audience were both bigger than his; for her part, Baez recognized songwriting genius when she heard it, and she had heard it when her manager sat her down and made her listen to an acetate of demos Dylan had recorded for his publishers, Witmark. This, she realized, was a talent that far outstripped all his contemporaries. "He wrote songs that hadn't been written yet," she said later. "There aren't very many good protest songs. They're usually overdone. The beauty of Bobby's stuff is its understatement."

The Newport Folk Festival, held over the weekend of July 26-28, 1963, was effectively Bob Dylan's coronation. He dominated the gathering, being name-checked constantly as performers covered his songs, and made several appearances of his own—a solo slot on the Friday night, followed by a group encore of 'We Shall Overcome'; a topical-song workshop event on the Saturday; and a guest slot during Joan's Sunday performance to duet on 'With God On Our Side', followed by another group encore, this time of 'This Land Is Your Land'. Every mention of his name was applauded by the audience, eager to acclaim the new star. Meanwhile, backstage and back at the Victory Motel where a coterie of young performers were staying, Dylan had begun to take on the character of a star, strolling around playing with a bullwhip which his rowdy friend Geno Foreman had brought him. It was as if he were assuming command of the genre, cracking the whip on the old guard.

Much to Suze's chagrin, following the festival Dylan accepted an offer of a guest slot on Joan Baez's summer tour, for which Grossman ensured he was paid more than the headline star. After recurring arguments about the state of their relationship, Suze finally moved out of the 4th Street apartment, shortly before Joan and Bob appeared at the August 28 March On Washington, at which Martin Luther King made his celebrated "I Have A Dream" speech. Bob took solace by making visits to Albert Grossman's place near Woodstock in upstate New York. A few weeks later, he took some more time out at Joan's place in Carmel, where he spent his days reading, writing and swimming. It may have seemed idyllic but, he later revealed, they never really talked that much. And though they remained in relatively close contact for a few more years, before too long they both realized they were too different to be together: to Bob, Joan was just too much of a clean-cut, straight-arrow goody-goody; and she, for her part, couldn't bear the nasty, spiteful tone that began to creep into his songs through 1964 and 1965. "Unlike other people, about whom I think I have some kind of sense," Joan explained three decades later, "I never understood him at all. Not a tweak."

Joan, however, wasn't the only one mistaken in her view of Dylan. The "spokesman of a generation" began to realize that this new position, foisted upon him by one magazine article after another, was actually more of an imposition, as

◀

DYLAN DUETS WITH JOAN BAEZ AT HER 1963 CONCERT IN CAMBRIDGE, MASSACHUSETTS.

this political group and that political group attempted to make claims on his time. In July, his friend Theodore Bikel had persuaded him to fly down to Greenwood, Mississippi, to perform at a voter-registration drive organized by the Student Non-Violent Coordinating Committee (SNCC, or "Snick") to increase the black vote in the state. Dylan was pleased to help out a cause he believed in, and he got on well enough with the local farm workers, but not for the first time, he found himself surrounded by activists who seemed to want to lecture him about his responsibilities to the civil rights movement—as if he hadn't shown his commitment by going down there in the first place! And after Joan Baez's concert at Forest Hills, New York, he had been buttonholed at the post-gig party by Clark Foreman, head of the Emergency Civil Liberties Committee (ECLC), who had made him listen to a recording of some screenwriter's speech about the social responsibility of writers! Who needed *that*?

What he wanted to do most in the world—write and sing songs—was increasingly being viewed as something in which other people felt they had a say. Plus, Dylan had started to be regarded as some kind of oracle, as if he had all the answers—which was flattering, certainly, but also worrying. Besides which, he was beginning to hate being typecast as just a "protest singer." "Man, I don't write protest

"Unlike other people, about whom I think I have some kind of sense, I never understood him at all. Not a tweak." **JOAN BAEZ**

songs," he claimed. "I just react. I got all these thoughts inside me and I gotta say 'em." And not all of these thoughts were exclusively about injustice. Some of them were about himself. "Because Dickens and Dostoevsky and Woody Guthrie were telling their stories much better than I ever could," he told one newspaper, "I decided to stick to my own mind."

His mind could be a lonely place, however, particularly for one with a natural aversion to crowds. Even at Newport, Dylan had seemed scared by his growing fame, telling friends, "The

attention is too much commotion for my body and head." He had long since realized the value of autobiographical fictions in protecting his real self from unwelcome attention, spreading all kinds of misinformation about himself ever since his earliest days in New York. None of his friends was unduly bothered by this, but they saw a streak of paranoia developing in Dylan around this time, possibly inculcated by Grossman, who assiduously stoked the notion of the "Dylan mystique" and encouraged Bob to think of himself as someone special, apart from the general run of performers. As if he needed any evidence that this was the case, there was an edge of adulatory hysteria about Dylan's triumphant Carnegie Hall solo concert on October 12, which concluded with him having to be whisked away from a crowd of screaming teenagers who thronged the stage door. By the end of the year, he would write, in a poetic letter to *Broadside* magazine explaining the pressures he had begun to experience, "I am now famous by the rules of public famiousity...it snuck up on me an' pulverized me... I never knew what was happenin'."

Things all came to a ghastly head in December, when Dylan was invited to accept the ECLC's Tom Paine Award at a gala dinner at the Americana Hotel in New York. It was a great honor, the kind he couldn't really refuse—the previous year's recipient had been Bertrand Russell, the philosopher and anti-nuclear campaigner—but Dylan's discomfiture was apparent from the start. "I looked down from the platform and saw a bunch of people who had nothing to do with my kind of politics," he told Nat Hentoff later. "They were supposed to be on my side but I didn't feel any connection with them." The audience was substantially made up of older liberals, balding veterans of the Thirties left-wing struggles and victims of the McCarthyite communist witch-hunts of the Forties and Fifties, but for the occasion, they had dressed up to the nines in furs and jewels. Dylan drank heavily and, when the time came for him to accept his award, he had to be collected from the men's room, somewhat the worse for wear.

His acceptance speech was disastrous, a nightmarish ramble which managed to offend just about everybody. He thanked them for the award on behalf of "everybody that went down to Cuba"

because they were, like him, young people. "I only wish that all you people who are sitting out here tonight weren't here and I could see all kind of faces with hair on their head and everything like that," he burbled, "...because you people should be at the beach." That drew a few laughs, so he warmed to his theme of hair, or lack of it: "Old people, when their hair grows out, *they* should go out. And I look down to see the people that are governing me and making my rules, and they haven't got any hair on their head. I get very uptight about it."

From there, he drifted on to the subject of race—"There's no black and white, left and right to me anymore; there's only up and down, and down is very close to the ground. And I'm trying to go up without thinking of anything trivial such as politics"—and his Negro friends, and then back to Cuba and then, in a classic *faux pas*, arrived by a roundabout route at the subject of Kennedy's assassination. "I have to be honest, I just have to be," he assured his audience, "as I got to admit that the man who shot President Kennedy, Lee Oswald, I don't know exactly...what he was doing, but I got to admit honestly that I, too, I saw some of myself in him... I got to stand up and say I saw things that he felt in me. Not to go that far and shoot..." By this time, the appalled silence had

▲

THE QUEEN OF FOLK ENJOYS A LONG, COOL GLASS OF DELICIOUS, HEALTH-GIVING MILK. MMM-MMM!

39

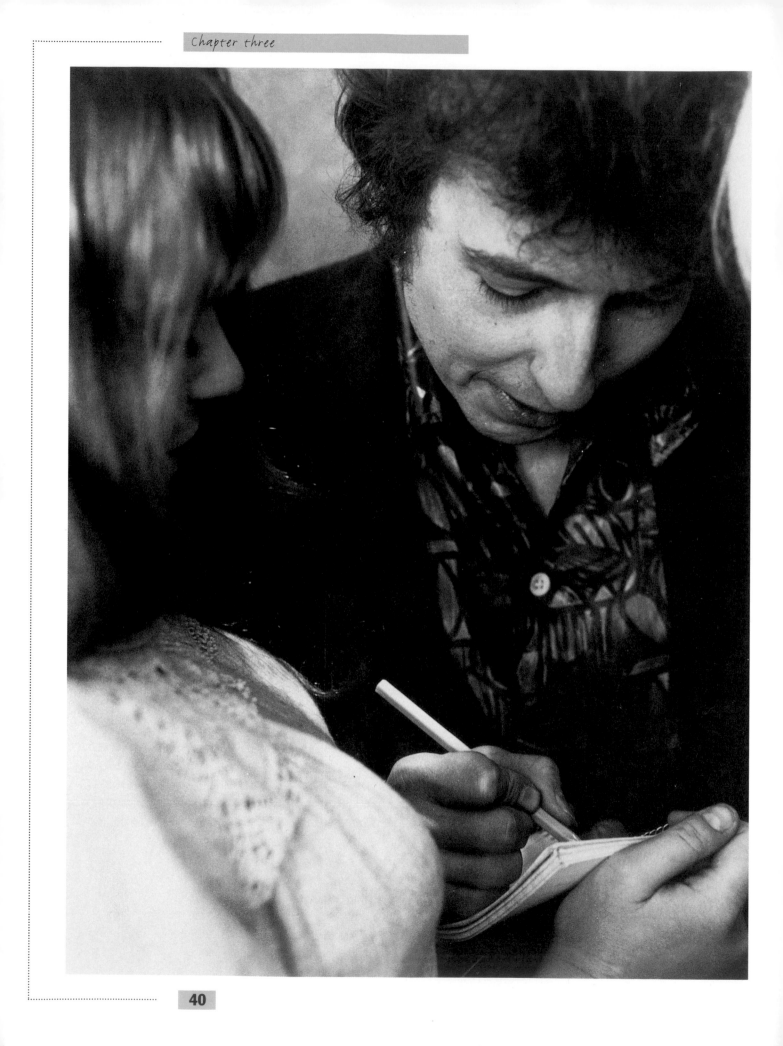

turned to a chorus of boos and hisses, which Dylan tried to counter by garbled recourse to the Bill Of Rights and free speech, before he was hustled off the stage and out of the place.

The audience was outraged. Was this youth saying he sympathized with the assassin? Why had *he*, of all people, been given the prestigious Tom Paine Award? Was *this* what the ECLC had sunk to? After the speech, the customary donations for the organization were taken from the audience. The depth of the crowd's anger can be gauged by the $6,000 drop on the previous year's donations.

When he sobered up, Dylan was torn between remorse and a desire to explain, and so composed a poem, entitled *A Message*, which he sent to the ECLC. In it, he outlined the circumstances surrounding the speech, and offered to make up to the organization any losses it may have sustained. His reference to Lee Harvey Oswald, he implied, was as a metaphor for the times, not a direct reference to the assassination: "...if there's violence in the times then/there must be violence in me/I am not a perfect mute/I hear the thunder an I can't avoid hearin' it..." It was some way short of an apology, and left intact his unflattering comparisons of the complacent old liberal audience with his young activist friends. A benefit concert was subsequently agreed, then postponed as Dylan's commitments snowballed over the ensuing years. Despite Clark Foreman's several attempts to collect on the offer of remuneration, Dylan never made up for the lost donations.

It was against a background of personal and public upheaval that Dylan went into the studio in August and October 1963 to record his aptly-titled third album. Where *Freewheelin'* had changed shape between its early sessions, which featured predominantly traditionally-influenced material, and its later sessions, as Dylan's songwriting matured, he was determined to record all original material, and mostly "finger-pointing" protest songs that reflected the social tenor of the times.

The same problems that he had experienced with John Hammond's production, however, recurred with Tom Wilson. Primarily a jazz producer, Wilson was uncertain about the qualities that made for a good folk performance. As a company man he was under pressure not to let the sessions take too long. Dylan felt that he wasn't

getting the feedback he needed and that Wilson was settling for inadequate takes. There was no chance of replacing him: the record company dictated that the job be done by a company producer.

Bob invited his friend Paul A. Rothchild, who produced Elektra's folk artists (and who would go on to produce many of The Doors' albums), to visit the studio and sit in front of the console where, unseen by Wilson, he would signal through the control-room window to Dylan if another take was required. With the weight of Rothchild's experience behind him, Dylan felt more secure when challenging

> "...if there's violence in the times then there must be violence in me I am not a perfect mute..." **BOB DYLAN**

his producer's opinions. Notwithstanding the problems, the sessions passed quickly, just three days in August and another two in October furnishing the bulk of the tracks, with another, final session hastily scheduled to record 'Restless Farewell' at the end of the month.

The album was released on January 13, 1964, in a sleeve with a rear taken up with a sequence of "11 Outlined Epitaphs," a series of poems in which Dylan dealt with his past, poetry, politics, accusations of plagiarism, the opinions of critics and the position in which he now found himself. The front cover, featuring Barry Feinstein's photo of a frowning Dylan in an open-necked shirt, told no lies about the album's contents. Compared to the smiling lovers of the *Freewheelin'* sleeve, this one spoke of grit and integrity, pain and hardship, injustice and truth. The intervening nine months, it said, had brought little to laugh about.

The reviews of the album were, to use the classic critical euphemism, "mixed," with some critics put off by its incessant gloom, while others applauded the artistry and concern—but Dylan's work had by now assumed a power and momentum of its own that rendered any criticisms redundant. The album cemented his reputation as the era's pre-eminent voice of protest, even as he was turning his back on that arena.

BOB MAKES HIS MARK FOR A LISSOME YOUNG FAN.

The Times They Are A-Changin'

The title-song of his third album effectively re-stated the message of Dylan's disastrous Tom Paine Award speech—that the old should get out of the way and let the young have their say—but in a manner that caused less offense to his audience, which was, in any case, rather younger than that at the award dinner.

The most explicit of what Dylan called his "finger-pointing" songs, 'The Times They Are A-Changin' ' is a deliberate anthem, in both intention and execution. It is steeped in a self-conscious gravitas, from the earnest sanctimony of Dylan's delivery to the archaic cast of the introductory lines, which carry the same air of impending declamatory moralism as Mark Anthony's "Friends, Romans, countrymen, lend me your ears" speech from Shakespeare's *Julius Caesar*, and which Dylan claimed were influenced by Irish and Scottish ballads such as 'Come All Ye Bold Highwaymen' and 'Come All Ye Tender Hearted Maidens'.

It's the battle-hymn of the new republic of youth, bursting with images of overturned order. The lines about the loser winning, and the slow becoming fast, echo the air of patient inevitability in such biblical promises of revolution as the Sermon on the Mount's suggestion that the meek would inherit the earth, and the lines from the Book Of Ecclesiastes which Pete Seeger adapted for 'Turn, Turn, Turn' (also echoed in the chorus of

▼
PRESIDENT KENNEDY'S ASSASSINATION IN DALLAS, NOVEMBER 23,1963.

Dylan's 'Percy's Song', which was recorded at the same session and originally intended for inclusion on *The Times They Are A-Changin'*). The climactic line about the first later being last, likewise, is a direct scriptural reference, to Mark 10:31: "But many that are first shall be last, and the last first."

The hypnotic delivery, and the references to curses being cast and wheels (of fate) still spinning, reinforce the sense of irrevocable historical momentum, as it applied to the changes then sweeping through the consciousness of Western youth. It would be five more years before the student protest movement that grew out of the civil rights struggles of the early Sixties would make its presence felt abroad, with riots in Paris and demonstrations in London, but the song's few specifically American references, to senators and congressmen, didn't prevent it from becoming the pre-eminent international anthem of the emergent youth culture.

The song's effectiveness resides in its dialectical union of personal and collective drives: each individual, it suggests, must make his or her own choice—but that choice could only be to join the rising tide of change, or be "drenched to the bone" by it. Conversely, aligning oneself with a tide of change should only be done through personal deliberation, not through herd instinct. Collectivity, Dylan implies, does not absolve one from individual responsibility.

For Dylan himself, the song's message was brought into frighteningly sharp, yet confusing, focus by the assassination of President John F. Kennedy on Friday, November 22, 1963. The next night, Dylan began a concert in upstate New York with the song. "I thought, 'Wow, how can I open with that song? I'll get rocks thrown at me,' " he later told biographer Anthony Scaduto. "But I had to sing it, my whole concert takes off from there. I know I had no understanding of anything. Something had just gone haywire in the country, and they were applauding that song. And I couldn't understand why they were clapping or why I wrote that song, even. I couldn't understand anything. For me, it was just insane."

In 1994, Dylan demonstrated just how much the times had changed when he allowed the accountants Coopers Lybrand to use a version of the song in a commercial.

Ballad Of Hollis Brown

In its attempt to raise sympathy for the plight of poor farm-workers, the wind-blown fatalism of 'Ballad Of Hollis Brown' represents perhaps the last gust of Woody Guthrie's direct influence on Dylan's songwriting. It's a vivid enough portrait of desperate rural poverty, with dark, looming portents in the images of dry wells, blackened grass, diseased horses and encroaching rats, but the intimations of pre-determined destiny in the final two verses' "seven breezes," "seven shots," "seven dead" and "seven new people born" undercut the song's impact as a social statement: is Dylan suggesting the farmer's awful plight was completely foredoomed in some way? And if so, doesn't that downgrade the tragedy?

The song is one of the least effective of Dylan's protest vignettes, not least for its weakness regarding causation: though the South Dakota farmer may have had a run of bad luck, it's ultimately hard to feel that much sympathy for someone reckless enough to have five children—one, we learn, a baby—which he clearly cannot support. In the end, Hollis Brown appears not just dirt-poor and tragic, but stupid, feckless (in letting his farm deteriorate in such a manner), ruthless and spiteful (in shooting his family, making them pay the price of his incompetence). As a heart-tugger on behalf of country folk, the song failed.

'Ballad Of Hollis Brown' did, however, come into its own later in Dylan's career, when it was one of the songs he performed at Live Aid, July 13, 1985, where he explained, "I thought that was a fitting song for this important social occasion... I'd just like to say that I hope that some of the money that's raised for the people in Africa, maybe they could take just a little bit of it—maybe one or two million maybe—and use it, say, to pay the mortgages on some of the farms, that the farmers owe to the banks." It was a typically contrary Dylan gesture, cutting through the event's overpowering air of smug self-satisfaction with a reminder that capitalism was quite happy to chew up its own heartland as well as the Third World.

With God On Our Side

This elegiac anti-war ballad was one of the most popular and widely-performed of Dylan's protest pieces in the early Sixties. Its mournful tune—taken from Irish writer Dominic Behan's rebel song 'The Patriot Game'—sounds like a funeral march for national integrity, which is effectively what the song comprises.

Adopting the persona of a nameless everyman from the American midwest, the narrator considers

> "Got no religion. Tried a bunch of different religions. The churches are divided. Can't make up their minds, and neither can I." **BOB DYLAN**

his country's military history, as he was taught in school—from the conquest of the native Indians, then the Mexicans and Confederates, on through two World Wars, up to the point where his country trembles on the brink of nuclear war with Russia—and realizes that on each occasion, the war-mongers have claimed they were fighting on God's behalf. The song concludes with him hoping that if God is indeed on our side, he'll stop the next war. It's an elegant, neatly-turned piece, complete with a sly, sardonic reference to how, despite the Holocaust, the forgiven Germans now have God (in the form of the US) on their side; but the penultimate verse, in which he wonders whether Judas Iscariot had God on his side too, disrupts the flow, a too-cute conceit which Dylan couldn't bring himself to leave out.

Dylan's attitude toward God—or at least, toward organized religion—has been ambivalent, to say the least. Only in his later career did he make overt statements of specific religious belief, and for many fans and observers they didn't gel too well with earlier statements on the subject, such as those in the interview he gave to Izzy Young of

Sing Out! magazine around the time he was recording his first album: "Got no religion. Tried a bunch of different religions. The churches are divided. Can't make up their minds, and neither can I. Never saw a god; can't say until I see one."

He has, however, always been keenly aware of biblical discourse as a useful storehouse of mythopoeic folk imagery, littering his songs with references to parables and prophets; and as he got involved with the civil rights movement, Dylan surely recognized the commitment of church leaders like Martin Luther King, and the strength King's followers drew from their faith. Indeed, many of his own songs from this period suggest his acknowledgment that protest anthems are, in effect, secular hymns, and his delivery frequently takes on a sermonizing cast.

Set against this understanding, however, was a deeply-rooted belief that God, in his role as publicity agent for the organized churches, was not on the side of the angels, but working for the system against the interests of the underdog. 'With God On Our Side' manages to articulate all these complex conflicts of interpretation, mocking the notion of a god that can be manipulated by politicians into justifying war, yet ultimately appealing to that same god to stop the next war. By comparison, the bullying fundamentalism of his later born-again Christian songs seems simplistic and small-minded, and more than a little mean-spirited.

One Too Many Mornings

This calm, reflective mood piece is clearly indicative of Dylan's increasingly problematic relationship with Suze Rotolo. There's a melancholy recognition that the protagonists are drifting slowly but irrevocably apart, and that it's Dylan's fault, just as much as Suze's—"You're right from your side, I'm right from mine."

While Suze had been away in Italy, Bob had used her absence as a creative spur, letting his

▲

**MARTIN LUTHER KING
HAS A DREAM,
AUGUST 28, 1963 AT THE
LINCOLN MEMORIAL,
WASHINGTON.**

muse feed off the emotional pain, while preserving her as an idealized memory. When she returned, it became apparent that they had both done a lot of growing-up in the intervening seven months, and, they slowly realized (Bob more reluctantly than Suze), a lot of growing apart, too. Bob had become something of a star, and Suze had become a more assertive young woman, but Bob still craved the attentions of the more supportive, "Bob-centric" girl who had left for Italy.

Though Suze moved back into the 4th Street apartment shortly after returning from Italy, the old magic had gone—friends reported that they didn't seem to talk as much and that they spent a lot of time just watching television. As the summer of 1963 wore on, with Dylan's star increasingly in the ascendant, the incessant rumors of a liaison

between him and Joan Baez took their toll on Suze. "What kind of rumors do you hear about Bobby and Joanie?" she asked Terri Van Ronk at the Newport Folk Festival that July. "The same kind of rumors you hear," replied her friend.

In September, Suze moved in to her sister Carla's East Village apartment, where Bob followed her, eventually moving in with the sisters—a situation which placed an intolerable burden on all three of them. A miserable Christmas with Suze's mother in New Jersey was followed by the embarrassment of a party at Carla's apartment during which Bob's outlandish friend Geno Foreman—son of the celebrated liberal activist Clark Foreman— burst in shouting, "Hey Bobby! Heard you're makin' it with Baez, man! She any good?" Bob's six-week road trip brought things to head: as the trip wound

45

on, he phoned Suze less and less, and when he got back to New York, he seemed meaner and more sarcastic than before. The final break-up came shortly after his return in March 1964, following a storming row at Carla's apartment (see entry for 'Ballad In Plain D').

'One Too Many Mornings' seems poised on the cusp of self-knowledge, a moment of contemplative stillness in the eye of an emotional hurricane. Some fans of Dylan's protest anthems found the song's introspective tone and personal subject-matter a betrayal of the "finger-pointing" principles underlying nearly all the rest of the album's songs. It is, however, more of a break-through than a betrayal, marking one of the earliest realizations in his work that simple black and white answers may not be applicable to more complex emotional issues.

North Country Blues

For the second time in the space of five tracks, listeners are invited to "Come gather round" the storyteller—a miner's wife in this instance—as she relates her mournful ballad of hard times in the iron-ore mining district of Minnesota.

As with so many of Dylan's protest songs, there is a resonance that goes beyond the imme-diate situation, returning to haunt subsequent similar events. Here the narrator, having already

"He'd come back and say 'Dad, these people haven't got any money'. And I'd say, 'some of those people out there make just as much money as I do, Bobby..." **ABE ZIMMERMAN**

lost a brother and father to mining disasters, suffers again when the mine is closed: her husband turns to drink and eventually disappears, leaving her alone to bring up their three children. In

the recession years of the late Eighties and early Nineties, particularly as the North American Free Trade Agreement (NAFTA) began to bite, the succinct seventh-verse explanation of free-trade economics—basically, that there's always some poor foreigner who can undercut your labor wage—took on a starkly premonitory tone, suggesting that the ravages of capitalism are both cyclical and inescapable.

The song is undoubtedly one of the more personal of Dylan's protest offerings, set as it is on the Iron Ranges where he lived as a child, among the endless acreage of spoil tips and strip-mines that made up the Eastern Mesabi Range. The town of Hibbing, where he grew up, started off in the 1890s as an iron-ore version of one of the Klondike gold-rush boom-towns of California. Following a slump in the early years of this century, John D. Rockefeller was able to buy up the entire range cheap and sell it on at a huge profit to US Steel, who pillaged the earth at an unprecedented rate, supplying a quarter of America's iron from vast open-cast mines. One such mine, the Hull-Rust Pit, measured almost four miles long and one mile across by the time young Robert Zimmerman was around to peer into it. More earth was dug from this hole, it's said, than was excavated for the entire Panama Canal.

By the early 1950s, most of the ore had been mined, and the area slipped into another localized depression. Dylan himself didn't come from a poor mining family —as he explains in the second of the "11 Outlined Epitaphs" which comprise the album's liner-notes, "my parents were not rich...an' my parents were not poor"—but it was impossible not to notice the effect of the mining slump in this "dyin' town." Bob's dad, Abe, ran a store, Zimmerman's Furniture & Electric, selling appliances and furniture to the town's 18,000 inhabitants. As soon as Bob was old enough, Abe would make him go out collecting hire-purchase payments in the poorer sections of town, even though he knew his customers wouldn't be able to pay. "I just wanted to show him another side of life," explained Abe. "He'd come back and say, 'Dad, these people haven't got any money.' And I'd say, 'Some of those people out there make just as much money as I do, Bobby. They just don't know how to manage it.' '

"Bob hated it most of all when he had to repossess stuff from people who couldn't pay," recalled his first girlfriend, Echo Helstrom. "I think that's where he started feeling sorry for poor people." Certainly, it's easy to imagine how the combination of, on the one hand, the heart-breaking poverty of redundant miners' families, and on the other, the huge gaping holes left by the earth-raping multinational mining companies, might have stirred the first sore flutterings of a sense of injustice in the young Bob Dylan's heart: these faceless corporations simply tore holes in every-thing, the human spirit just as easily as the ground. Hardly surprising, then, that he did exactly as the miner's wife advises in the song, barely waiting till he was grown before he fled the town, there being nothing left there to hold him.

Only A Pawn In Their Game

The National Association for the Advancement of Colored People (NAACP)'s chief organizer in Mississippi, Medgar Evers, was murdered in his front yard in June 1963, possibly an enraged racist's response to the enrollment of two black students at the University of Alabama (where Governor George Wallace made a token attempt at obstructing their entry to the premises) earlier that day.

▲ BEFORE HIS MURDER, ACTIVIST MEDGAR EVERS (CENTER) AND COLLEAGUE ROY WILKINS ARE ARRESTED WHILST PICKETING THE JACKSON, MISSISSIPPI BRANCH OF WOOLWORTHS.

47

Ironically, as Evers was being shot that evening, President John F. Kennedy was celebrating the successful demolition of another bastion of segregation in a televised speech which claimed, "This is one country; it has become one country because all of us and all of the people who came here had an equal chance to develop their talents. We cannot say to ten percent of the population that...the only way they are going to get their rights is to go into the streets and demonstrate." He was, of course, wrong: further racist outrages stained that year, culminating in the murder of four young girls at worship when Birmingham, Alabama's 16th Avenue Baptist Church was bombed at the end of the summer.

Evers' death baffled and infuriated Kennedy, who had tried to compromise with the segregationists. He admitted to Arthur Schlesinger, "I don't understand the South...when I see this sort of thing, I begin to wonder how else you can treat them." To show solidarity, Kennedy had his brother, Attorney General Robert F. Kennedy, attended Evers' funeral, and he invited Evers' family to the White House; his policy of appeasement, meanwhile, was consigned to the garbage, as he sought to impose desegregation on the South.

Protest singers were quick to respond to the murder, in drearily didactic songs like Phil Ochs' 'The Ballad Of Medgar Evers', a typically quotidian account of Evers' life and death which did little to rouse spirits, rally energies or inspire thought. 'Only A Pawn In Their Game', which Dylan first performed at a voter-registration rally in Greenwood, Mississippi, on July 6, 1963 (captured in footage included in D.A. Pennebaker's film *Don't Look Back*), was a more telling, elegant work, establishing Evers' death in the very first line and then, rather than just condemning the killer, considering the underlying causes—institutionalized poverty, the divide-and-conquer policies of demagogic Southern politicians —which had led a pathetic white man to commit such a cowardly act.

This method, of moving from the detail to the larger picture, was one that Dylan had recently used in another song, 'Who Killed Davey Moore?', debuted in April 1963 but never recorded. Both works take specific events as the central core of songs which quickly spin out to more generalized conclusions, the first implicating fight officials,

promoters and audiences in the death of boxer Davey Moore, and the second consigning Evers' killer to a marginal role as a tiny cog in the huge machine of institutionalized racism. While Evers was buried "as a king," Dylan concludes, his killer's epitaph will state that he was "only a pawn in their game."

The song's intelligence and deft design set standards none of Dylan's contemporaries could match, marking him out as not simply a journalistic protest singer, but a political philosopher too. But, ironically, the increased depth at which Dylan was starting to work, both technically and imaginatively, would soon lead him to a style of composition which effectively reversed this process of deriving general conclusions from particular events: in his later Sixties work, the turbulent, multifarious characteristics of an entire cultural *zeitgeist* would be boiled down into some of the most inscrutably personal songs ever written.

Boots Of Spanish Leather

Dylan himself has described 'Boots Of Spanish Leather' succinctly as "This is girl leaves boy," and that just about covers it, though not quite as tenderly and elegantly as the song itself. It's yet another song inspired directly by the absence of Suze Rotolo on her Italian trip, though here Dylan transposes the location to Spain in order to accommodate the punchline. A girl, about to depart for Spain, asks her lover what sort of gift he'd like her to send back to him; nothing, he answers, but her safe return. When, shortly after, she sends a letter from the ship telling him she may be gone for longer than planned, he realizes she doesn't feel for him as he does for her, and decides that, yes, she can send him something: a pair of boots —the suggestion being that even if she does return, he will likely have traveled on himself, rambling off down the road that figures in so many of his songs.

'Boots Of Spanish Leather' was written while Dylan was on a visit to Italy in the first week of

1963 with the black folk singer Odetta. Bob had hoped to meet with Suze in Italy, but his expectations were dashed when he learned that she had left for New York a few weeks earlier. Like another song he wrote in Italy, 'Girl From The North Country', the tune to 'Boots Of Spanish Leather' leans heavily on the traditional folk song 'Scarborough Fair', which he had recently learned from the English folk singer Martin Carthy.

When The ship Comes In

This was the earliest and most explicit example of the religious imagery that would continue in Dylan songs through the Eighties. Though 'With God On Our Side' mentions the deity, it is not built of religious images, the way that 'When The Ship Comes In' is.

The ship is the Ship Of God, or Noah's Ark—a vessel of salvation protecting its passengers from the storms which will wreak God's vengeance upon unbelievers and the wicked. The opening lines echo Revelations 7:1, where "no wind might blow on earth or sea or against any tree," though Dylan's Judgment Day contains the spookily surreal additions of laughing fishes and smiling seagulls.

It's a hymn of victory over the immoral and iniquitous, to lift hearts saddened by the roll-call of injustice that makes up most of *The Times They Are A-Changin'*. It's as close as folk protest gets to happy-clappy Christianity, with a vindictiveness to its self-righteous apocalyptism, particularly in the final verse, where the drowning of the foes is greeted with distasteful triumphalism. The bitter tone arises from the circumstances of the song's birth. According to Joan Baez, the pair arrived at a hotel where the desk clerk snubbed Bob, but when Joan went in to check, the staff responded, "Hello Miss Baez, we've been waiting for you." Bob poured his anger into the song. "He wrote it that night," she recalled to Anthony Scaduto, "took him exactly one evening to write it, he was so pissed...I couldn't believe it, to get back at those idiots so fast."

The Lonesome Death Of Hattie Carroll

William Zantzinger, a Maryland socialite and scion of a wealthy farming family, did indeed kill poor Hattie Carroll, a 51-year-old barmaid, at the Spinsters' Ball at the Emerson Hotel in Baltimore, early in the morning of Saturday February 8, 1963. Zantzinger hit the mother of 11 children around the head and shoulders with a cane when she was slow delivering a drink. "When I order a drink," he is reported as saying, "I want it now, you black bitch." She collapsed and was taken to Baltimore Mercy Hospital, where she died of a brain hemorrhage shortly after 9 o'clock that morning.

Zantzinger, who had tried to dispose of the cane by snapping it into several pieces, resisted arrest when policemen tried to charge him with assault, and was accordingly also charged with disorderly conduct and held overnight. Released on $600 bail, he was re-arrested and charged with homicide when police learned of Hattie Carroll's death—the first white man in Maryland ever to be accused of murdering a black woman. In June

▼

"WHO KILLED DAVEY MOORE?" ASKED DYLAN AFTER THIS FIGHT. THE BOXER IS SEEN HITTING THE ROPES AFTER BEING FATALLY STRUCK BY SUGAR RAMOS (RIGHT).

1963, three judges found Zantzinger guilty only of manslaughter and, adding insult to injury, in August he was sentenced to six months imprisonment.

The shameful inequity of such "justice" stung Dylan into a swift response and—either in Joan Baez's Carmel home (according to Baez) or in a 7th Street cafe in New York (according to Dylan's own annotations to the Biograph box set)—he composed this epic of deferred outrage, using a verse pattern based on Brecht's *The Black*

> "...the strange intensity of Bob Dylan's climbing up the meter of his song-poem as if he were on all fours, wailing at the world he never made but understood too well" **ANDREW SARRIS**

Freighter. As with 'Only A Pawn In Their Game' and 'Who Killed Davey Moore?', Dylan tries to broaden the issue to reflect upon a system that enables such an act to occur, rather than the act itself. Here, he does it by referring repeatedly to the violent act through three verses (the second and third compare the relative social positions of the two protagonists), ending each verse with a request that the liberal listener should save their tears, before revealing the injustice which truly merits those tears in a devastating final verse, with what the *Village Voice*'s Andrew Sarris splendidly described as "...the strange intensity of Bob Dylan's climbing up the meter of his song-poem as if he were on all-fours, wailing at the world he never made but understood too well."

The rhyme scheme shows how Dylan was maturing technically as a poet: apart from repeating "table" in three consecutive lines of the third verse to evoke the tedium of Hattie Carroll's servility, the only rhyming lines are the "fears" and "tears" of the chorus—until the last verse. This opens with the quasi-assonance of "gavel" and "level" to suggest subtly the imbalance in the scales of justice, and concludes with the sucker-punch of "repentance" and an understated "six-month sentence," which finally bursts the dam of tears. According to Phil Ochs, the song was one of Dylan's favorites.

Restless Farewell

The last of the album's songs to be recorded, 'Restless Farewell' bears out the message of the title-track, but not in a way most fans would have expected. A weary *mea culpa* fittingly set to a melody reminiscent of the traditional song 'The Parting Glass', it features Dylan effectively walking away from his past, apologizing to those he may have harmed, admitting his frustration at others' claims upon his time and muse, and fretting at the distorting-mirror effect of fame. In its apparent rejection of commitment, and its stress on personal over public values, it seems to go against all that the rest of the album stands for.

Two days after what he had thought was the final recording session for the new album, Dylan played an October 26, 1963 concert at Carnegie Hall, which demonstrated how far his fan-base had grown beyond the narrow confines of the folk audience, taking in a less sophisticated but equally enthusiastic teenage crowd. After the concert, he had been frightened by the intensity of the mob of screaming fans around the stage door, but he recovered his buoyancy at an after-show party held at the 96th Street apartment of Woody Guthrie's manager Harold Leventhal.

The very next day, however, his parade was rained upon by *Newsweek* magazine, which ran an exposé, by journalist Andrea Svedburg, of Dylan's middle-class Jewish roots. When a promised interview had not materialized, Svedburg had rooted around in Hibbing and Minneapolis and dug up the truth about his childhood. Faced with the prospect of his client's carefully-nurtured image being cracked, Albert Grossman relented and the interview finally went ahead. But not for long: Dylan quickly became riled and terminated the interview, and Svedburg went ahead and wrote a sharply iconoclastic profile, featuring the embarrassing juxtaposition of Dylan's claim to have lost contact with his parents with an account of how Abe and Beatty Zimmerman had, at Bob's expense, actually attended the Carnegie Hall concert to see their son perform.

In itself, that would not have been too damaging; indeed, a competent PR person could

50

easily have put a different spin on the story, to make it appear as though kindly Bob was simply trying to protect his family from the corrosive effect of fame (which was probably partly true anyway). But the article also included the rumor—since utterly disproven—about how Dylan had either stolen or bought his most famous song, 'Blowin' In The Wind', from a New Jersey high school student (see the entry for 'Blowin' In The Wind'). Understandably furious, Dylan raged at everyone around him, castigating his parents for talking to Svedburg, and Columbia press officer Billy James (to whom he would not speak for two years) for setting up the interview. He raged about journalists in general, who would henceforth be given as rough and unrevealing a ride as possible whenever he was forced to communicate with them. "Man, they're out to kill me," he complained bitterly. "What've they got against me?"

His immediate response, though, was to seek vengeance the only way he knew how: through words. He wrote the ninth of the album's "11 Outlined Epitaphs" liner-note poems, in which he ridicules magazines in general—"I do not care t' be made an oddball/bouncin' past reporters' pens"—and pointedly describes an interview exchange in which the inquisitor sinisterly

threatens unspecified rumor as punishment if he refuses to co-operate. He also wrote 'Restless Farewell', in which he set his face against the "false clock" trying to "tick out [his] time" and obscure his purpose with the "dirt of gossip" and the "dust of rumors"—a clear reference to the *Newsweek* article—as all the misgivings he was currently experiencing about the direction of his life, his work and his career brimmed over into a wistful *adieu* to his former friends and foes.

Five days after the Carnegie Hall concert, on October 31, 1963, another recording session was scheduled specifically to record 'Restless Farewell', which was added as the album's final track—probably at the expense of the vastly superior 'Lay Down Your Weary Tune', which had been recorded the previous week, and which shares its album-closing air of reflective resignation. (If so, it would not be the last time his judgment in such matters would prove fallible, as anyone who has heard his 'Blind Willie McTell' would attest.) Nevertheless, it provides a fitting epilogue to Dylan's protest period, even though he would continue to be viewed predominantly in that light for another year or two. There would be no "finger-pointing" songs on the next album, other than ones aimed at himself.

▲
BOB FONDLES HIS BASS
AT COLUMBIA'S NEW
YORK STUDIOS, 1965.

ALL I REALLY WANT TO DO

BLACK CROW BLUES

SPANISH HARLEM INCIDENT

CHIMES OF FREEDOM

I SHALL BE FREE NO.10

TO RAMONA

MOTORPSYCHO NITEMARE

MY BACK PAGES

I DON'T BELIEVE YOU
(SHE ACTS LIKE WE NEVER
HAVE MET)

BALLAD IN PLAIN D

IT AIN'T ME, BABE

Another side Of Bob Dylan

Dylan's words were coming home to roost, faster than he had anticipated. By the time *The Times They Are A-Changin'* was released in January 1964, he was already feeling estranged from his former self, and the people and events which had influenced him.

He was becoming increasingly convinced that the quick and easy answers demanded by the protest movement were not answers at all, merely slogans, and that the search for real answers lay within oneself. It was a search, moreover, which raised the possibility that what was needed was not actually answers, but a whole new set of questions. Simply by answering the old questions, he believed, one was already playing on somebody else's pitch. "Nobody in power," he told a friend, "has to worry about anybody from the outside...because he's not in it anyway, and he's not gonna make a dent. You can't go around criticizing something you're not a part of, and hope to make it better." Accordingly, one could either opt in and criticize, or opt out and keep one's counsel.

In the aftermath of the Kennedy assassination, Dylan had every reason to keep his own counsel. "If somebody *really* had something to say to help somebody out," he told friends, "well, obviously, they're gonna be done away with." Already scared by the impact of his own mounting fame, Dylan had now found the horrifying justification that rendered his paranoia more than just an egotistical indulgence, that brought the fear on to a very real plane indeed. He needed to get away, he told friends, needed to see more of the world. He had already taken refuge from the public pressures of New York City by spending more and more time at the Woodstock home of his manager Albert Grossman, but now he wanted to travel further afield. "I wanna get out and ramble around," he told Pete Karman, a journalist friend of Suze's. "Stop in bars and poolhalls and talk to real people. Talk to farmers, talk to miners. That's where it's at. That's real."

Accordingly, a cross-country road trip was set up for February, on which Dylan was accompanied in his new Ford station-wagon by Karman, folk singer Paul Clayton—the one from whom Bob had "borrowed" the melody for 'Don't Think Twice, It's All Right'—and his new road manager Victor Maimudes, who did the bulk of the driving.

Ostensibly underwritten as a promotional tour for Dylan's new album, the trip quickly turned into a drunken, drugged debauch, Bob's very own *On The Road* and *Bound For Glory* combined, as he was able to compare, first-hand, the virtues of Guthrie's ethical activism with the thrills of Kerouac's experientialism.

From New York, the gang headed to Hazard, Kentucky, where they delivered a stack of donated secondhand clothing to striking miners. They also picked up a package of marijuana that had been mailed ahead to the local post office, the first of several such deliveries; at a cafe, Dylan bought a spice-jar humorously labeled "marijuana," which, full of dope, was proudly displayed on the car's dashboard as they sped through the South. The next stop was Flat Rock, outside of Hendersonville, North Carolina, where they visited the poet Carl Sandburg. Though he was difficult to track down— the locals knew Sandburg primarily as a goat farmer, not a poet—they eventually made it to his farm, where Dylan gave him a copy of his new record and spent a short while trying to converse with Sandburg, poet-to-poet, before departing, apparently slightly peeved that the older poet had not heard of him.

Without the secondhand clothing taking up space, Dylan was able to move into the rear of the station-wagon, which he used as a study, pecking out lyrics on a portable typewriter. Punctuating the trip with occasional performances at places like Emory College, they eventually arrived in New Orleans in the middle of the Mardi Gras celebrations, into which they threw themselves with gusto. Dylan seemed determined to make gestures against the city's separatist social policies, visiting a black bar, Baby Green's—where the bartender, not needing trouble with the local police, threw them out—and incurring the wrath of sailors by sharing his bottle of wine with a black performer in the carnival procession. After two nights, they headed off for Denver, where Bob had a concert scheduled, by way of Dallas. As they pulled away from New Orleans, Dylan sat in the back, transforming the magic swirlin' ship of the carnival procession into 'Mr Tambourine Man'.

In Dallas, they wanted to see for themselves the site of Kennedy's assassination, and were shocked when, while asking for directions to

◄

BOB DYLAN: "THERE'S SO MANY SIDES TO HIM, HE'S ROUND," SAID A FRIEND.

Dealey Plaza, a local said, "You mean where they shot that sonofabitch Kennedy?" Continuing on to Denver, they stopped off to pay respects at Ludlow, Colorado, scene of a legendary labor massacre in 1914 when over 30 striking miners were shot by strike-breaking National Guardsmen. After the Denver gig, they headed across the Rockies, in a hurry to get to California. At one point, Victor gunned the station-wagon past a funeral cortege on a narrow mountain road, only to find a police car at the head of the procession; the resulting confrontation, which they survived by claiming to be a group "like The Kingston Trio" en route to a show, sobered them up quickly.

After the initial euphoria of the trip had worn off, however, the road took its toll on their nerves. By the time they hauled into the Bay Area for a show at the Berkeley Community Theater, a rift had developed between the non-doper Karman, who increasingly felt as if he was trapped with a trio of

► DYLAN FINDS HIS OLDEST FAN IN LONDON, 1965.

lunatics, and the others, who had grown tired of his nit-picking straightness and his habit of sneering at Bob's poetic imagery, which he thought was meaningless jive-talk. "I was beginning to feel crazy when they were crazy," he recalled later. "Victor, a freaky nut, and Dylan very weird, and Clayton always high on pills—I just had to break away from them." He was replaced for the final leg of the trip by Bob Neuwirth, an extrovert artist/musician who would become one of Dylan's closest confidantes over the next few years.

After the Berkeley show, the portable party moved on to Joan Baez's place in Carmel, then to Los Angeles, where Bob made a late February appearance on *The Steve Allen Show*. When he eventually got back to New York, relations between Bob and Suze deteriorated further until, following a furious row one night in March (see entry for 'Ballad In Plain D'), they finally broke up for keeps. Bob was devastated, but had plenty to occupy his time and thoughts: after a short April concert tour of the North-East, he flew to England in early May, where he played at London's Royal Festival Hall to a sellout audience that included the Beatles, the Stones and various other members of the new British pop aristocracy, before moving on, via Paris and Berlin, to the Greek village of Vernilya. During his brief holiday there, he wrote many of the songs he would record on *Another Side Of Bob Dylan*, boiling down his experiences of the last six to nine months into his most personal album yet, a mixture of reactions to his split from Suze and reflections upon his art and position, leavened with a few moments of sharp humor. "There ain't any finger-pointing songs in here," he told journalist Nat Hentoff as he was recording the album. "I don't want to write *for* people any more—you know, be a spokesman. From now on I want to write from inside of me..."

Another Side Of Bob Dylan was recorded in a single session on the evening of June 9, 1964, in order to be ready for the record company's fall sales conference. Attending the session, besides Dylan, Nat Hentoff and producer Tom Wilson, were a handful of Bob's buddies, including Ramblin' Jack Elliott, with whom he recorded an (unused) early version of 'Mr Tambourine Man'. Working his way steadily through a couple of bottles of Beaujolais, Dylan got seven songs down between

"I don't want to write for people anymore — you know be a spokesman. From now on I want to write from inside of me" **BOB DYLAN**

▲

CARNIVAL TIME IN NEW
ORLEANS, WHERE DYLAN
ATTENDED THE MARDI
GRAS FESTIVAL IN 1964.

7.30 and 10.30, and had completed the album by 1.30 in the morning, finishing up with the song most indicative of his new mood, 'My Back Pages'.

Wilson, who had tried to drum some microphone technique into Bob—to get him to stop moving around so much—knew that he had to capture as much as he could as early as he could, and was reluctant to press Dylan beyond three takes of any song. Though he had not known exactly what Bob was going to record that evening, Wilson was aware of the changes that were occurring in Dylan's writing. "Those early albums gave people the wrong idea," he told Hentoff. "Basically, he's in the tradition of all lasting folk music...he's not a singer of protest so much as he is a singer of *concern* about people." And the people concerned here, the songs suggested, were rather closer to home than on his previous releases. "The songs are insanely honest," Dylan later admitted, "not meanin' to twist any head, and written only for the reason that I myself, me alone, wanted and needed to write them. I've conceded the fact that there is no understanding of anything—at best, just winks of the eye—and that is all I'm looking for now, I guess."

The album title, much against Bob's better judgment, was Wilson's idea. Dylan felt it was over-stating the obvious, placing too great an emphasis on its implied negation of the ideals of his protest songs. That is certainly how a lot of his old supporters felt when the album was released early in August, a mere seven months after *The Times They Are A-Changin'*. Irwin Silber, editor of *Sing Out!* magazine, was moved to write an open letter to Bob in the magazine, in which he denigrated Dylan's new songs as "all inner-directed now, inner-probing, self-conscious—maybe even a little maudlin or a little cruel on occasion." All, of course, completely true: but what Silber failed to realize was that, years before the notion became common currency, Dylan had effectively made the personal political, too.

All I Really Want To Do

'A ll I Really Want To Do' opens the album on a light note, the most overt suggestion that there were to be no "finger-pointing" songs this time around: not only is the song about a personal relationship, rather than protesting a more political issue; it's also downright funny, from the hilariously busy rhyme scheme to the ludicrous falsetto yodel with which Dylan transforms the final word of the title in each chorus. This last effect may have started as a light-hearted parody of Jimmie "Singing Brakeman" Rodgers, a favorite of Bob's, and taken

" The songs are insanely honest, not meanin' to twist any head, and written only for the reason that I myself, me alone wanted and needed to write them" **BOB DYLAN**

on a more flamboyant life of its own as the session progressed and the bottles got emptier.

Compared with most of the other songs on the album that were inspired by the break-up with Suze Rotolo, this is a relatively generous expression of Dylan's mood, as he tries to convince his girl that there are no ulterior motives to his desire, that he has no intention of attempting to alter or confine her. Yet even as he gives these fulsome assurances, the sheer clutter of disavowed intentions in each verse suggests the over-bearing, domineering side of Dylan which Suze found so restricting. It's almost as if he's trying to pre-empt her complaints, rattling off up to nine examples in each verse of things he knows she might object to, before she can voice those objections. Ultimately, the song denies itself.

Nevertheless, the following year 'All I Really Want To Do' would furnish a sleek, albeit less successful, follow-up to The Byrds' 'Mr Tambourine Man', and the same year provided a winsome enough start to Cher's solo career.

Black Crow Blues

T his moody, stalking blues represents the first time that Dylan played piano on one of his records—quite a surprise for those who considered him a guitar troubadour, pure and simple. Performing on an old upright piano, Dylan's technique is shaky in places, particularly in the third verse, as he offers a simplified version of the stride piano style of such boogie giants as Cow Cow Davenport and Meade "Lux" Lewis. What makes the track all the more unusual are the punctuating stabs of harmonica which he inserts into the second and third verses and between the penultimate and final verses, stressing the already heavily-accented syncopation.

It seems second nature now, but up until this point his audience had regarded Dylan's use of "blues" as referring more to his lyric modes than actually to the music, and this sudden outbreak of R&B rhythms in the folk arena came as a great shock in 1964, providing dyed-in-the-wool folkies and committed protesters alike with further misgivings to set alongside their more general complaints about Dylan's new direction. Lyrically, it's the most basic of responses to his emotional situation following the split with Suze, the first verse's reference to a "long-lost lover" he wishes would tell him "what it's all about" being followed in subsequent verses by further non-specific expressions of his resultant distraction.

Spanish Harlem Incident

T he shortest song on the record, 'Spanish Harlem Incident' offers a slight counterbalance to the album's generally bitter tone as regards love. Where songs like 'It Ain't Me Babe', 'All I Really Want To Do' and 'To Ramona' find Dylan struggling with women whose responses and demands are fatally mediated by modern neuroses and external pressures, here he is exultant, completely fulfilled, swept off his feet by the "wildcat charms" of an earthier, more primal female force who, the imagery suggests, responds with physical immediacy and a welcome absence of psychological debate.

After singing the song at the recording session, he asked a friend if he understood it. The friend nodded enthusiastically, whereupon Dylan responded with a laugh, "Well, I didn't!" It doesn't look as though the song became any clearer for him, either: in the version published in *Lyrics 1962–1985*, the penultimate lines of the second and last verses are mysteriously altered from those sung, the turbulent (and clearly superior) "I'm nearly drowning" and "where you surround me" replaced by the more prosaic "I got to know, babe" and "will I be touching you"—surely a mistake?

◄

DYLAN AT THE PIANO DURING THE BRINGING IT ALL BACK HOME SESSIONS.

Chimes Of Freedom

Marking a pivotal moment in Dylan's songwriting, 'Chimes Of Freedom' is the song which first signals his move away from straight protest songs to more allusive "chains of flashing images." It's his own *Tempest*, a compelling account of a visionary epiphany experienced during an electric storm, rendered in a hyper-vivid poetic style heavily influenced by the French Symbolist poet Arthur Rimbaud. As Dylan and his companion dive into a doorway to avoid the thunderous downpour, a church bell begins tolling, and the synaesthetic combination of these two elemental forces—the sound and the fury—inspires in him a vision of universal redemption.

The song is Dylan's Sermon On The Mount: having spent the last couple of years supporting this or that specific cause, his chimes of freedom here toll for all of life's downtrodden and unjustly treated folk—unmarried mothers, refugees, outcasts, the disabled, conscientious objectors, the unfairly jailed and "For the countless

▶

19TH CENTURY FRENCH SYMBOLIST POET ARTHUR RIMBAUD, ONE OF THE GREATEST INFLUENCES ON DYLAN'S MID-SIXTIES LYRIC STYLE.

> *"For the countless confused, accused, misused, strung-out ones and worse. And for every hung-up person in the whole wide Universe"* **BOB DYLAN**

confused, accused, misused, strung-out ones and worse/And for every hung-up person in the whole wide Universe." It's a veritable army of underdogs and peaceniks in uplifting collusion, an anthem as generous and inclusive as 'The Times They Are A-Changin' ' was divisive and exclusive.

'Chimes Of Freedom' was written during the cross-country road trip of February 1964. Another song begun on that same trip was 'Mr Tambourine Man', a version of which was also recorded (though not used) at the *Another Side...* session, with Ramblin' Jack Elliott adding backing vocals on the choruses; it's not difficult to see, in both songs, vivid echoes of the Mardi Gras festival which Dylan and his pals had entered into with such drunken gusto a few days before, transmuted into images of dynamic salvation through a process analogous to the prolonged disordering of the senses which Rimbaud recommended as the means whereby a poet might become a seer.

From this point on, social reality would not be carved up into strictly black and white issues in Dylan's songs, but transformed by a razor-sharp satirical surrealism into a parallel universe in which the underlying forces were more subtly revealed.

I Shall Be Free No. 10

Amid the unremitting doom and gloom of *The Times They Are A-Changin'*, Dylan presumably felt it might be prudent to lighten things up with a comedy number after the *sturm und drang* of 'Chimes Of Freedom', especially since the main creative spur for this new album—his break-up with Suze—left a melancholy, rather bitter edge to several of the remaining songs.

Accordingly, 'I Shall Be Free No. 10' is pure play, a burst of intellectual hillbilly humor whose light sparring with conservative values echoes the fancy footwork of Cassius Clay—who finds his own poetic efforts satirized in the second verse. The humorous punchline status accorded to contemporary bogeymen like the Russians and hawkish right-winger Senator Barry Goldwater demonstrates how determined Dylan was to change the way he was expected to deal with such subjects. Derision, he's suggesting, has just as much a place in his work as debate and declamation.

Dylan had some trouble recording the song, stumbling over some of the later verses. He wanted to leave it for a while and record something else, but Tom Wilson insisted he finish it, suggesting Dylan simply record an insert of the last section—less common practice then than now, but no great problem. To Wilson's annoyance, one of Dylan's friends in the control-room advised him to let Bob start again from the beginning, on the grounds that "you don't start telling a story with Chapter Eight." "Oh man," said Wilson, "what kind of philosophy is that? We're recording, not writing a biography." Dylan did the insert, as requested.

In Dylan's collected *Lyrics 1962-1985*, 'I Shall Be Free No. 10' is printed in pale gray text, a format used mainly for liner-notes and additional prose poems—suggesting perhaps that the author wouldn't try to defend it as a sterling example of the songwriter's art. Even the original 'I Shall Be Free' from *Freewheelin'* is given full black text, though this comic doggerel is no less deserving of it.

To Ramona

'To Ramona' is part of the extended canon of Dylan songs—including 'Don't Think Twice, It's All Right' and 'It's All Over Now, Baby Blue'—in which departure or severance accompanies some momentous sea-change in the narrator's attitude. It's fundamentally a break-up song in which the singer reluctantly takes his leave of a girl ensnared by the phoney aims and pointless opinions of her acquaintances, the "worthless foam" pumped out by "fixtures, forces and friends." Though not quite

"Basically, he's in the tradition of lasting folk music...he's not a singer of protest so much as he is a singer of concern about people" **TOM WILSON**

as blunt as 'Ballad In Plain D', it deals fairly directly with the basic issues behind Bob and Suze's split, softened by the wistful lilt of the melody and reaching a moving resolution in which he comes to accept the inevitability of the change, while refusing to shut the door completely on any future possibility of reunion.

It's by far the most elegant of the many songs on the album that were inspired by the split, and it offers, by extension, an insight into Dylan's changing attitude toward his old finger-pointing, protesting self. The key lines are those in which he equates the eponymous Ramona's belief that she is "...better 'n no one/And no-one is better than you" with having "...nothing to win, and nothing to lose," a characterless position of stagnant ambition and minimal risk quite at odds with his own recent lifestyle. Always convinced that he was a special talent (and encouraged to think that way by a manager who deliberately fostered the Dylan "mystique"), Dylan was starting to consider more deeply those notions of "equality" and "freedom" he had recently espoused with such assurance, a subject to which he returned in 'My Back Pages'.

Motorpsycho Nitemare

Another slice of nonsense to sweeten the record's predominantly bitter tang, 'Motorpsycho Nitemare' takes the talkin' blues form which Dylan learned from Woody Guthrie into areas his one-time idol might not recognize—although he'd doubtless appreciate the humor. The main difference is that, in his day, Guthrie would have made up the song, performed it a time or two, then forgotten it, while Dylan has to live alongside his for posterity. The forerunner of 'Bob Dylan's 115th Dream' on *Bringing It All Back Home*, 'Motorpsycho Nitemare' is an absurdist development of the old joke about the traveling salesman, the farmer and the farmer's daughter, filtered through a sensibility informed in roughly equal parts by leftist sympathies, movies and jive-talk—a perfectly-gauged summation, in other words, of his collegiate audience's interests.

In Dylan's version of the joke, the farmer's daughter, Rita, a pulchritudinous sort who "looked like she stepped out of *La Dolce Vita*," takes on the sinister character of Anthony Perkins in *Psycho*, necessitating the salesman—who's actually a doctor, born at the bottom of a wishing well (go figure!)—to make a pro-Castro statement in order to get out of milking the farmer's cows, as he'd promised. Or something like that. It could, at a stretch, be read as a broad satire on the antagonism between bohemian urban cool and reactionary rural conservatism, but why bother? The track's little more than a throwaway, a means of injecting some light-hearted pace into an otherwise more than usually lugubrious album. Dylan's laconic delivery here, however, offers the record's most marked change from the tone of earnest profundity which characterized *The Times They Are A-Changin'*, prefiguring the air of sardonic, offhand genius that would dominate his next few albums.

At the recording session, Dylan apparently experienced some problems reading his lyrics, and had to do several fresh starts. One of his friends in the control room advised Tom Wilson, "Man, dim the lights—he'll get more relaxed." Wilson declined the suggestion. "Atmosphere is not what we need," he explained, "legibility is what we need."

My Back Pages

The clearest statement of Dylan's changing attitude—and the single greatest justification of the album's title—'My Back Pages' is his *mea culpa*, an apology for the stridency of his earlier social prose-lytizing in which the paradoxical refrain "Ah, but I was so much older then, I'm younger than that now" attests to the rejuvenation of spirit the song-writer feels, having removed the blinkers of protest from his creative urges.

Within the song's six verses can be found sketched out the essential core of the debate which all left-wing activists inevitably have to confront, concerning the extent to which individual desires and aspirations must be curtailed in pursuit of a more universal social "good." The youthful certitude of his protest period, Dylan suggests, was indicative of an autocratic conser-vatism almost as detrimental to the progress of the human spirit as those forces it condemned; having abandoned it, he now felt younger, more open to the sheer variety of possibilities. It was only later, he realized, "that I'd become my enemy in the instant that I preach[ed]."

For Dylan, the nub of the matter is as much literary as political: though he would never totally abandon the tradition of social commentary (merely change his mode of address), the extent of his disaffection with the direct-address style

▼

WHAT AN ABSOLUTE SHOWER: ANTHONY PERKINS IN HITCH-COCK'S PSYCHO, 1961.

demanded by the protest-song movement can be gauged by the virulent, dramatic imagery with which he disdains his former self: the "half-wracked prejudice" he felt; the "corpse evangelists" of the left; the "mongrel dogs who teach"; and the "mutiny" his change of attitude entailed. "I'm not really a social critic," he said to a friend. "I knew where to put the song back then, I knew where the slot was, that's all. When I wrote those songs, they were written within a small circle of people. I took time out to write those things... stopped to write them consciously. The other stuff I was doing, resembling more what I'm writing today, they came from inside of me and I didn't have to stop to write them... I was me back then, and now I'm *me*. I can't ever be the me from back then, I can only be *me*, from today. And the me from today is involved in a bigger circle of people."

This seems a more honest explanation than the bravado with which he greeted Joan Baez's retrospective query about what he was thinking when he wrote his protest songs. "Hey, news can sell, right?" he claimed, cynically. "You know me. I knew people would buy that kind of shit, right? I was never into that stuff." Others have claimed that all along, Dylan's motives were driven more by ambition than empathy, that he was simply using the topical-song movement to achieve stardom.

Ignoring for the moment the obvious fact that, until Dylan transformed it, the topical-song movement was hardly a guaranteed route to success, this view of him does not match that held by friends like Phil Ochs, Dave Van Ronk and John Hammond, who later stressed, "When he first came here he was thinking and talking about injustice, and about social problems... He was uptight about the whole set-up in America, the alienation of kids from their parents, the false values." Ochs, a fervently political songwriter who frequently found himself on the receiving end of Bob's jibes, was generous enough to vouch for Dylan's integrity during that period: "He was just going on to bigger things when he started denying it, that's all." Ochs was right: for Dylan himself, 'My Back Pages' would be the *auto-da-fé* from which would rise, phoenix-like, the rejuvenated modern artist of the electric trilogy. "I used to think I was smart," he said around this time, "but I don't know any more. Don't even know if I'm normal."

I Don't Believe You
(She Acts Like We Never Have Met)

R eversing the usual sexual roles of the time, 'I Don't Believe You' finds a male lover bewildered by his one-night-stand's disavowal the morning after. It seems equally as likely to have been written about Joan Baez as about Suze Rotolo—though it could just as easily be about a literal one-night stand. Whichever it is, the theme of emotional bewilderment reflects the increasing complexity of his private life, as it trailed in the slipstream of his accelerating celebrity.

Dylan's phrasing, and the uptempo swirl of the strummed guitar, expertly evokes the heady abandon of momentary, drunken infatuation, but serves to render each verse's subsequent deflation less convincing. There's also a snort of tipsy laughter in verse three—one of the humanizing

> "Hey, news can sell right? You know me. I knew people would buy that kind of shit right? I was never into that stuff." **BOB DYLAN**

moments Dylan likes to leave in his songs—which, besides making him sing the wrong lines, also adds to the song's curiously chipper tone. It's as if, even as he sings, the bewilderment is being sloughed off, allowing him to conclude the song with one of his better deadpan jokes, responding to a query about whether it's easy to forget with a sardonic "It's easily done/You just pick anyone/And pretend that you never have met."

The song was written during Bob's summer 1964 stay in Vernilya, a village outside of Athens, Greece. It also provided him with a sharp riposte, caught for posterity on the legendary 1966 UK concert bootleg: as The Band counts into 'Like A Rolling Stone', Dylan responds to an outraged folkie's cry of "Judas!" with "I don't believe you—you're a liar!" This was a clear reference to the fickleness of his folk fans' affections, so flimsy they might be shocked by mere electricity.

61

Ballad In Plain D

The title is particularly apt: written and recorded at a time when Dylan was leaving behind his straight-shooting protest-song mode in favor of a more allusive lyric style featuring chains of resonant, surreal imagery, this is perhaps the plainest song from his mid-Sixties canon, and one of the least satisfying. For while he could wax lyrical about more abstract philosophical concerns, such as the state of society and the nature of freedom, the specifics of personal trauma proved less permeable to artistic interpretation, as demonstrated by this self-pitying, one-sided account of the final traumatic night of Dylan's long-standing romance with Suze Rotolo.

The only girl with whom he had experienced any sort of extended relationship, Suze was duly rewarded for her constancy by being pictured with Dylan on the front sleeve of *The Freewheelin' Bob Dylan*, although it was, annoyingly for him, a relationship on which Suze's older sister Carla and her mother Mary seemed to exert unwelcome influence. In Dylan's maudlin song, Suze is a clumsily idealized figure ("With the innocence of a lamb, she was gentle like a fawn"), the constant scapegoat of her family's jealousies, while Carla is viciously characterized as a pretentious, social-climbing parasite. Dylan was gaining a reputation

> "I used to think that I was smart, but I don't know anymore. Don't even know if I'm normal" **BOB DYLAN**

for waspish put-downs of friends and acquaintances, and it's possible that where most of his victims, not wishing to jeopardize their relationship with the rising star, were easily cowed, Carla may have been less ready to accept his acid tongue. He did, after all, live in her apartment. The showdown between Bob and Carla late in March 1964 is rendered here in a portentous, melodramatic

manner, full of heavy-handed, violent imagery.

The two of them had had a flaming row the previous summer at a record company sales conference in Puerto Rico, Bob blowing his top when Carla chafed at his rebellious rudeness. Ever since then, their relations had become so abrasive that Carla was made to feel a stranger in her own Avenue B home after Bob followed Suze there from the 4th Street apartment. The couple were bound by a sort of fatalistic Catch-22: Bob desperately craved Suze's attention and support, and Suze desperately wanted to be more than Bob would let her be. Increasingly, their time together became mired in sullen funks, with television replacing communication. At the conclusion of Dylan's previous romantic liaisons, he usually preferred to avoid outright confrontation, affecting disinterest until the relationship atrophied and the girl simply left him. Carla, however, was clearly not prepared to let her kid sister be treated this way, demanding resolution when the rumors about Dylan's perpetual on/off romance with Joan Baez grew too strong to ignore.

In February 1964, Dylan's stoned cross-country road trip was scheduled to end up in San Francisco, where Joan would be the "surprise" guest at his Berkeley concert —and, the Rotolos suspected, further insinuate herself into his affections. As the tour progressed, Bob's phone calls to Suze became more and more infrequent and she suspected the worst. The truth was probably that the hopped-up Dylan was on a creative roll, completely caught up in his work—it was on this trip that he wrote 'Mr Tambourine Man' and 'Chimes Of Freedom'—and he simply couldn't be bothered sustaining the bourgeois pretense of a stable relationship. Ironically, one of the poetic images that Pete Karman had, on the car journey, denigrated as meaningless jive-talk—"No-one's free, even the birds are chained to the sky"— found its eventual home in the last line of 'Ballad In Plain D'.

The affair between Suze and Bob finally came to a head in the last week of March 1964, with a major argument. Carla returned home to the apartment late one night to find Bob and Suze rowing loudly. She asked Dylan to leave, but otherwise decided not to get involved, retiring to bed. An hour later, she asked him to leave again, whereupon

Dylan turned on her, unleashing a vitriolic outburst. Angry and distracted, Suze threatened suicide, but fainted before she could cut her wrists. Carla tried to push Dylan out of the door and the two ended up brawling, before he eventually left at around four in the morning.

Though he attempted reconciliation later that day, his relationship with Suze was finally over, but its collapse stained several of the songs on *Another Side Of Bob Dylan*, where it was positioned between 'I Don't Believe You' and the concluding 'It Ain't Me Babe', two of his most cynical relationship songs. It remains the only song which Dylan regrets writing—though happily, Bob and Suze later became just friends.

"People have asked how I felt about those songs that were bitter, like 'Ballad In Plain D'," Suze later told Victoria Balfour. "I never felt hurt by them. I understood what he was doing. It was the end of something and we both were hurt and bitter... His art was his outlet, his exorcism. It was healthy. That was the way he wrote out his life...the loving songs, the cynical songs, the protest songs...they are all part of the way he saw his world and lived his life, period."

▲

It Ain't Me, Babe

'I t Ain't Me, Babe' was reportedly begun in outline form early in 1963 in Italy, while Dylan was on the European trip that would also see him playing a small role in the BBC drama *Madhouse On Castle Street*, though its tone suggests it may have been completed later.

It's yet another song inspired by Suze Rotolo, reflecting both the bitterness of Dylan's feelings in the immediate aftermath of their break-up, and a kind of damage-limitation exercise whereby he might salvage some of his wounded pride. A rebuttal of the notion of true love, it finds the song's narrator unable to fulfill his beloved's demands, unwilling to perform the roles of protector, healer, loyal lover and gallant gentleman with which society has saddled the male suitor. Its curt tone—"leave at your own chosen speed," "everything inside is made of stone"—stood in stark contrast to the gross sentimentality of the contemporary Tin Pan Alley-dominated pop song tradition, which, then as now, trafficked in the illusory bliss of love.

It's a sharply cynical piece of work—indeed, though essentially an admission of weakness on the singer's part, it thrusts blame on to the object of his disaffection, implying that her conservative demands are an imposition which could hold him back from some unspecified goal. Accordingly, some have viewed the song as an allegorical reflection of Dylan's relationship with his audience, against whose restrictive demands he was beginning to kick. Though lacking virtually all the necessary characteristics for mainstream pop success, in the immediate aftermath of The Byrds' hit with 'Mr Tambourine Man', it gave close-harmony pop group The Turtles their breakthrough hit in 1965.

Chapter five

SUBTERRANEAN HOMESICK BLUES

SHE BELONGS TO ME

MAGGIE'S FARM

LOVE MINUS ZERO/NO LIMIT

OUTLAW BLUES

ON THE ROAD AGAIN

BOB DYLAN'S 115TH DREAM

MR TAMBOURINE MAN

GATES OF EDEN

IT'S ALRIGHT, MA (I'M ONLY BLEEDING)

IT'S ALL OVER NOW, BABY BLUE

Bringing it all back home

ob Dylan's *annus mirabilis* was 1965, the year he would transform popular music with two extraordinary albums that brought a new wit and literacy to rock'n'roll, and an electric immediacy to poetry.

At the time, however, the presence of an amplified rock band on *Bringing It All Back Home* was widely viewed more as a defection from folk music than a breakthrough to an exciting new mode of expression. Eyebrows were raised and letters were written within a folk-singing community lulled into pessimism by the sort of dreary protest balladry that Bob had grown out of a couple of years before. Rather than acknowledge his ambition, they denounced him as a sell-out.

In one sense, they were right: *Bringing It All Back Home* would be Dylan's first million-seller, reaching the US Top Ten and going on to top the LP charts in Britain, where Bob-mania reached such a pitch that in May 1965 he would achieve the rare feat of having three albums in the Top Ten (the others being *The Freewheelin' Bob Dylan*, which also reached the top, and *The Times They Are A-Changin'*). But what old folkies saw as an abject surrender of commitment to commerce, Dylan viewed more in terms of his constituency, which suddenly expanded exponentially, and his own artistic needs, which were being satisfied more completely than before.

Others were able to view the situation from a more revealing perspective than the insular folk community. Through much of 1964/5, the photographer Daniel Kramer had the opportunity to spend time with Dylan, photographing him intermittently over the course of several months—mostly unposed stuff, but including both the recording sessions for Bob's next album, and its cover photo. As the months passed, he grew astonished at the changes in Dylan. "In just one year, not only his songs but his very appearance changed radically," Kramer noted. "He was new all the time."

Most of late 1964 was taken up with Dylan's Fall Tour—on which Joan Baez appeared frequently as a "surprise" guest—though his burgeoning celebrity increasingly brought him into contact with the era's glitterati. He attended a party for Robert Kennedy at Miles Davis's house; and in August, Bob and journalist Al Aronowitz introduced The Beatles to the enigmatic charm of marijuana while

▲

THE BEATLES IN AMERICA. DYLAN WAS IMPRESSED BY THEIR RADICAL APPROACH TO ROCK'N'ROLL.

◄

DYLAN IN ONE OF HIS LIGHTER MOODS, 1965.

the Fab Four were staying at New York's Delmonico Hotel. The group had had a profound influence on Dylan earlier that year, when they dominated the nation's airwaves during his cross-country trip. "They were doing things nobody was doing," he told biographer Anthony Scaduto later. "Their chords were outrageous, and their harmonies made it all valid. You could only do that with other musicians... I knew they were pointing the direction of where music had to go."

This conviction grew during the Fall Tour, as Bob grew increasingly bored with the cozy conventions of his acoustic shows. "Out front it was a sure thing," he explained in a summer 1965 interview with Nora Ephron and Susan Edmiston. "I knew what the audience was gonna do, how they would react. It was very automatic. Your mind just drifts unless you can find some way to get in there and remain totally there." To a friend, he admitted his dissatisfaction with what had become a routine: "I play these concerts and I ask myself, 'Would *you* come to see me tonight?'—and I'd have to truthfully say, 'No, I wouldn't come. I'd rather be doin' something else, really I would.' That something else is rock. That's where it's at for me. My words are pictures, and the rock's gonna help me flesh out the colors of the pictures."

The future, clearly, was electric. Bob had started to feel the tremors of a new rock approach in the Greenwich Village scene when he played (as "Bob Landy") on an album of blues covers by old

65

friends like Dave Van Ronk, Ric Von Schmidt and "Spider" John Koerner. Called *The Blues Project*, it featured an electric backing band which included Al Kooper, Danny Kalb and Steve Katz, who later took the album's title for their band name. And in June 1964, Dylan had been mightily impressed when he attended some sessions at which John Hammond Jr.—the bluesman son of the legendary Columbia A&R man—recorded his album *So Many Roads* with a backing band that included guitarist Mike Bloomfield of the Paul Butterfield Blues Band, and several members of a Canadian band, The Hawks, who had once backed rockabilly singer Ronnie Hawkins. The clincher, though, came in August, when the English R&B group The Animals—who had already had a hit in Britain with what was basically a souped-up version of 'Baby Let Me Follow You Down' from Bob's first album—topped the charts on both sides of the Atlantic with an electrified version of 'House Of The Rising Sun', too. If they could do it, why not Bob himself?

Tom Wilson felt much the same way, and without Dylan's knowledge, went into the studios that December to overdub rock backing on to three of Bob's old songs: 'Mixed Up Confusion', the unreleased 'Rocks And Gravel', and 'House Of The Rising Sun' itself. The results were not as successful as he had hoped, though he would later experience spectacular success when he employed the same approach to modernize Simon & Garfunkel's 'The Sound Of Silence', which kickstarted the duo's career after they had all but given up. (Simon only learned of his chart-topping success while on a solo tour of England.) But the sessions undoubtedly helped Wilson get some idea of the dynamics of rock-group recording, which were put to devastatingly effective use when Bob and a band of musicians cut *Bringing It All Back Home* over three days in mid-January 1965.

Dylan had retired to the relative seclusion of Woodstock to finish writing some new material a few weeks before the sessions, arriving with 18 songs ready to record. Some, though, had been longer in gestation: at his Halloween concert at New York's Philharmonic Hall on October 31, 1964, he gave standout performances of 'Mr Tambourine Man', 'Gates Of Eden' and 'It's Alright, Ma', three of the upcoming album's highlights.

These new songs were unlike anything he had

written before, packed with images which sparked back and forth between anti-authoritarian cynicism, existentialist immediacy and ribald satire, offering up a surrealist distorting mirror to modern life, American history and interpersonal relations. There were stories in some of them, but not the straightforward kind his fans were used to; these stories took absurd twists and turns, and seemed to mock the listener's desire for strict narrative continuity. And while it was obvious that 'Gates Of Eden' and 'It's Alright, Ma', in particular, were offering considered critiques of society, their "messages" seemed diffuse and poetic, rather than cut-and-dried. As one reviewer wrote of a 1965 Dylan concert: "Dylan used to sound like a lung cancer victim singing Woody Guthrie. Now he sounds like a Rolling Stone singing Immanuel Kant."

Dylan had devised a new mode of expression which took his primary poetic influences—the Symbolist poetry of Rimbaud and Villon, the folk vernacular of Woody Guthrie, the immediacy of beat writers like Ginsberg and Kerouac, the visionary awareness of William Blake, and the hipster slang of beat comics like Hugh ("Wavy Gravy") Romney and Lord Buckley—and lashed them to a driving rock beat. Even the songs which didn't feature the full rock backing seemed somehow informed by it, hovering over their

► **DYLAN'S FRIEND, BEAT POET ALLEN GINSBERG, AMERICA'S UNOFFICIAL POET LAUREATE.**

ostensible subjects like ghostly allusions to a more powerful presence. "I don't call myself a poet because I don't like the word," he told Nora Ephron and Susan Edmiston. "I'm a trapeze artist." And to Robert Shelton, he said, "What I write is much more concise now than before. It's not deceiving."

The first day of the recording sessions featured just Dylan with, on a couple of songs, John Sebastian on bass (later leader of The Lovin' Spoonful); none of these acoustic takes made it on to the album. The next two days, 14 and 15 January, he re-recorded several of the same tracks, plus the rest of the album, accompanied by a band that comprised Bobby Gregg on drums, Paul Griffin on piano, Bruce Langhorne and Kenny Rankin on guitars, and either Joseph Macho Jr. or William E. Lee on bass. Though Tom Wilson was the producer, the arrangements were very much down to Dylan, who passed from one musician to another, explaining what he wanted, sometimes demonstrating parts on the piano, until the pieces came together as he desired. "Dylan worked like a painter," reported Daniel Kramer, "covering a huge canvas with the colors that the different musicians could supply him, adding depth and dimension to the total work."

Most of the tracks needed only three or four takes, during which time the song might mutate slightly in terms of tempo or phrasing. Sometimes they got it first time out. Other times, things didn't go quite that smoothly. At one point, distracted by the "obstacle course" of microphone stands and bits of furniture that Wilson had secretly arranged around the microphone to try and keep him stationary while he was doing his vocals, Dylan blew up in mid-take, storming across the room with a chair, before acknowledging his momentary peevishness with a self-deprecatory smile. 'Outlaw Blues', an overnight re-write of the previous day's acoustic 'California', took some time to crystallize into its final form, but that was very much the exception. On the final day of the sessions, Dylan recorded 'Mr Tambourine Man', 'It's Alright, Ma' and 'Gates Of Eden' in one long take, without stopping to hear a playback between tracks. (Before he started, he instructed the engineers not to make any mistakes, because they were long numbers and he didn't want to do them more than once.)

With 'Subterranean Homesick Blues' put out as a trailer a few weeks before, *Bringing It All Back Home* was released in late March 1965, in a sleeve which indicated how far Dylan had moved on from the denim-clad troubadour of his early records, and hinted at the complexity of the new album's contents. With Daniel Kramer, Bob devised a cover photo featuring himself and an elegant brunette dressed in red (Albert Grossman's wife Sally) reclining, unsmiling, upon a

> "*Dylan worked like a painter, covering a huge canvas with the colors that the different musicians could supply him...*" **DANIEL KRAMER**

chaise-longue amid a clutter of bric-a-brac, magazines and long-playing records (by Lotte Lenya, The Impressions, Eric Von Schmidt and Robert Johnson) which Kramer arranged so as to have them "move" around Dylan. Bob's last album *Another Side Of Bob Dylan* is toward the back of the shot, almost in the fireplace.

Above the mantelpiece is a colored-glass collage of a clown face which Dylan had made for Bernard Paturel, the owner of Bernard's Cafe in Woodstock, where Bob played chess and frequently took refuge from the pressures of fame in an upstairs room which the Paturels kept vacant for him. The cute gray kitten Bob is cuddling is his pet, Rollin' Stone—though there is a pronounced feline grace about all three of the photo's subjects, who share a disquieting air of luxuriant sensuousness which might at any moment reveal its claws. On the rear sleeve, a spread of Kramer's photos depicting Dylan with artists such as Baez, Allen Ginsberg (in a top hat), Peter Yarrow (of Peter, Paul & Mary) and filmmaker Barbara Rubin (giving Bob a head-massage) hint at the growing hubbub surrounding the singer, while the discursive sleeve-note features his musings upon life, poetry and song in a chunk of beat-styled prose indicative of the book he was working on, which would be published some years later as *Tarantula*. It all made for a package of great mystique and sophistication, a giant step beyond anything which the pop world had encountered before.

Subterranean Homesick Blues

As the earliest example of his new electric sound, 'Subterranean Homesick Blues' marks a pivotal moment in Dylan's career. Together with the accompanying extract from D.A. Pennebaker's documentary film *Don't Look Back*, which served as one of the first (and still the best) pop promo clips, its effect was seismic, gaining Dylan his first American Top 40 entry and his second UK Top-Ten hit (hot on the heels of 'The Times They Are A-Changin' ', which had belatedly stormed up the charts in March 1965), and securing his reputation as the hottest cat on two continents.

Stylistically, the song is a three-way cross between Chuck Berry, Jack Kerouac and a Woody Guthrie/Pete Seeger song called 'Taking It Easy', whose repetitive structure ("Mom was in the kitchen, preparing to eat, Sis was in the pantry

► **FILM POSTER FOR PENNEBAKER'S CLASSIC DYLAN DOCUMENTARY, DON'T LOOK BACK.**

"So we dropped an acid on Bob...If you ask me that was the beginning of the mystical sixties right there." **PAUL ROTHCHILD**

looking for some yeast...") Dylan parodies both here and in the next album's 'Tombstone Blues'. Injected with R&B energy, the machine-gun patter of words tumbling after each other takes as its closest precedent the rock'n'roll poetry of Chuck Berry, in particular 'Too Much Monkey Business'— though it's perhaps the eponymous hero of 'Johnny B. Goode' whose hopped-up, streetwise doppelganger we find "mixing up the medicine" at the beginning of 'Subterranean Homesick Blues'. Subsequent references to drug busts and police surveillance, and the generally paranoiac tone of the song, suggest that our Johnny is a drug chemist, synthesizing his wares in the basement.

Dylan was by this time no stranger to drugs. Pot-smoking had been commonplace on the folk scene long before his arrival in Greenwich Village, and was an essential element of that February's cross-country trip. According to producer Paul Rothchild, he and Victor Maimudes had themselves introduced Dylan to LSD a few months earlier, following a Spring 1964 concert at the University of Massachusetts in Amherst. "I looked at the sugar cubes and thought, 'Why not?' " Rothchild told Bob Spitz. "So we dropped acid on Bob. Actually, it was an easy night for Dylan. Everybody had a lot of fun. If you ask me, that was the beginning of the mystical Sixties right there."

It was certainly the beginning of a new phase of Dylan's career, although, despite his "pro-chemistry" outlook, he later denied that drugs had that much of an influence on his songwriting, but had simply served to heighten his "awareness of the minute." Rather than write sermons for tomorrow, he chose to focus on the present, a choice which manifested itself in a restless search for kicks and a refusal to try and shoehorn experience into tidy moral platitudes.

Not that he had completely abandoned protest. Far from it: 'Subterranean Homesick Blues' remains the most concise compendium of anti-establishment attitude Dylan ever composed, just over two minutes crammed with beat cynicism and drug paranoia, in which virtually every couplet can be abstracted as a slogan. (Most have been.) Indeed, so powerful was its effect that a group of militant underground activists, the Weathermen, chose their name from one such slogan, "You don't need a weatherman to know which way the wind blows." What was different from his earlier message-song style was the cynical, streetwise nihilism of the song, whose third and fourth verses condense a generation's disquiet with the American Dream lifestyle into a few succinct phrases, while offering only the most nugatory, absurd advice on how to deal with it. There was no specific victim in the song, and no message other than the recurrent "Look out kid" to warn of society's manifold traps and dead-end diversions.

For Joan Baez, this was a step in the wrong direction, as too was what she viewed as his negative, "death-trip" lifestyle at the time. "He criticizes society and I criticize it," she explained to Robert

Shelton, "but he ends up saying there is not a goddamned thing you can do about it, so screw it. And I say just the opposite. I am afraid the message that comes through from Dylan in 1965 and 1966 is: 'Let's all go home and smoke pot, because there's nothing else to do...we might as well go down smoking.' " But what Baez viewed as defeatist actually proved inspirational for a much wider audience than the one to which she and Dylan had previously been preaching: faced with the apparent absurdity of modern life and its institutions, an entire generation recognized the zeitgeist in the verbal whirlwind of 'Subterranean Homesick Blues'.

The track made a fitting opening to *Don't Look Back*, in a classic sequence where Dylan, standing in an alleyway alongside London's Savoy Hotel, drops cards bearing words and phrases from the song, trying to keep pace as the declamatory deluge pours forth. (The cards had been marked up the previous evening, by Dylan, Donovan— who crashed on the floor of Bob's suite for a few nights during his stay—Allen Ginsberg and Bob Neuwirth. At the song's conclusion, the latter pair stroll across the alley, following Dylan out of the frame.)

Written at the apartment of John Court, an associate of Albert Grossman's, 'Subterranean Homesick Blues' was recorded on January 14, 1965, after Dylan had done a solo acoustic run-through the day before. Though he was working with a band for the first time, he seems remark-

ably at ease—indeed, compared with the nagging, monotonous delivery of the previous day, when Dylan (like so many since) experienced some difficulty making all the lines scan, he sounds audibly freed up by the band, effortlessly riding the R&B bounce of Bobby Gregg's drums while Kenny Rankin pierces the song's fabric with little exclamation-mark stabs of electric guitar. Amazingly, it was done in one take.

She Belongs To Me

The two love songs on *Bringing It All Back Home* are decidedly different in character from Dylan's earlier romantic compositions. Just as the wistful longing of early songs like 'Girl From The North Country' had been replaced by the bitter recrimination and melancholy of 'It Ain't Me Babe' and 'To Ramona' on *Another Side Of Bob Dylan*, so that is in turn supplanted here by an ambivalent tribute that veers between acquiescent devotion and subliminally mild contempt, the latter cunningly concealed by the gentleness of Dylan's delivery and the sensitivity of the backing. The key to the song is the bluntly possessive title, which runs so counter to Dylan's anti-materialist attitude that it can only be intended ironically, suggesting that the song's apparent affection should likewise be taken with a pinch of salt.

The references in 'She Belongs To Me' to the subject's status as an artist and her ownership of an Egyptian ring suggest that it was written for

"I'm scared, I think what it means is that you'll be the rock 'n' roll king, and I'll be the peace queen" **JOAN BAEZ**

Joan Baez, to whom Bob had once given just such a ring. The song pays due tribute to her self-assertiveness and unbreakable moral conviction ("She never stumbles/She's got no place to fall"), but characterizes her interest in the narrator as that of a dilettante art collector whose gaze effectively transforms the object of her affections into an antique—presumably a reference to Baez's patronage of Dylan, her desire to keep him as her pet protest singer, rather than let him develop according to his own desires. Even the apparently obsequious devotion of the final verse masks a condemnation of a lover whose obsessive demands for compliments and attention have fatally wearied the relationship.

Bob and Joan's relationship had been eroding for the past year, but as with the earlier situation between Bob and Suze, he had not been able to call it quits. Instead, he allowed the relationship to deteriorate slowly, until she could stand no more and was forced to break things off. Joan had had misgivings for some time about the divergent direction their careers appeared to be taking, which were crystallized when he suggested to her that they play at Madison Square Garden. "I'm scared," she told him. "I think what it means is that you'll be the rock'n'roll king, and I'll be the peace queen." Dylan scoffed at her fear, but she was right: while her sense of liberal concern expanded to accommodate the diverse needs of her audience, he had come to the realization that to accept responsibility for "those kids" would stifle his muse, that he would become a walking antique unless he cast off all responsibilities except for those he had for his art.

Baez dates the watershed point of their relationship to a bi-coastal telephone conversation they had in 1964 during which, while they were joking about getting married, she had demurred, saying it would never work out. From that point, she claims, Dylan's attitude toward her changed, eventually coming to a head on the 1965 tour of England covered in *Don't Look Back*. She had accepted his invitation to accompany him to Europe, believing it would be a reciprocation of her American shows, at which she had introduced him to her audience. But Dylan never invited her up on stage with him, leaving her forlornly in the wings as he basked in adulation. In the film, the distance between the two of them is plain to see in the hotel-room scenes where Joan vainly serenades Bob while he, oblivious, continues working on his book.

Worse still, the vicious banter that Dylan and Bob Neuwirth dealt in was increasingly aimed in her direction. In one of the film's cruelest scenes, after the three of them have traded Hank Williams songs in a backstage dressing-room, she admits to feeling tired. "I'm fagging out," she explains. "Let me tell you, sister," ripostes Neuwirth, quick as a flash, "you fagged out a long time ago!" Then, stepping further over the mark of propriety, he says to Dylan, "Hey, she's got one of those see-through blouses that you don't even wanna!" Unable to keep up with such insults, Joan flounces out of the room. Shortly afterward, things came to a head between Joan and Bob and, distraught, she left the tour and flew on to her parents' place in Paris.

Maggie's Farm

At the final day of the *Bringing It All Back Home* recording sessions, according to photographer Daniel Kramer, Bob and his musicians were elated when they managed to kick off proceedings with a storming version of 'Maggie's Farm'. This, combined with the simplicity of its blues structure, may explain why Dylan chose the song to open his ill-fated performance with the Butterfield Blues Band at the 1965 Newport Folk Festival.

'Maggie's Farm' was probably inspired by 'Penny's Farm', a song from Pete Seeger's first album which criticized the meanness of a landlord, George Penny. In Dylan's song, the criticism is less specific and, crucially, less earnest: the eponymous farm has expanded to take in the entire country's system of labor relations, which are ridiculed through the three-fold impact of the song's imagery, Dylan's bitingly sardonic delivery, and the rebellious ebullience of the backing.

The song is virtually a shorthand précis of the Marxist analysis of the alienating condition of capitalism upon the workers—indeed, so alienated from the fruits of his labor is the narrator that we never learn exactly what kind of work it is that he's

involved in. What we do learn about, in a series of cartoonish vignettes, is the small-minded nepotism and petty officialdom of most company organizations; the old ties between capital, the institutions of government and the church; and the grinding

"He criticizes society and I criticize it, but he ends up saying there's not a goddamned thing you can do about it, so screw it." **JOAN BAEZ**

boredom of manual labor, especially when inflicted upon those workers who still retain a little imagination and a few ideas of their own.

The final verse concludes with a damning indictment of the way that, post-Henry Ford, modern assembly-line manufacturing methods impose uniformity on the labor force just as much as on the goods manufactured. Of course, Dylan is not fool enough to believe he is exempt from such forces, and so the last verse also becomes an explicit condemnation of all those folk fans and commentators who criticized his various changes of lyrical style—including, ironically, Pete Seeger himself, who had to be restrained from taking an ax to the power-cables that fed Dylan's electric band at the Newport Folk Festival that year.

Love Minus Zero/ No Limit

The second of the album's love songs is more straightforwardly devotional than 'She Belongs To Me', despite the dark, looming energy of much of its imagery. The first verse is as close as Dylan gets to amorous infatuation, marveling at a lover of elemental constancy and rock-like imperturbability, one whose emotional strength is not dependent on overt displays of emotion, but on some deeper, inner fortitude. The three remaining verses then offer a parade of the

◀ **JOAN BAEZ'S INCREASING DISAFFECTION WITH DYLAN WAS VISIBLE DURING HIS 1965 TOUR OF BRITAIN, THE LAST TIME THEY SPOKE FOR MANY YEARS.**

inauthentic chaos which routinely assaults the narrator's sensibilities, from which his lover's devotion provides him with necessary refuge: critics dissect, rich girls presume, bridges tremble, statues crumble—but through it all, she remains untouched, unaffected, smiling with the knowing, Zen-like calm of the Mona Lisa. By the song's conclusion, she occupies his thoughts as completely as the eponymous bird obsesses the hapless protagonist of Poe's *The Raven*—although the closing image of the bird with the broken wing tapping at the narrator's window could simply be an expression of her essential vulnerability, despite that inner strength he so admires.

In its admiration for a lover who "knows too much to argue or to judge," the song is surely inspired by Sara Lowndes, the former model and *Playboy* bunny with whom Bob had become involved some time in late 1964, and whom he would marry in a secret wedding ceremony in November 1965. A divorcee friend of *Bringing It All Back Home* cover-star Sally Grossman, Sara was a frequent visitor to the Grossmans' Woodstock spread, but lived with her young daughter Maria in New York's Chelsea Hotel, where Bob took an apartment in order to be close to her. It was Sara, through her work connections at Drew Associates, a film-production company, who introduced Bob and his manager to the young cinema-verité film-maker Donn Pennebaker, who would go on to make the *Don't Look Back* documentary.

Apart from her great natural beauty, what probably attracted Bob to Sara was her Zen-like equanimity: unlike most of the women he met, she

"You gotta read the I Ching... You read it and you gotta know it's true. It's something to believe in." **BOB DYLAN**

wasn't out to impress him, or to interrogate him about his lyrics. An adherent of Eastern mysticism, she possessed a certain ego-less quality which dovetailed neatly with Bob's more pronounced sense of ambition. Indeed, so self-effacing was she that for a long time their relationship remained

a secret even to Dylan's friends, most of whom learned about their marriage several months after it had occurred.

Encouraged by his Buddhist friend, the poet Allen Ginsberg, Dylan was at this time becoming increasingly interested in Eastern mysticism himself, particularly the *I Ching*, the ancient oriental Oracle Of Change. "You gotta read the *I Ching*," he told friends. "I don't wanna talk about it, except to say it's the only thing that's fantastically true. You read it, and you gotta know it's true. It's something to believe in. Of course," he added with a Zen-like touch of self-contradiction, "I don't believe in anything."

Outlaw Blues

Originally rehearsed in acoustic form as 'California'—under which title it appeared on several bootlegs—'Outlaw Blues' is the most raw and basic of Dylan's early electric outings, a churning twelve-bar blues grind of rhythm guitars that just chugs onward, over and over, like a runaway sixteen-wheeler truck barreling down a highway, leaving gusts of harmonica and slivers of lead guitar trailing like leaves in its wake.

As a performance, it could have been designed specifically to raise the hackles of his discomfited folkie fans, while the studied absurdity of the lyrics might also have been devised to annoy those who demanded meaning from his songs—and, increasingly, from Dylan himself. Hardly an interview or press conference would pass without Bob being asked to explain his songs, which is probably why the second verse finds Dylan watching his back, refusing to hang any specific opinions out in public view for fear of being shot down, the way Jesse James was shot in the back by Robert Ford while putting up a picture.

Two verses later, he returns to the same theme, with a damning vernacular finality that cuts both ways, through both his own oracular ability and his interrogators' motives: "Don't ask me nothin' about nothin'/I just might tell you the truth." And that, he implies, would be the last thing anyone would want.

On The Road Again

As the first side approaches its end, Dylan slips into the parade of comic grotesques that would increasingly populate his songs over the course of the next few albums. A paranoid, nightmarish version of the in-law dread that affects every courting couple, 'On The Road Again' opens with the most standard of blues beginnings—the narrator waking up in the morning—but instead of the string of clichés that are usually on a bluesman's mind, he's plunged here into a surreal netherworld where the mother-in-law lives in the refrigerator, father-in-law wears a mask of Napoleon, grandfather-in-law carries a sword-stick, and frogs inhabit his socks. Even the simplest tasks—eating, stroking a pet—become laden with pitfalls, while the most mundane and innocent of delivery-men and servants are imbued with a sinister, premonitory presence. No wonder, then, that Bob refuses to move in on a permanent basis.

Bob Dylan's 115th Dream

The mutant rock'n'roll offspring of 'Motorpsycho Nitemare', 'I Shall Be Free No.10' and his various humorous talking blues, 'Bob Dylan's 115th Dream' bears no relation at all to the wistful reverie of the original 'Bob Dylan's Dream'. Over the course of the intervening 113 dreams, Dylan's dream-world has presumably become less personal but much more frantic, judging by the pace of this recording and the vitality of its imagery.

The song is a satiric dream vision of the discovery of America in which images, scenes and references dissolve into each other, so that the *Mayflower* can be captained by a cartoon version of *Moby Dick*'s Captain Ahab—here re-named "Arab" for dumb comic effect—who, upon sighting America, abandons his quest for the whale in favor of buying up the land with beads and imposing the principles of property ownership upon a people for whom it has no meaning. Jailed alongside the rest of the crew for carrying harpoons, the narrator breaks out and goes in search of help for his ship-mates, who remain unaccountably imprisoned.

From there, the narrative rattles along with the berserk logic of dreams (at one point, a foot bursts out of a telephone), while riding roughshod over such sacred establishment cows as the flag, police, religion and capitalism. Like the dysfunctional family of 'On The Road Again', this dream-America is fraught with ludicrous dangers and inexplicable sights: exploding desserts, runaway bowling-balls, talking cows, predatory French girls, paranoid coast guards and, of course, naval traffic wardens, all of whom exert their influence on our hero. Eventually tiring of his ordeal, the narrator returns to the ship and sets off back across the ocean, passing *en route* a ship bearing a certain Christopher Columbus, to whom he offers, more in sympathy than hope, "Good luck."

The surreal imagery of 'Bob Dylan's 115th Dream' led many to suppose that this was one of the first "drug songs" for which Dylan and his peers would become notorious. There were, however, precedents for the song's loopy, extempore style in Bob's youth, according to his teenage buddy John Bucklen, who recalled that the pair of them would pass many evenings ad-libbing nonsense songs. "We'd get a guitar and sing verses we made up as we went along," he told Robert Shelton. "It came out strange and weird. We thought we'd send them in somewhere, but we never did."

The song's false start came about when the backing musicians missed their cue, but Bob kept on singing, cracking up with laughter a line or two into the song, along with producer Tom Wilson and everyone else—though only Dylan's hilarity was caught on tape. He insisted the mistake should be retained on the album, telling Wilson he would even be prepared to pay for its inclusion. Edited on to the beginning of a bona-fide band take, the laughter sets up the tenor of the song, and makes the band's entrance all the more dynamic.

73

Mr Tambourine Man

fter the sardonic absurdity of 'Bob Dylan's 115th Dream', Dylan chose to start the second side of the album with his most luminous, meditative song yet. Begun on the 1964 cross-country trip, as his station-wagon left New Orleans for Texas on February 12 and completed a month or two later at the New Jersey home of his journalist friend Al Aronowitz (who claims to have rescued Bob's discarded false starts from the waste-basket), 'Mr Tambourine Man' had been considered for inclusion on *Another Side Of Bob Dylan*. It had been recorded, with Ramblin' Jack Elliott providing harmonies on the choruses, at the June

▲

DYLAN ON STAGE IN BRITAIN, 1965.

9 session which produced that entire album, but was ultimately left off the record because Dylan "felt too close to it to put it on."

While there's no doubt that it would have sat well within *Another Side Of Bob Dylan*'s prevailing mood of ruminative melancholy, the song has an added strength and power on *Bringing It All Back Home*, where its plea for artistic liberation underlines the first side's break with tradition. Not for nothing did Dylan choose to play this song and 'It's All Over Now, Baby Blue' when he was called back to perform solo for a crowd who'd just booed his backing band offstage at the 1965 Newport Folk Festival: what the audience, relieved at the sight of Dylan toting an acoustic guitar again, took as a *mea culpa* recanting of his rock experiment, was actually an implicit statement that,

whatever *they* desired of him, he must follow his muse wherever it led him.

At the time, 'Mr Tambourine Man' was widely considered to be a drug song, its exultant imagery and urge for transcendence seen as analogizing the psychedelic experience. What, such interpreters demanded, could "smoke rings of my mind" refer to, if not marijuana? And that request to "Take me on a trip..."—an LSD trip, surely? For most listeners, their first encounter with the song came via The Byrds' hit single, and it's easy to understand how the sleek, euphoric rush of their version might lead one to such a conclusion. But to impose such a narrow interpretation on the song is to miss its wider meaning, which has more to do with the artist's invocation of his/her muse (here confusingly cast as a male figure, rather than the more usual female). That much is clear from Dylan's own more haunted delivery, in which the desired transcendence is always slightly out of reach, an aim and an ideal, rather than an indulgence. It's one of Dylan's most mesmerizing performances, burnished with a wistful, gently swaying harmonica break which perfectly evokes the sense of lonely aesthetic reverie.

The first verse finds the writer, late at night, tired but unable to sleep, facing the blank page again. (The Clancy Brothers' Liam Clancy, a folk-singing friend of Dylan's from his early years in New York, told journalist Patrick Humphries that when he first heard Dylan sing the line about the "ancient empty street [that's] too dead for dreaming," he *knew* Bob was referring to "Sullivan Street on a Sunday"). In the second verse, the writer appeals for inspiration, "ready to go anywhere" his muse might lead, if s/he should only "cast your dancing spell" his way. The third verse offers reassurance that any "vague traces of skippin' reels of rhyme" the muse might hear echoing his tambourine would merely be a "ragged clown" (the writer himself) chasing the elusive shadow of poetic perfection cast by the muse. Finally, in the fourth verse, the writer appeals again for an artistic experience outside the realms of memory and fate, beyond the bounds of time and place: a visionary experience in which the overwhelming immediacy of the aesthetic *now* obliterates more mundane, ego-directed notions of past, present and future.

Several sources have been claimed as the inspiration for the central pied-piper image of the tambourine man, though Dylan himself, in the liner notes to his *Biograph* box set, cites guitarist Bruce Langhorne, who attended an earlier recording session (presumably for *The Freewheelin' Bob Dylan*) with a gigantic tambourine, "big as a wagon-wheel." Fittingly, it's Langhorne who provides the floating droplets of electric guitar which are the only accompaniment to Dylan's own voice and rhythm guitar here.

Gates Of Eden

Dylan admitted to Nora Ephron and Susan Edmiston that his writing style was influenced by William Burroughs ("a great man") and claimed that, like the beat author, he too collected photographs which illustrated his songs. "I have photographs of 'Gates Of Eden' and 'It's All Over Now, Baby Blue'," he said. "I saw them after I wrote the songs. People send me a lot of things and a lot of the things are pictures, so other people must have that idea too."

It's hardly surprising that 'Gates Of Eden' should inspire visual responses, as the song contains some of Dylan's most vivid, unsettling dream imagery, and may itself have been inspired by William Blake's pictorial sequence *The Gates Of Paradise*. Like 'A Hard Rain's A-Gonna Fall', each verse—virtually each couplet—stands on its own as a discrete tableau, combining to offer a devastating evocation of societal entropy. The song sets up hopeful expectations with the title 'Gates Of Eden', but it's actually about an Eden from which paradise has been eroded: there is a terrible stench of decay and corruption about the imagery, and Dylan's portentous delivery of each verse's closing line offers a warning rather than a welcome. This Eden is a place to be avoided, where the best that can be expected is oblivion.

When he debuted the song at his New York Philharmonic Hall concert on October 31, 1964, Dylan introduced the song as "a sacrilegious lullaby in G minor," a light-hearted description nevertheless borne out by the depiction of "Utopian hermit monks" sharing a saddle on the

Golden Calf with "Aladdin and his lamp." Religion, he seems to be suggesting, is composed of equal parts piety and magic, an unhealthy combination of morality, smoke and mirrors, whose protagonists' "promises of paradise" raise only hollow laughter from Eden's inhabitants.

Elsewhere in the song, small-minded, gray-flanneled citizens are shocked by biker molls, impotent paupers chase materialist goals, industrialized cities remain impervious to babies' cries, secretive kingmakers determine power relations and "friends and other strangers," in an elegant twist on the notion of resignation, "from their fates try to resign." Throughout, the catalogue of hardship and debasement is recurrently wiped clean at the end of each verse, rendered meaningless by the looming specter of the Gates Of Eden. Finally, the narrator is woken from his nightmare visions by his lover, who, like the beatific woman of 'Love Minus Zero/ No Limit', reports her own dreams without trying to decipher them; perhaps, he

▼
WILLIAM BURROUGHS, DOYEN OF THE BEAT MOVEMENT AND AN IMPORTANT INFLUENCE ON DYLAN'S WRITING STYLE.

thinks, that is the best way to deal with his own visions, which seem somehow truer, more revealing of life, than strict narrative interpretations. After all, as he concludes, "there are no truths outside the Gates Of Eden."

With its ponderous delivery, methodical strumming and bare arrangement—the only embellishment is a single windswept wheeze of harmonica planting a full-stop at the end of each verse—'Gates Of Eden' is the closest Dylan had come to an outright sermon since 'The Times They Are A-Changin' '; but compared with the clarity of that song's well-targeted attack, this one offers only a troubling perception of general unease, a glimpse of a hell which we may already inhabit.

At almost six minutes long, the song was the perfect B-side partner for 'Like A Rolling Stone', adding extra layers of dense imagery to the A-side's oblique character-assassination, and making it, at nearly 12 minutes in total, by far the longest single that had ever been released—a factor which added to the perception of Dylan as a serious young man with a lot to say.

It's Alright, Ma
(I'm Only Bleeding)

T hough more direct in its imagery, 'It's Alright, Ma' shares the same sense of societal entropy as 'Gates Of Eden'. But rather than disguise his critique behind clouds of allusion, here Dylan unsheathes his verbal dagger and plunges it squarely into the breast of contemporary American culture, in lines requiring little or no deciphering. The title itself is a sly multiple pun, recalling both Dylan's own 'Don't Think Twice, It's All Right' and 'That's All Right, Mama', the Arthur Crudup song which provided Elvis Presley with his breakthrough first single.

The opening image, of "Darkness at the break of noon," echoes the title of Arthur Koestler's anti-communist novel *Darkness At Noon*, suggesting that the human spirit can be cast into shade just as much by the rampant consumerism of a capitalist society in which manufacturers can make "everything from toy guns that spark/To flesh-

▶
SCOTTISH FOLK SINGER DONOVAN, THE MOST SUCCESSFUL OF THE VAGABONDS RAPPING AT DYLAN'S DOOR.

colored Christs that glow in the dark," as by the dead hand of communism. The machinations of corporate America and its Madison Avenue advertising industry thought-police, the song claims, are just as effective as communist brainwashing and show-trials in determining peoples' attitudes and mapping out their psyches.

There follows a catalogue of capitalist shame in 15 verses, punctuated by four cautionary choruses. As with 'Subterranean Homesick Blues', many lines were subsequently abstracted as slogans of the burgeoning counter-culture: "Money doesn't talk, it swears" became the favored catch-phrase of any scuffling hustler on the wrong end of a deal, while "even the president of the United States sometimes must have to stand naked" was pronounced with grim glee at the time of Richard Nixon's resignation. Most tellingly of all, "he not busy being born is busy dying" offered an update of the theme of 'The Times They Are A-Changin' ' in which the target was switched, from the old and out-of-touch, to the young listeners themselves: only through the perpetual rebirth of new experience, the song suggested, could the pervasive entropy be staved off.

Like 'Gates Of Eden', the stripped-bare backing offers little distraction (or protection) from the words, which cut through the parade of hypocrisy and deceit like a machine-gun. Following the descending chord-sequence as it spirals abjectly away down the plughole, Dylan's deadpan, declamatory delivery here is surely one of the most potent precursors of rap, though the occasional tug of nihilism glimpsed in lines like "There is no sense in trying" and "I got nothing, Ma, to live up to" is nowhere near as hopelessly final as the nihilism of Nineties hip-hop culture. Despite this, 'It's Alright, Ma' was undoubtedly one of the songs to which Joan Baez was referring when she criticized Dylan's supposed nihilism and lack of (what she regarded as) commitment during this period. She later admitted that, in the sour aftermath of their split, she couldn't listen to his records from this period very often; if she had, she might have recognized that, far from abandoning the search for a solution to society's problems, Dylan was laying the groundwork for that decade's momentous changes of heart and mind with songs like 'It's Alright, Ma'.

It's All Over Now, Baby Blue

A s with his last two albums, Dylan chooses to close *Bringing It All Back Home* with a song casting off old allegiances, bidding farewell to attitudes and acquaintances that have slipped irrevocably from his orbit as he spins off in a new direction. At the time, some thought it was written about Bob's blue-eyed old friend Paul Clayton, though Dylan later denied this. The inspiration, he claims in the annotations for the *Biograph* box set, came from a much more innocent source, the Gene Vincent song 'Baby Blue', which had stuck in the back of his memory since he used to sing it back at Hibbing High School. "Of course," he adds with droll superfluity, "I was singing about a different Baby Blue."

That different Baby Blue is most probably Joan Baez, judging by the retinue of dispossessed orphans, empty-handed painters and pestering vagabonds whose fates occupy so much of her concern. Alternatively, it could be a self-directed piece, the singer coming to terms with the great changes occurring in his life and career, drawing new inspiration from the *I Ching* ("take what you have gathered from coincidence"), and attempting to escape from the pursuing hordes of followers and imitators "standing in the clothes that you once wore." This last line took on a devastating pertinence when, in a scene captured in the *Don't Look Back* documentary of Dylan's May 1965 tour of England, he played the song for Donovan during a party in his suite at the Savoy Hotel.

Whoever the song's subject is, its resigned finality is streaked with tremendous pain and sadness, reflecting the strength of the ties being broken. Finally, after all the images of traumatic sunder, the song concludes with the invocation to "Strike another match, go start anew"—an acknowledgment that, whatever the pain involved, this end is but the start of a new chapter.

LIKE A ROLLING STONE

TOMBSTONE BLUES

IT TAKES A LOT TO LAUGH, IT
TAKES A TRAIN TO CRY

FROM A BUICK 6

BALLAD OF A THIN MAN

QUEEN JANE APPROXIMATELY

HIGHWAY 61 REVISITED

JUST LIKE TOM
THUMB'S BLUES

DESOLATION ROW

singles:

POSITIVELY 4TH STREET

CAN YOU PLEASE CRAWL OUT
YOUR WINDOW?

Highway 61 Revisited

Things continued to move fast for Dylan. After the release of *Bringing It All Back Home*, he played a few more American shows before departing in late April for Britain, for the tour that would be featured in Donn Pennebaker's revealing documentary *Don't Look Back*. At the time, Dylan was far more popular in Britain than he was in America, and the film captures the adrenaline rush of fame better than any subsequent attempt.

"I wanted to hear him sing, and I wanted to watch him with people," Pennebaker told me. "Beyond that, I had no expectations. It's the process of being there that's interesting. The one sure thing in life is that you never know what's going on in somebody's head—that's what the novel was invented for. You can't point a camera at someone and find out what's in their head. But it does the next best thing: it lets you speculate. The process of looking, if you look sharply and well, is a stunning process—people make lifetime generalisations based on a glance, and I think in a sense that's what the camera's doing with Dylan. And that's probably the best you can hope for."

"With Dylan, what you see is what you get," Pennebaker believes. "And for everybody who says, 'You really savaged that bastard,' somebody else says, 'God, he's wonderful, I love him.' It's clear that people see what they set out to see. And I'm no different—I guess I tried to make that film as true to my vision of him as I could make it. But as a storyteller, I wanted there to be stories in it."

Pennebaker had been introduced to Dylan's people by Sara Lowndes, and was immediately intrigued when Dylan and Neuwirth tried out their assassin routine on him. "I recognised instantly, when I met Dylan and Neuwirth, that they had the same sense about what they were up to as we did about what we were up to, which was a kind of conspiracy," he recalled. "We felt as if we were out conning the world in some kind of guerrilla action and bringing back stuff that nobody recognized as valuable and making it valuable."

Accompanied by an entourage including side-kick Bob Neuwirth and an increasingly estranged Joan Baez, Dylan cut through the country like a whirlwind, from his first press conference on arrival at Heathrow—where he carried an outsize light bulb and answered the inevitable question about his "message" with the advice, "Keep a good head

and always carry a light bulb"—through his none-too-private life at the Savoy Hotel, and on to his concerts in provincial cities like Sheffield, Liverpool and Leicester. Significantly, the brief moments of concert footage are vastly outweighed by the fascinating backstage cinema-verité, which features, a drunken Alan Price opening a bottle of Newcastle Brown on a dressing-room piano; Dylan losing his rag when a glass is thrown out of a window at a party in his Savoy suite; Bob Neuwirth and Dylan ruthlessly mocking Joan Baez; Albert Grossman and UK promoter Tito Burns playing off two television companies against each other; and Dylan verbally cutting a variety of interviewers and sundry other inquisitors into shreds.

One of the more enjoyable aspects of the film is the running gag about Donovan, the young Scottish Dylan imitator who was experiencing his first flush of success with the single 'Catch The Wind'. Everywhere he went in Britain, Dylan kept coming across Donovan's name, in the papers, on peoples' lips, and even announced over the concert-hall PA systems at his shows. At his Leicester concert, he made fun of his imitator's omnipresence by altering a line of 'Talkin' World War III Blues' to "I turned on my radio—it was *Donovan*," adding as an afterthought, "Whoever Donovan is…" Later on, the two troubadours would meet at Bob's hotel, in a crushing scene during which Donovan played Bob his song 'To Sing For You', and Bob responded in kind with 'It's All Over Now, Baby Blue'. Nevertheless, Dylan liked Donovan enough to let him sleep on the floor of his suite for a few nights, during which time he helped (along with Baez and Alan Price) in the writing of the lyric cards which Bob would discard during the film's famous opening scene. Other visitors to the suite—though not filmed—included The Beatles, who spent an afternoon of cheery badinage in the company of Dylan, Ginsberg and Neuwirth. (Dylan later reciprocated by visiting the Lennons' home.)

During his stay, Dylan made a drunken attempt at recording a version of 'If You Gotta Go, Go Now' with John Mayall's Bluesbreakers, but the session

▲
ALAN PRICE OF THE ANIMALS TEMPTS DYLAN WITH HIS FAVOURITE TIPPLE.

◄
DYLAN CONTEMPLATES A LIFE MEASURED OUT IN PRESS CONFERENCES.

proved unfruitful, to put it mildly—after a single verse and chorus, Dylan shouted at producer Tom Wilson, "Fade it out! Fade it out!"; then, when the music stopped, "Didja fade it out?" Equally as amusing was the message he taped for Columbia Records' Miami Sales Convention—"Hi! Thanks for selling so many of my records! I'll see you next year in New York. God bless you."

Unfortunately, the tour ended on something of a low note, with Dylan having to spend several days in hospital with a viral complaint. By the time he returned to America, in early June, The Byrds' version of 'Mr Tambourine Man' was heading for the top of the charts. A couple of weeks later, he went into the studio to start recording his next album, beginning with 'Like A Rolling Stone'. Before any further sessions could take place, however, he was booked to appear on the Sunday evening show at the 1965 Newport Folk Festival, where he stunned the crowd by appearing with an electric band comprised of members of the Butterfield

Blues Band, a hot young outfit from Chicago.

Sam Lay, who had played on many of Howlin' Wolf's classic Chess tracks, was the band's drummer. "The first time I played with Dylan was at the Newport Festival," he recalls. "I don't think we even rehearsed for it! He wanted to try the electric sound, but the people didn't go for that. It was a stormy reception, without a doubt. When they're used to that acoustic sound and all of a sudden you break out with all that power and stuff, people don't like that. They weren't exactly liberal-minded that day!" After only three songs—'Maggie's Farm' and the live debuts of 'Like A Rolling Stone' and 'It Takes A Lot To Laugh, It Takes A Train To Cry'—during which the sound quality was allegedly so bad few could make out the shape of the songs, let alone their lyrics, the band were booed off; but Dylan was persuaded to return with his acoustic guitar, to play 'Mr Tambourine Man' and, pointedly, his swansong to

the Festival, 'It's All Over Now, Baby Blue'. Some among the crowd considered this a victory.

Pete Seeger, who was infuriated by the electrical intrusion into what he considered his own personal acoustic oasis (but who would later succumb, like everyone else, to the lure of amplification, by recording an album with The Blues Project), had crassly opened that night's show with the sound of a new-born baby crying, asking the evening's artists to sing to that baby to tell it what kind of a world it would grow up in. Ironically, of all the performers, only Dylan's supercharged electric approach offered anything approaching an accurate representation of the world to come.

So it was too with *Highway 61 Revisited*, which was completed at three or four days' more sessions on the cusp of July and August. Impressed by John Lennon's mansion during a visit there, Dylan had gone out and bought himself a 31-room house upon his return to America, where he holed up and wrote the rest of the album. (Within a year, he had put the place up for sale and moved back into Albert Grossman's place, explaining to Robert Shelton, "I don't believe in writing some total other thing in the same place twice. It's just a hang-up, a voodoo kind of thing… I just can't stand the smell of birth. It just lingers, so I just lived there and tried to go on, but couldn't.") The new material was mostly of a piece: streamlined, sardonic, surrealistic and bulging with raw blues power, particularly as rendered by his new studio band. "I can't tell you how disorganised it was," says organist Al Kooper of the sessions. "*Highway 61* has a very raw edge to it, because half the people involved were studio musicians, and half weren't, so it's got that rough thing which Dylan loves."

"I've stopped composing and singing anything that has either a reason to be written or a motive to be sung," Dylan explained to Nat Hentoff in a *Playboy* interview later that year. "What I'm going to do is rent Town Hall and put about 30 Western Union boys on the bill. Then there'll *really* be some messages!" This was, however, so much jesting: Dylan hadn't really stopped offering messages, only obvious ones. His new messages were more a matter of implication and inference than direct statement, and needed more deciphering than his old ones. *Highway 61 Revisited*, for instance, suggests that ours is an absurd world navigable only from the position of an outsider—from which vantage one may, like Chaplin, attack life's drawbacks with wit and clowning; brute reality is consequently dismissed as "useless and pointless knowledge," compared with the life of the spirit. As Dylan acknowledged around this time, "Philosophy can't give me anything that I don't already have."

Released at the end of August, just as the colossal 'Like A Rolling Stone' was sending shockwaves through the music industry, *Highway 61 Revisited* followed the single into the Top Five on both sides of the Atlantic. Though the rear sleeve featured the singer's now familiar stream-of-consciousness beatnik screed, the front offered the clearest indication yet that Dylan's folkie days were but a distant memory. With Neuwirth's lower half visible behind him dangling an SLR camera on its strap, a sleek, epicene Dylan sits on the steps of a white-fronted building, fixing the viewer with an enigmatic expression that's neither smile nor frown, but some gestalt combination of both. His blue and pink silk shirt is unbuttoned to reveal a white Triumph Motorcycle T-shirt underneath. The hand clutching his sunglasses, however, has clearly not been near the business end of a motorbike engine in quite some time. If there was a cooler person on the planet—Beatles and Stones included—no one had told Bob Dylan.

No one had told the old folkies, either. They were still too busy singing 'The Times They Are A-Changin' ' to realise just how much the times had actually changed. Dylan's switch to rock'n'roll triggered off a furious correspondence in the letters columns of *Sing Out!* magazine between detractors and supporters of the new style, not all as prescient as one Loren D. Schwartz, who pointed out that "The oral tradition you so cherish is now in the hands of Top 40 radio. It is its logical heir... Dylan is bringing his personal distillation of hundreds of years of liberal and enlightened thought to the youth of America and the world in the greatest number possible... His drive, I'm sure, is not to 'create art', but to communicate at all costs and to as many as will listen. The fact is, he has caught the general ear while you have yet to be heard above a whisper."

Others were less impressed. "Dylan is to me the perfect symbol of the anti-artist in our society," pontificated traditional singer Ewan MacColl, with

no discernible trace of irony, in *Melody Maker*. "He is against everything—the last resort of someone who doesn't really want to change the world... I think his poetry is punk. It's derivative and terribly old hat." Some could even get it wrong while getting it right, such as *Sing Out!* editor Irwin Silber, who wrote of the "essentially existentialist" philosophy of *Highway 61 Revisited*: "Song after

> "It's the kind of music that plants a seed in your mind and then you have to hear it several times" **PHIL OCHS**

song adds up to the same basic statement: Life is an absurd conglomeration of meaningless events capsuled into the unnatural vacuum created by birth and completed by death; we are all living under a perpetual sentence of death and to seek meaning or purpose in life is as unrewarding as it is pointless; all your modern civilization does is further alienate man from his fellow man and from nature." True enough, of course—but it's exactly this emptiness and absurdity that furnishes the freedom which gives the album its unique potency.

The younger singers, though, recognised Dylan's achievement for what it was. "I knew he'd produced the most important and revolutionary album ever made," acknowledged his friend, the singer Phil Ochs. "It's the kind of music that plants a seed in your mind and then you have to hear it several times. And as you go over it you start to hear more and more things. He's done something that's left the whole field ridiculously in back of him." Eric Anderson, too, tipped his hat in Dylan's direction: "He may be the greatest influence on the generation," he said. "I think the seeds of the future were laid down by him right there. I don't see any force quite like what Dylan did. Keats said the artist is the antenna of the race. Dylan is the antenna of the race."

Even Dylan himself, normally his own harshest critic, was impressed. "I'm not gonna be able to make a record better than that one," he claimed. "*Highway 61* is just too good. There's a lot of stuff on there that *I* would listen to!"

◄

AL KOOPER, FIRST-TIME ORGANIST ON 'LIKE A ROLLING STONE'.

Like A Rolling Stone

'L ike A Rolling Stone' was unlike any rock-'n'roll record that had been heard before. At one second short of six minutes, it was far longer than any previous single, and its rippling waves of organ, piano and guitar formed as dense and portentous a sound as anyone had dared to offer as pop, smothering listeners like quicksand, drawing them inexorably down into the song's lyrical hell. Dylan's performance, too, was utterly gripping, a semi-spoken blues rap delivered in a sour, offhand monotone which curled occasionally at the ends of lines, like a sneer twisting the corner of his mouth as he gloated over a hipster's downfall. At a time when three-minute declarations of love were still the pop norm, this vicious tirade of recrimination was quite simply without precedent, a strange but compelling experience made all the more troubling by the

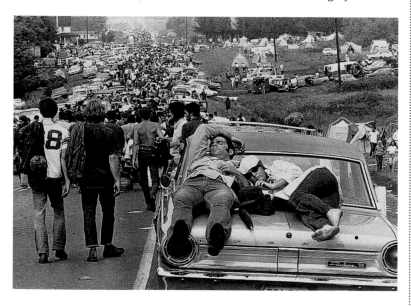

incursions of surreal imagery into its damning flow. Who, fascinated fans debated, were Miss Lonely, Napoleon in rags, and—most bizarre of all—the diplomat who rode a chrome horse while balancing a Siamese cat upon his shoulder? What on earth was going on here?

For an industry whose optimum single length—between two and three minutes—had been set during the Forties and Fifties by jukebox operators intent on maximising the number of

plays per hour, 'Like A Rolling Stone' was far too long to secure blanket radio coverage, but it still managed to become Dylan's biggest hit so far, reaching number two on the American charts (and number four in Britain) in August 1965. Its effect was simply stunning: fans, peers and rivals alike realised that he had raised the bar way beyond anything they had heard or done before.

More importantly, a whole new army of teenagers, for whom Dylan had previously meant little or nothing, were profoundly moved in ways they couldn't quite explain. At Dylan's Rock'n'Roll Hall Of Fame induction on January 20, 1988, Bruce Springsteen described hearing 'Like A Rolling Stone' for the first time, while out in the car with his mom. "I knew that I was listening to the toughest voice that I had ever heard," he recalled. "It was lean and it sounded somehow simultaneously young and adult...it made me feel kind of irresponsibly innocent—it still does—when it reached down and touched what little worldliness a 15-year-old high-school kid in New Jersey had in him at the time. Dylan was a revolutionary. Bob freed your mind the way Elvis freed your body."

The song was written upon Dylan's return from England, in what he described as a "vomitific" manner, at a Woodstock cabin he and Sara rented from Peter Yarrow's mother. "It was ten pages long," he told journalist Jules Siegel. "It wasn't called anything, just a rhythm thing on paper all about my steady hatred directed at some point that was honest. In the end it wasn't hatred, it was telling someone something they didn't know, telling them they were lucky. Revenge, that's a better word. I had never thought of it as a song, until one day I was at the piano, and on the paper it was singing, 'How does it feel?' in a slow motion pace...it was like swimming in lava. In your eyesight, you see your victim swimming in lava. Hanging by their arms from a birch tree. Skipping, kicking the tree, hitting a nail with your foot. Seeing someone in the pain they were bound to meet up with."

Exactly who this "someone" was has long been a matter of conjecture. Joan Baez believes it is about Bobby Neuwirth, Dylan's partner in char-acter-assassination; others suspect it refers to the recently-dumped Baez herself—and certainly, there are distinct parallels between the well-off, well-schooled, slumming princess pilloried in the song, and that most saintly of folk-singers. Yet another theory contends that the song could, like so many of Dylan's writings from this period, be self-referential—after all, Bob's mother's maiden name was Stone, and he had, by this time, certainly rolled some distance from home. "I don't dislike them or anything," he said of his family around this time, "I just don't have any contact with them. They live in Minnesota, and there's nothing for me in Minnesota." Later, in the same interview, he admitted he found it "easier to be disconnected than to be connected."

Over the previous couple of years, Dylan's world view had altered drastically from the youthful socialist spirit that informed his early albums, to a position which could loosely be described as existentialist. 'Like A Rolling Stone' reflects this new attitude, arguing that truly to know yourself and find fulfilment, you must face the world alone, mould your future and your philosophy from your own experiences, without relying on the comforts of favour or patronage; instead, one has to push off from shore, head out into uncharted waters with "no direction home." Accordingly, the song's climactic assessment that "you're invisible now, you got no secrets to conceal," ostensibly a triumphalist sneer of *schadenfreude*, can be read as a positive breakthrough, applauding a revelatory moment of self-awareness.

Dylan wrote the song on an upright piano in the key of G sharp, using the riff from 'La Bamba' as a jumping-off point, then transferred it to the key of C on guitar before recording it on June 15, 1965. "The chorus part came to me first," Dylan said later in *Rolling Stone* magazine. "I'd sorta hum that over and over, then later figured out that the verses would start low and move on up." The song's time signature wasn't figured out until he got to the studio; on the rehearsal fragment included in *The Bootleg Series Vols 1-3*, Dylan and Paul Griffin can be heard trying to work their way through a waltz-time setting of the song, before the hit single version crystallised later in the session.

Crucial to the session's success was the introduction of Al Kooper, a musician Dylan had never met before, on organ, an instrument Kooper had never played before. "I was very good friends with Tom Wilson, who invited me to the session to watch, because he knew I was a Bob fan," Kooper explained to me. "But I was very ambitious then,

and planned to play! The session was booked for two in the afternoon, so I got there early, about 1.20, with my guitar—because at the time I had been doing sessions as a guitar player—sat down, plugged in and warmed up, and at about a quarter to two, Dylan came in with Mike Bloomfield, who I didn't know. I heard Bloomfield warming up,

> " 'Like A Rolling Stone' changed it all. After that I didn't care about writing books or poems or whatever. " **BOB DYLAN**

packed up my guitar and went back into the control room. I'd never heard anybody play like *that*!"

Salvation came for Kooper's ambitions when, midway through the session, organist Paul Griffin was moved to piano. "I said to Tom, Why don't you let me play the organ, I've got a really good part for this," continues Kooper. "He said, 'Oh man, you're not an organ player!' But then he was called to the telephone before he could refuse, so I went out and sat at the organ. In fact, on the *Highway 61 Interactive* CD-ROM, they include some of the different takes of the song, with the between-takes chatter, and you can hear Tom Wilson saying, 'OK, this is Take 7, 'Like A Rolling Stone'...hey, what are *you* doing out there?', and you can hear me laugh. At that moment, he could have pulled me out of there, but he didn't, and that was the moment I became an organ player!"

With Kooper's organ swathing Dylan's lines in brooding, exultant chords while Bloomfield's guitar arpeggios and Griffin's piano circled menacingly around each other, the song developed an animated, claustrophobic atmosphere which Dylan tried to recapture several times afterwards, though rarely with the same impact. " 'Rolling Stone' is the best song I wrote," he told journalist Ralph Gleason. "When I was writing it I knew I had to sing it with a band. I always sing when I write, even prose, and I heard it like that."

" 'Like A Rolling Stone' changed it all," he told Nat Hentoff around that time. "I didn't care anymore after that about writing books or poems or whatever. I mean it was something that I myself could dig."

◀

THE WOODSTOCK FESTIVAL, AUGUST 1969: THREE DAYS OF LOVE, PEACE AND MUD. BUT NO BOB DYLAN.

Tombstone Blues

Despite the success of 'Like A Rolling Stone', Dylan was dissatisfied with Tom Wilson as producer. For the rest of the album he was replaced by Bob Johnston, best known as a songwriter for some of Elvis Presley's movies. Al Kooper was unimpressed with his abilities, compared to Wilson's more hands-on style.

"Tom was musically inclined, and the only quality Bob Johnston really has as a producer," Kooper claims, "is that he knows how to pat the artist on the back. He made that into an art form! He says things like, 'Can you *believe* these songs? This is the *greatest* record that I ever made in my *life*!', whatever record he's working on, and that pumps the artist up tremendously." Then again, in the case of *Highway 61 Revisited* and the ensuing *Blonde On Blonde*, at least, Johnston's assessment would have been 100% accurate—though given that his previous

> "I wrote this either in that place [a bar frequented by off-duty cops] or remembering some conversations." **BOB DYLAN ON 'TOMBSTONE BLUES'**

greatest production success had involved the resuscitation of Patti Page's career, it needn't have been that great a record to exceed his personal best.

Whatever the reason for changing producers, there would be an hiatus of six weeks before the musicians gathered for the next session, on July 29, when three more tracks were recorded, including the thrilling 'Tombstone Blues'. A fast blues shuffle with Chuck Berry's tyre-tracks all over it, 'Tombstone Blues' was the second song of Dylan's (after 'Subterranean Homesick Blues') to parody the repetitive structure of Woody Guthrie and Pete Seeger's 'Taking It Easy', updating lines like "Mom was in the kitchen/ preparing to eat" for its chorus. In Dylan's song, the matriarch has been freed from the role of cook and housekeeper, but it's a pyrrhic emancipation which finds her working in a factory, shoeless, while

her husband hustles on the streets and the narrator is stuck in the kitchen (or in trouble) with the eponymous Tombstone Blues—probably a reference to police. In the annotations to the *Biograph* box, Dylan recalls playing in a bar frequented by off-duty cops, whose salty, violent conversation he mimics here. "I think I wrote this either in that place or remembering some conversations," he admits. "I don't know, I had it for a while before I recorded it." Also included in the *Biograph* box is a 48-second fragment of the previously unreleased 'Jet Pilot'—a throwaway boogie about a woman who "weighs more by the foot than she does by the inch" and who turns out to be a transvestite—which Dylan regarded as the original 'Tombstone Blues'.

With comic panache, the song uses a parade of historical characters—American hero Paul Revere's horse (reincarnated), vaudeville artiste Belle Starr, biblical temptresses Delilah and Jezebel (the latter now a nun), Jack The Ripper (now a successful businessman), John The Baptist (now a torturer), a Philistine king, Galileo, Cecil B. DeMille, and the intriguing musical double-act of blueswoman Ma Rainey and classicist Beethoven (here caught sharing a sleeping bag)—to sketch an absurdist account of contemporary American ills. In these verses, church, state, college and commerce collude to squander both the country's history and its future, most notably in the lines where the Philistine king (surely President Lyndon Johnson) "Puts the pied pipers in prison and fattens the slaves/Then sends them out to the jungle"—a reference to the country's treatment of draft-dodgers and the inequitable proportion of black Americans sent to fight in Vietnam.

Written in paired four-line stanzas to the rhyme-scheme a/a/a/b, c/c/c/b, the song allows Dylan to indulge in some outrageous rhyming—never more so than in the opening couplet, where "endorse" follows "of course" in a daring leap from the demotic to the bureaucratic. This parallels Dylan's take on American society, in which ordinary folk are in constant struggle with the authorities' attempts to control them through their desires. After every second verse, the chorus rolls around to remind us that, whatever the high-falutin activity of the verses, with their star-studded cast of characters, life just goes on as normal for the scuffling ordinary Joes and Janes confined to life's chorus-line. In the official version included in Dylan's *Lyrics 1962-1985*, the variations in the chorus ("I'm in the kitchen..." and "I'm in trouble...") have been flattened into the dull uniformity of "I'm in the streets..." which may give a more street-wise/underclass interpretation to the choruses, but don't sing anywhere near as colourfully.

After the sour recrimination of 'Like A Rolling Stone', Dylan's delivery is delightfully offhand, with a wry comic nonchalance punctuated between verses by some of guitarist Mike Bloomfield's greatest work, which may have been decisive in choosing which take to release. "I know we cut a version with The Chambers Brothers singing on the chorus, almost like a gospel backing," recalls Al Kooper. "I often wonder what happened to that version, and if it could be resurrected at all—I thought it was great. But I think the deciding criterion was that Mike Bloomfield was great on the take they used."

It Takes A Lot To Laugh, It Takes A Train To Cry

On a couple of levels, 'It Takes A Lot To Laugh, It Takes A Train To Cry' provides a succinct illustration of Dylan's creative processes in action. Firstly, it shows he was still keen on borrowing from old blues songs, the second verse being an adaptation of lines ("Don't the clouds look lonesome shining across the sea/Don't my gal look good when she's coming after me?") from Brownie McGhee and Leroy Carr's 'Solid Road' —which, as 'Rocks And Gravel', had been one of the tracks Dylan recorded for *The Freewheelin' Bob Dylan* but pulled at the eleventh hour. (Ironically, Dylan's own song then went on to provide similar second-hand inspiration for Steely Dan, Dylan fans who borrowed the line "Can't buy a thrill" as the title of their debut album.)

Secondly, 'It Takes A Lot To Laugh, It Takes A Train To Cry' offers a glimpse of the malleability of Dylan's material and the improvisational nature of his recording methods. Two different versions of the song were recorded, sharing the same lyrics, though completely separate in mood and approach. The first version, since included on *The Bootleg Series, Vols 1-3*, was recorded the same day as 'Like A Rolling Stone', along with an unreleased track which later turned up on various bootlegs (and eventually on *The Bootleg Series, Vols 1-3*) called 'Sitting On A Barbed Wire Fence' (aka 'Killing Me Alive'). The latter's tart, bluesy sound seems to have provided the basic inspiration for this first, uptempo run-through of 'It Takes A Lot To Laugh, It Takes A Train To Cry', a sleek R&B groove dominated by Mike Bloomfield's quicksilver guitar, one of whose breaks is punctuated by an exhilarated "Aaah..." from Dylan. At that time, the song was called 'Phantom Engineer', but by the next sessions, six weeks later, it had been transformed in both title and style into the slow, loping, piano-based blues that was included on *Highway 61 Revisited*.

Al Kooper, who played one of the two pianos on the song, liked the original, faster version so much he later recorded the song that way on the Super Session album he made with Mike Bloomfield and Stephen Stills. "I don't want to put down the version that's on *Highway 61*, though," he assures me, "because it's a wonderful mood—you can slice the mood on that song. All these songs went through incredible metamorphoses, like 'Like A Rolling Stone' being in 3/4 originally. 'Phantom Engineer' was done fast at first, then slow a day or two later, after Bob had had a chance to think about it. It might just have happened, but I suspect it was premeditated."

◀

LUDWIG VAN BEETHOVEN: ONCE UNWRAPPED A BEDROLL WITH BLUES SINGER MA RAINEY, APPARENTLY.

From A Buick 6

As with 'Like A Rolling Stone', 'From A Buick 6' sails in on the back of a declarative snare-shot from Bobby Gregg, but thereafter the mood is quite different, being loose and goosey motorvating rock'n'roll striding along on the back of Harvey Brooks' bass and crowned with a soaring harmonica break. It's great, simple fun, just like the song itself, which is basically another of Dylan's paeans to his female ideal, the unpretentious, undemanding earth-mother type who'll be there to take care of him when he falls apart. References to her as a "soulful mama" who "don't make me nervous, she don't talk too much" suggest the role model may be Sara, though the various descriptions of her as "graveyard woman," "junkyard angel," "steam shovel mama" and "dump truck baby" seem somewhat less than completely flattering. As for the claim that "She walks like Bo Diddley," what woman could resist such enigmatic blandishment?

Ballad of a Thin Man

After the light-hearted frolic of 'From A Buick 6', the stern, sententious opening piano chords (played by Dylan himself) of 'Ballad Of A Thin Man' sound more like the theme to a courtroom drama series like *Perry Mason*. And so it proves: this is one of Dylan's most unrelenting inquisitions, a furious, sneering dressing-down of a hapless bourgeois intruder into the hipster world of freaks and weirdoes which Dylan now inhabited. Al Kooper remembers that when the musicians listened to a playback in the control room, drummer Bobby Gregg said, "That is a *nasty* song, Bob... I don't know about this song!" to which Bob chuckled, "*Nasty* song!" "We all had a good laugh at that," Kooper recalls. "Dylan was the King of the Nasty Song at that time."

Since its appearance, 'Ballad Of A Thin Man'—and particularly the identity of the denigrated "Mr Jones" figure—has probably prompted more debate among Dylan fans than any other song. Bob's insecure friend Brian Jones, who suffered badly from Dylan and Neuwirth's badinage, was convinced it was him; some have suggested it might refer to Ms Joan (Baez), or others among Dylan's uncomprehending folkie friends; Judson Manning, the *Time* reporter savaged so mercilessly by Dylan in *Don't Look Back*, fits the part as well as any other candidate—as indeed does Terry Ellis, the student inquisitor mocked by Dylan in the same film (who would, by the by, become co-founder of the Chrysalis record label a few years later); and of course, anyone searching for drug references would instantly recognise a "jones" as a junkie's habit.

And the longer the song remains inconclusively explained, the weirder the explanations get. As recently as April 1998, a fascinating, albeit slightly tenuous, interpretation of the song as "outing" a closet homosexual's repressed desire to perform fellatio (based on the cumulative inference of references to "your pencil in your hand," "raise up your head." "hands you a bone," "contacts among the lumberjacks," "sword swallower" and "give me some milk") was posted on one of the many Internet web-sites devoted to Dylan's work, though this is probably more indicative of the pitfalls of interpretation than Dylan's intentions with the song, which itself condemns the urge to interpret pruriently that which we don't immediately understand.

At the time the song was written, Dylan was routinely plagued by journalists demanding explanations of his songs—to which he would offer routinely condescending, nonsensical replies such as (in the case of Mr Jones' occupation), "He's a pinboy. He also wears suspenders." Even to reputable reporters like Nora Ephron and Susan Edmiston, he would offer no clues about the victim's identity. "He's a real person," Dylan told them. "You know him, but not by that name... I saw him come into the room one night and he looked like a camel. He proceeded to put his eyes in his pocket. I asked this guy who he was and he said, 'That's Mr Jones'. Then I asked this cat, 'Doesn't he do anything but put his eyes in his pocket?' And he told me, 'He puts his nose on the ground'. It's all there, it's a true story." Which leaves everyone right back where they started, chasing a chimerical character round another man's imagination. To Robert Shelton, he claimed, more openly but no more revealingly, "It's not so incredibly absurd and it's not so imaginative to have Mr Jones in a room with three walls and a midget and a geek and a naked man. Plus a voice…a voice coming in his dream."

So notwithstanding all other claimants upon the dubious title, Mr Jones is most likely to be a journalist; indeed, Dylan himself admitted as much when he introduced the song at a 1978 concert by saying, "I wrote this for a reporter who was working for the *Village Voice* in 1963." Three years earlier, however, Jeffrey Jones had already "outed" himself as "Mr Jones" in *Rolling Stone* magazine, explaining that as a student journalist on assignment for *Time* magazine, he had embarrassed himself at the 1965 Newport Folk Festival when attempting to interview Dylan for a piece on the proliferation of the harmonica in contemporary folk music (!). Later that day, in the hotel dining-room, he had been unfortunate enough to bump into Dylan again, this time with entourage in tow. "Mr Jones!" shouted Dylan, mockingly. "Gettin' it all down, Mr Jones?" The poor youth, unskilled in even the basic rudiments of verbal duelling, let alone a blade as sharp as Dylan wielded, was forced to sit and squirm silently as he was cut to pieces for the entertainment of Dylan's table. When, a few months later, the song appeared on *Highway 61 Revisited*, he knew instantly it referred to himself. "I was thrilled," he admitted, "in the tainted way I suppose a felon is thrilled to see his name in the newspaper."

Queen Jane Approximately

When asked "Who is Queen Jane?" Dylan responded with typical panache, "Queen Jane is a man." This seems sardonic at best, a sarcastic denial of the obvious. The prime candidate would, again, seem to be the queen of folk music, Joan Baez, whose stable and secure family life Dylan probably regarded as a brake on her creative development. The song is a double-edged missive, criticising its subject's immersion in an inauthentic world of superficial attitudes and acquaintances, yet offering a sympathetic invitation, should she break free of these diversions and require a more honest, authentic experience with "somebody you don't have to speak to," to come up and see him sometime. It's the least interesting track on the album, although the piano cantering up the scale through the harmonica break neatly evokes the stifling nature of an upper-class existence reduced to the level of dressage.

Highway 61 Revisited

Highway 61 is one of the great North American arteries, originating across the border in Thunder Bay, Ontario, and snaking down through Dylan's native Minnesota and on South through Wisconsin, Iowa, Missouri and Arkansas, hugging the western bank of the Mississippi River, which it crosses at Memphis, continuing on down through the state of Mississippi into Louisiana, where it hits the Gulf Of Mexico at New Orleans. To the young Bob Zimmerman, growing up in chilly Minnesota with an urge to ramble, it must have seemed a romantically tight connection to the Southern homeland of R&B, blues and rock'n'roll, a tarmac Mississippi river leading to the music's heart.

Appropriately enough, it's celebrated in the album's most raucous blues boogie, a railroad shuffle scarred with Mike Bloomfield's razor-slashes of slide guitar and boasting the most flip and sacrilegious of Bible studies, as befits such a slick example of the Devil's music. In the album's opening lines, Dylan cheekily invokes his own father's name by having God refer to Abraham as "Abe," which effectively makes Bob himself the son whom God wants killed. The fourth verse extends the tone of theological satire through the mathematically precise nature of the family relations outlined with such biblical pedantry, while the remaining three verses broaden the vision of Highway 61 as a site of limitless possibility populated by a string of highly dubious gamblers, drifters and chancers called things like "Mack the Finger," and "Louie the King." It's perhaps indicative of Dylan's increasingly cynical attitude towards the entertainment business that the last, and most venal, of these is a promoter who seriously considers staging World War III out on Highway 61.

The song marks the only appearance on the album of drummer Sam Lay, who had backed Howlin' Wolf for six years, playing on most of his classic Chess recordings, before hooking up with young white blues-harp sensation Paul Butterfield to form the Butterfield Blues Band. "We recorded it in one night, pretty quickly," Lay recalls. "He knew what he was doing. The little police whistle in that track was mine, a little thing I had on my keychain. I had it in my drum case, and between takes I picked it up and blew it, and Dylan heard it and reached out his hand for it—didn't say nothin'—then when we went back over the track, he blew it a couple of times."

Al Kooper, who played the galloping electric piano on the track, remembers things a little differently, however. "I was wearing that siren around my neck at the time," he claims, "and I don't know exactly how Bob got hold of it, but he stuck it in his harmonica holder and it became immortalised on that track."

Just Like Tom Thumb's Blues

As the album nears its close, Dylan takes a right turn from his trip down Highway 61, heading off down Mexico way. Ciudad Juarez is a Mexican border town just across the Rio Grande from El Paso, the kind of place Americans go to let their hair down and their morals slide. It's used here in much the same way pulp novelist Jim Thompson and film maker Sam Peckinpah have used Mexico, both as a symbol of escape from the strict regimentation of American society, and as an index of how far down a person might have been forced to go—fallen so low, they've literally dropped out of America into the Third World.

The song opens to reveal the singer washed up, lost in the rain after an Easter vacation binge, with literal alienation hardening into its spiritual equivalent in the rank and humid atmosphere. Weak with mysterious ailment, drained by his excesses with hookers and booze, he assesses his own situation, and realises there's no place for the civilised side of him in a place so riddled with venality that its authorities brag of their corruption. Finally, abandoned by his friends, he decides to head back to New York City, a place which may be a sump of human depravity, but which still retains the vestiges of basic civilised contact.

The song has been likened to T.S. Eliot's portrait of 20th century alienation, *The Love Song Of J. Alfred Prufrock*, but it's probably more accurate to view it as depicting the downside of Dylan's attempt to escape such alienation (and boost his own creative powers) through intense sensory derangement and bohemian experientialism. Don't try this, he's saying, unless you're prepared for the worst. The presence of the eponymous nursery-rhyme character in the title probably refers to Rimbaud's *Ma Bohème* (aka *Wandering*), which finds the French Symbolist engaged in similar dropout pursuits: "I tore my shirt; I threw away my tie/Dreamy Tom Thumb, I made up rhymes/As I ran…in dark and scary places/And like a lyre I plucked the tired laces/Of my worn-out shoes, one foot beneath my heart."

The song's enervated tone is perfectly captured in the weary, reflective trudge of the music, which makes innovative use of two different pianos, Al Kooper playing the electric Hohner Pianet while Paul Griffin adds a lovely bar-room feel on tack piano.

▶

JUAREZ, MEXICO: DON'T GET LOST IN THE RAIN HERE, PARTICULARLY AT EASTER.

▶

ALBERT EINSTEIN: NOT DISGUISED AS ROBIN HOOD, SADLY.

Desolation Row

The south-of-the-border slant continues with 'Desolation Row', an 11-minute epic of entropy set to a courtly flamenco-tinged backing. Often described as a latterday equivalent of Dante's Inferno, it takes the form of a Fellini-esque parade of grotesques and oddities, in which equilibrium can only be maintained through immersion in the absurdity of the situation, acceptance of one's position in Desolation Row.

It could serve as Dylan's alternative State Of The Nation Address, an increasingly surreal update of the America depicted in 'Gates Of Eden'. From his vantage point on the Row, the singer describes the futile activity and carnival of deceit indulged in by a huge cast of iconic characters, some historical (Einstein, Nero), some biblical (Noah, Cain and Abel, The Good Samaritan), some fictional (Ophelia, Romeo, Cinderella, Casanova), some fantastic (The Hunchback Of Notre Dame, The Phantom Of The Opera), some literary (T.S. Eliot, Ezra Pound), and some who fit into none of the above categories, notably Dr Filth and his dubious nurse. Detached from their historical moorings, abandoned in this cultural wasteland, these figures serve mainly as shorthand signifiers for more complex bundles of human characteristics, allowing Dylan to cram extra layers of possible meaning into the song's already tightly-packed absurdist imagery.

As a result, the song is open to a plethora of interpretations, virtually impossible to decipher in detail with any degree of certitude. (The English poet Philip Larkin, reviewing the album in *Jazz Review*, described 'Desolation Row' as having "an enchanting tune and mysterious, possibly half-baked words.") Certain stanzas obviously offer implied criticisms of familiar Dylan targets: venal bureaucrats, bloodless academics, soulless theologians, loveless bourgeoisie, and the full stifling panoply of industrialised society in general, against which he posits the enduring power of creativity, love and freedom. Much of the song's enduring power derives from the way in which many of its characters are locked in symbiotic (but unfulfilling) balance with one another: the sex-fearing Ophelia

and the sex-obsessed Dr Filth; the blind commissioner and the tightrope walker to whom he is tied; Einstein and his friend, "a jealous monk," trapped in an insoluble debate between science and religion; Eliot and Pound, glimpsed arguing over arcane poetical points while pop singers steal their audience; and lustful Romeo and casual Cinderella, a cancellation of desire.

Like much of Dylan's material from this period, the song makes a mockery of accusations that he had betrayed or abandoned "protest" music; rather, what he has done is to broaden the scope of his protest to reflect more accurately the disconcerting hyper-reality of modern western culture. It's clear that he regarded the song as one of his best—he is reported to have spent some time discussing it with Allen Ginsberg, and when Nat Hentoff asked him what he would do if he were President, the least absurd part of Dylan's response was that he would "immediately re-write 'The Star-Spangled Banner', and little school children, instead of memorizing 'America The Beautiful', would have to memorize 'Desolation Row'."

Musically, the song is completely different from the rest of *Highway 61 Revisited*, abandoning the guitar/double keyboards set-up that gives the album its distinctive tone, in favour of a more stately, ruminative setting of just two guitars, with no rhythm section at all.  "I just think Bob wanted to set it apart in some way, shape or form," believes Al Kooper, "and instrumentation was just the way he chose. Bob Johnston had Charlie McCoy come up from Nashville to play electric guitar on that one, but there was a version on which Bob played acoustic guitar, Harvey Brooks played bass and I played electric guitar, with no drums on it."

"...an enchanting tune and mysterious, possibly half-baked words" **PHILIP LARKIN**

Positively 4th Street

T he follow-up single to 'Like A Rolling Stone', 'Positively 4th Street' (which reached US No. 7, UK No. 8 in September 1965) gave the impression of being simply the second wind of a one-sided argument, so closely did it follow its predecessor's formula, both musically and attitudinally. Such differences as there

"Dylan was very hostile, a mean cat, very cruel to people" DAVID COHEN

are between the two are marginal at best: Al Kooper's organ is poppier and better defined after a month's practice, and Dylan's delivery is slightly less caustic—an unconscious counterbalance, perhaps, to his most brutal condemnation yet.

The title offers a pretty clear indication of who (in general) the song was aimed at: Dylan once rented a flat on 4th Street in Greenwich Village, and the targets of his disdain are most likely to be the folkie in-crowd among whom he swam upon first relocating to New York from Minneapolis. As he admits in the fifth of twelve short verses, "I used to be among the crowd you're in with." Clearly, someone offended him deeply, judging by the song's contemptuous tone and its magisterially dismissive final lines, in which the victim is told, "I wish that for just one time you could stand inside my shoes/You'd know what a drag it is to see you."

Judging by the references to his having let someone down and caused them to lose their faith, the song's target is probably one of those folk-music authorities who rounded on Dylan first for "abandoning" protest songs, then again for picking up an electric guitar—in some cases, only to follow the same path themselves shortly afterwards, when they glimpsed the fortune and fame available. Which narrows the field down to a few hundred or so. If Dylan's intention was to inflict a more generalised guilt, he succeeded perfectly: everyone in the Village had the feeling he was

talking about them specifically, and quite a few felt deeply hurt by the broadside.

Dave Van Ronk—who, despite having had his arrangement of 'House Of The Rising Sun' stolen without permission or credit, had defended his friend when the folkies had turned on him a few years earlier, claiming that "The folk community is acting toward Dylan like a Jewish mother"—felt that Dylan's riposte was a righteous hit. "People from the early 1960s are very bitter about [Dylan]," he told Robert Shelton. "Although Bobby did treat most of them rather cavalierly, their reactions are largely their own fault. They just wanted to bask in the light of an obvious talent, to reflect a little glory on them... I think that 'Positively 4th Street' is a great song. It was high time Bobby turned around and said something to [*Sing Out!* editor] Irwin Silber and all those Jewish mothers. It's Dylan's farewell address."

Others, like folk archivist Israel (Izzy) Young, were more bemused at what they considered Dylan's cheek. "I don't know if it was [about me]," he told Anthony Scaduto, but it was unfair... Dylan comes in and takes from us, uses my resources, then he leaves and *he* gets bitter? He was the one who left!"

At the time, however, Dylan had raised bitterness to the level of an art form. Surrounded by a group of cronies that included Bob Neuwirth, Victor Maimudes, and the folk-singers Phil Ochs, Eric Anderson and David (Blue) Cohen, he would hold court at one of New York's bars or nightclubs—mostly the Kettle Of Fish—where those foolish or brave enough to try and intrude would be systematically demolished in the verbal crossfire. David Cohen became particularly close to Dylan, whose defensive, suspicious nature he shared. "Dylan was very hostile, a mean cat, very cruel to people," he admitted to Scaduto. "But I could see the reasons for it. It was very defensive, for one thing. Just from having to answer too many questions. The big thing was that his privacy had been invaded... He was a street cat, man, and he lost his freedom."

The verbal artillery was not just trained on outsiders, either. In the wake of his success, folk-singing had become something of a competitive sport, and Dylan realized that his cronies were picking crumbs from his table, trying to pick up clues that might bring them the same level of success. Cruelly, he rubbed their noses in their

► RICK DANKO (LEFT) AND ROBBIE ROBERTSON, THE FIRST OF THE HAWKS TO PLAY ON A DYLAN RECORDING.

opportunism, telling them they would never make it the way he had, and suggesting to Phil Ochs that he should find a new line of work, since he wasn't doing very much in his current career. "It was... very clever, witty, barbed and very stimulating, too," recalled Ochs, the most talented of the also-rans. "But you really had to be on your toes. You'd walk into a threshing machine if you were just a regular guy, naive and open, you'd be torn to pieces."

Can You Please Crawl Out Your Window?

The release of 'Can You Please Crawl Out Your Window?' in December 1965 proved a turning point in Phil Ochs' relationship with Dylan, when he made the mistake of being less than flattering at a playback of the new single. "It's okay," said Ochs, as a limousine arrived to ferry the entourage to an uptown disco, "but it's not going to be a hit." They had travelled but a few blocks when Dylan, no longer able to contain his mounting fury at this sacrilegious response, told the driver to pull over and ordered Ochs out of the car. "Get out, Ochs," he said. "You're not a folk-singer. You're just a journalist." Their friendship was over, consigned to history.

As it happens, both men's assessments were pretty much on the mark. Hidebound by the kind of protest issues that Dylan had deliberately thrown off, yet unable to animate them in anything like a comparable manner, Ochs *was* limited to a kind of sung journalism. And 'Can You Please Crawl Out Your Window?' was indeed nothing like as successful as Dylan's recent singles, scraping into the British Top 20 at No.17, but failing to crack the American charts at all.

The reasons are several. In the first place, it's not one of Dylan's better efforts, being basically yet another put-down song, but placed at one remove further from its target—Dylan's attempt to persuade a girl to elope being just a flimsy pretext to pick away at her current lover's faults, which seem to reside in a tight-assed materialism and lack of spirituality. The only line which compares with the verbal pyrotechnics of 'Like A Rolling Stone' is the scorching "If he needs a third eye he just grows it," and too many others seem like over-crafted exercises, excuses to work in polysyllabic oddities like "preoccupied" and "businesslike."

In the second place, the single's release was dogged by confusion and incompetence. Since neither song contains the actual words "positively fourth street," Columbia mistakenly issued an early version of 'Can You Please Crawl Out Your Window?' as 'Positively 4th Street', before quickly withdrawing it; and then, when 'Can You Please Crawl Out Your Window?' was itself released in the UK, the record company again initially put out the early version, before replacing it with the later version which constituted Dylan's first recording with members of The Band.

Al Kooper was fortunate enough to play on both. "There's a version of that on which I play celeste," he recalls, "which was done at the *Highway 61 Revisited* sessions. The other version was cut quite some time after that in New York, with Paul Griffin, Bobby Gregg on drums, and Rick [Danko] and Robbie [Robertson] from The Band, at the same time as 'One Of Us Must Know'—possibly the very same night." Again, Kooper's ambitious streak served him well. "I wasn't booked for the session," he admits, "but I visited the studio and ended up playing on it."

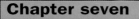

RAINY DAY WOMEN #12 & 35

PLEDGING MY TIME

VISIONS OF JOHANNA

ONE OF US MUST KNOW
(SOONER OR LATER)

I WANT YOU

STUCK INSIDE OF MOBILE WITH
THE MEMPHIS BLUES AGAIN

LEOPARD-SKIN PILL-BOX HAT

JUST LIKE A WOMAN

MOST LIKELY YOU GO YOUR
WAY AND I'LL GO MINE

TEMPORARY LIKE ACHILLES

ABSOLUTELY SWEET MARIE

4TH TIME AROUND

OBVIOUSLY 5 BELIEVERS

SAD EYED LADY OF THE
LOWLANDS

Blonde on Blonde

espite the disastrous Newport Festival appearance, Dylan was convinced he should continue his new rock'n'roll direction, particularly given the success of *Highway 61 Revisited*. But it would have to be better planned than at Newport. Accordingly, acting on the advice of Albert Grossman's secretary Mary Martin, he checked out a Canadian rock band, Levon & The Hawks, who had recently split from '50s rockabilly singer Ronnie Hawkins. Tight and disciplined, without sacrificing any of their essential wildness, the band's chops had been honed to a fine cutting-edge by years of one-night stands in clubs and juke-joints around the South and up in Canada, which native Arkansan Hawkins had made his base. Dylan was impressed, and midway through August he called them at Tony Mart's Nite Spot at Somers Point on the Jersey Shore, with an offer to back him at the Hollywood Bowl. "Who else is on the bill?" asked the drummer, Levon Helm. "Just us," answered Dylan.

"We had just come from Arkansas," recalls guitarist Robbie Robertson. "We were in a place near Atlantic City, a nice resort place to play, and we were going to try and do some stuff with Sonny Boy Williamson, even though it was a pretty off-the-wall idea for blacks and whites to be playing together at the time. So we went up to play this resort, to cool out a little, and it was there that we were contacted to meet with Bob. I went and met him and we talked about the possibilities and played a little music, and one thing led to another."

Initially, only Robbie and Levon were hired, joining Al Kooper and organist Harvey Brooks for a late August concert at Forest Hills Stadium, New York. The reaction was mixed—not as virulent as at Newport, but with a substantial proportion of dissenters. To silence the catcalls, Dylan had his band play the intro to 'Ballad Of A Thin Man' for what seemed like an eternity, and eventually most of the crowd were won over, rushing the stage during 'Like A Rolling Stone' and knocking Kooper's chair out from under him. "Kooper and I just looked at each other and laughed," recalls Harvey Brooks. "We were having the time of our lives. It was fun, gleeful, from the heart, exciting—an experience we'd never had before." Onstage, a laughing Dylan turned round to Levon Helm and shouted, "Looks like the attack of the beatniks

around here!" The Hollywood Bowl show a few days later was even better received, but following that, both Brooks and Kooper were replaced by the rest of the Hawks. The whole band decamped for a week of rehearsals in Toronto, where the Hawks' tailor, Lou Myles, ran up an outrageous brown houndstooth check suit for Dylan.

Through the rest of that Fall, Dylan and The Hawks toured the American heartland with a series of pioneering shows that brought high-volume rock-'n'roll to the country's old sports arenas, where Robertson's guitar would "reverberate around the big concrete buildings like a giant steel bullwhip," according to Levon Helm's autobiography *This Wheel's On Fire*. But the constant booing finally got to Helm, who quit the group prior to the 1966 world tour, being replaced by Mickey Jones (later to play the role of Tim Allen's ZZ Top-lookalike TV-show sidekick in the situation comedy *Home Improvement*). Things didn't improve outside America, however.

"We traveled all over the world, and people booed us everywhere we went," recalls Robbie Robertson. "What a strange concept of entertainment! We'd go on to the next town, and they'd boo us again, and we'd pack up our equipment and go on to the next place, and they'd boo us again. All over the world! I'll tell you what...it thickens the skin a little! After some of the places that we played with Ronnie Hawkins, and some of the rough joints we'd played when we were young— places where it's really a wonder anyone's left alive—after that, *this* was supposed to be success! You can get a little sadistic in these situations, turn up the volume that little bit louder!"

Dylan was particularly enamored with Robertson's guitar-playing, describing him as "the only mathematical guitar genius I've ever run into who does not offend my intestinal nervousness

◀ DYLAN FACES TOUGH QUESTIONING FROM THE FRENCH PRESS ON HIS WORLD TOUR.

▲ CHARLIE MCCOY, NASHVILLE SESSION LYNCHPIN OF DYLAN'S LATE SIXTIES ALBUMS; PLAYED BASS AND TRUMPET AT THE SAME TIME.

with his rear-guard sound," and using him as a sounding-board when working out new songs. "When we were on tour," explains Robertson, "a lot of times we would get a two-bedroom suite so we could play music. We were able to play most because we had guitars, but sometimes the other

"Nobody bitched or complained or rolled their eyes. That was the tempo of the sessions in Nashville, that anything could happen and these guys were fine with that" **AL KOOPER**

▶
DYLAN IN LONDON, 1966.

guys would bring their drums in, or an organ or something. It was just having fun with music, really." But the sound wasn't really gelling as Dylan wanted when he tried cutting more tracks in the New York studio—after several sessions between October 1965 and January 1966, he had only a couple of workable songs finished, and then only when Al Kooper dropped by the studio to add his organ. Accordingly, when Bob Johnston suggested going down to CBS's Nashville studio to record, Dylan agreed, taking along only Kooper and Robertson to augment a session crew comprised of the finest musicians money could hire, notably a nucleus of guitarists Wayne Moss, Jerry Kennedy and Joe South; drummer Kenny Buttrey; multi-instrumentalist Charlie McCoy; and the blind pianist Hargus 'Pig' Robbins.

"It was Bob Johnston's decision to record it in Nashville," recalls Kooper. "I gotta give him credit for that. Bob was a little reticent, but he thought it might be an interesting idea, so he took Robbie and I along to increase his comfort level." Like Kooper, the Nashville musicians were used to being booked by the hour, in three-hour slots, during which time they would usually expect to record three tracks. "These guys came from that mentality," Kooper acknowledges, "but they were booked open-end, and they had no preconceptions, so there was no pressure put on Bob at all. So they would sit there all day and maybe record four songs, sitting there for maybe ten hours while he went into the studio and wrote. No one disturbed

him, he was completely catered to, and whatever happened, happened. Nobody bitched or complained or rolled their eyes. That was the tempo of the sessions in Nashville, that anything could happen, and these guys were fine with that. Their temperaments were fabulous—they were the most calm, at-ease guys I'd ever worked with. New York people are very *New York*, and these guys were very country, and it was great to work with that kind of relaxation. But there was no way they would have heard of Bob at that time—as Dan Penn says, it was off the radar!"

"We hadn't really rehearsed the songs before we got to Nashville," admitted Robertson. "Sometimes Bob would be working out the ideas, and I'd play along and see if I could think of any ideas. The songs were just going by—once we had a set-up organized in the studio, Bob had a lot of material he wanted to experiment with, so they were just going by very quickly. Making a record, a lot of times you go in and record a song a day, laying down the tracks and overdubbing on them, but on this one we were just slamming through the songs."

At sessions snatched in between further tour dates in February and March, Dylan searched for what he called "that thin, wild, mercury sound," a more refined blend of the guitars/bass/drums/piano/organ/harmonica formula that had proven so effective on *Highway 61 Revisited*. To facilitate proceedings, Al Kooper translated Bob's ideas for the local musicians. "Bob had a piano put in his hotel room, and during the day he would write," Kooper recalls. "And as there were no cassette machines in those days, I would sit and play the piano for him, over and over, while he sat and wrote. We did this to prepare for the sessions at night, as well: he would come in an hour late, and I would go in and teach the first song to the band. Then he would arrive, and the band would be ready to play. He liked that, rather than have them sitting and learning the songs—although we did do that over the course of the night. After that, it was business as usual, though these guys were a crew, not dissimilar to Spector's Wrecking Crew—these were guys that played together, knew how to play together, and were incredibly versatile. I'd never seen anything like that."

The results were extraordinary, even by Dylan's previous standards, and he knew it. "...the last three things I've done on records [are] beyond criticism," he told Robert Shelton. "I'm not saying that because I think I'm any kind of god. I'm just saying that because I just know." Released as the first ever rock'n'roll double-album in May 1966, while Dylan and The Hawks were on tour in Britain, *Blonde On Blonde* was widely acclaimed for its musical sophistication, controlled power and subtle lyricism. Some thought that it was more approachable than his recent albums, finding its string of love songs less esoteric than the texts of *Highway 61 Revisited*, and everyone who heard it was struck by the way the album's overall dark, stifling mood was sustained through such a diverse range of musical approaches.

The gatefold cover photo, taken by Jerry Schatzberg, featured a slightly out-of-focus Dylan leaning against a wall wearing a brown suede jacket with a scarf knotted around his neck, frowning slightly at the camera from beneath a tangled halo of hair; inside, a suite of photos offered suitably shadowy glimpses of his life, along with an enigmatic posed shot of Dylan holding a small portrait of a woman in one hand and a pair of pliers in the other: they all contributed further to the album's air of reclusive yet sybaritic genius. Despite its hefty size (and price tag), *Blonde On Blonde* was another huge commercial success too, climbing into the American Top Ten and, upon its UK release three months later, reaching the British Top Three.

"I think *Blonde On Blonde* is my favorite album of all time," reflects Al Kooper, more than three decades later. "It's an amazing record, like taking two cultures and smashing them together with a huge explosion. I know that at one time, one of the jokier things considered was putting a paper band around the album saying 'Recorded in the South'— that was one of the late-evening control-room conversations between Albert Grossman and Bob Johnston. Because it was a very bizarre move at the time for Dylan to go to Nashville to record that album. It was unthinkable, actually—we lose sight of that because of *Nashville Skyline* and other things. He was the quintessential New York hipster—what was *he* doing in Nashville? It didn't make any sense whatsoever. But you take those two elements, pour them into a test-tube, and it just exploded."

Rainy Day Women #12 & 35

 eleased as a single in April 1966, 'Rainy Day Women #12 & 35' furnished the biggest shock yet for Dylan's old folkie fans, sounding as it did like a demented marching-band rehearsal staffed by crazy people out of their minds on loco-weed. The lyric, while not his most cryptic, was Dylan's most audacious yet, a unique mix of good-natured paranoia and nudge-nudge wink-wink bohemian hedonism in which the five verses' lists of persecution are each capped with the redemptive invocation "Everybody must get stoned."

The song was probably inspired by Ray Charles' famous recording of 'Let's Go Get Stoned', which Dylan had heard a few months earlier while visiting a Los Angeles coffee-shop with Phil Spector. In that short space of time, however, the argot had shifted slightly, so that the "stone" in question referred not to booze but to dope. The immediate effect was that the song had difficulty being playlisted by radio stations in both America and Britain, which didn't prevent the song becoming Dylan's biggest hit yet, garnering his second US No. 2 (or perhaps that should be US #2) and reaching the UK Top 10.

Nevertheless, the accusations did spur Dylan to denials. "This next song is what your English musical papers would call a 'drug song,' " he

"I never have and never will write a 'drug song'. I don't know how to. It's not a 'drug song', it's just vulgar." **BOB DYLAN**

announced at his Royal Albert Hall concert later in 1966. "I never have and never will write a 'drug song.' I don't know how to. It's not a 'drug song,' it's just vulgar." In another interview, he expanded on the theme: "People just don't need drugs," he said. "Keep things out of your body. We all take medicine, as long as you know why you're taking it. If you want to crack down on the drug situation, the criminal drug situation takes place in suburban housewives' kitchens, the ones who get wiped out on alcohol every afternoon and then make supper. You can't blame them, and you can't blame their husbands. They've been working in the mines all day. It's understandable." And to Nat Hentoff he explained, "I wouldn't advise anybody to use drugs —certainly not the hard drugs; drugs are medicine. But opium and hash and pot—now, those things aren't drugs; they just bend your mind a little. I think everybody's mind should be bent once in a while. Not by LSD, though. LSD is medicine—a different kind of medicine. It makes you aware of the Universe, so to speak; you realize how foolish objects are. But LSD is not for groovy people; it's for mad, hateful people who want revenge."

The truth, of course, was rather different. He had been using several different types of drugs for different reasons—primarily marijuana, to fuel both creativity and relaxation, and amphetamines, to withstand the hectic pace of the his touring schedule, during which he would routinely stay awake for days on end, continuing to play music in hotel rooms after shows, and working on songs constantly. "It takes a lot of medicine to keep up this pace," he told Robert Shelton between tour dates in March 1966.

The effect of stronger "medicine" was discernible to others. "Dylan is LSD on stage, Dylan is LSD set to music," gushed Phil Ochs, who knew him better than most, while his old friend from Greenwich Village, Dave Van Ronk, told Bob Spitz that although he knew Dylan was no junkie, he believed he had dabbled on occasion with heroin. "A lot of people *think* that I shoot heroin," Dylan acknowledged to Robert Shelton. "But that's *baby talk*. I do a lot of things, man, which help me... And I'm smart enough to know that I don't depend on them for my existence." But whatever he was doing to himself, he had the integrity to keep it to himself. When an Australian actress,

Rosemary Gerrette, spent some time with Dylan and The Band on their tour of Australia, he refused to turn her on to the dope he was smoking. "No, I'm not gonna give you any," he explained. "I'm not gonna start you off on anything."

For 'Rainy Day Women #12 & 35', recorded at the final Nashville session, Dylan wanted to try something a little different, and suggested recording the song out in the studio parking lot with a Salvation Army band. Drummer Kenny Buttrey felt that the local Salvation Army band might be a little more disciplined than Dylan expected, and suggested that, if Bob was after a more ramshackle sound, the musicians already assembled could "play pretty dumb if we put our minds to it." Accordingly, he dis-assembled his drum kit, laying the bass drum flat across two chair-backs and deadening his snare-drum to approximate the sound of a marching-band drummer. Al Kooper switched from organ to tambourine, augmenting his part with assorted yelling and whooping. And despite the late hour—it was the early hours of the morning—a trombonist friend of Charlie McCoy's, called Wayne Butler, was brought in to play at a moment's notice.

"They called him in the middle of the night," recalls Al Kooper, "and in half an hour he was there, in a shirt and tie and suit, immaculately groomed! He played for no longer than 20 or 30 minutes, and then graciously left! That's all he was required for —called at three o'clock, and he was back home at four-thirty. Charlie McCoy played bass and trumpet on that track at the same time—the bass with one hand, and the trumpet with the other—because we didn't overdub on that album at all, Dylan was adamant about that. So all the vocals were done live and, catering to that, Charlie McCoy played two instruments at once. I almost fell on the floor when I saw that. It's like Roland Kirk, except they're not all wind instruments! That was the most awesome display of musicality I'd seen in my life, just 'Bam!' right on the spot."

The song was cut in just two or three takes—too fast for Robbie Robertson, who blinked and missed it completely. "On 'Rainy Day Women', I think I went out to get some cigarettes or something," he believes, "and they'd recorded it by the time I returned!"

Pledging My Time

After the good-time goofing of 'Rainy Day Women #12 & 35', the slow blues 'Pledging My Time' sets the humid, emotionally oppressive tone for the rest of *Blonde On Blonde*. Slithering in on the back of Kenny Buttrey's enervated snare-roll, it slouches along, streaked by Robbie Robertson's spindly Chicago blues guitar lines and Dylan's harmonica, with some of Hargus 'Pig' Robbins' finest blues piano holding it all together. Lyrically, references to "a poison headache" and the room being "so stuffy, I can hardly breathe" combine vividly with the music to evoke a smoky, late-night club ambiance whose few remaining patrons have slipped beyond tipsy to the sour, sore-headed aftermath of drunk. Like much of the album, it's a beautifully-sustained exercise in mood, notable mainly for the remarkable predictive prescience of the final verse, in which "Somebody got lucky/But it was an accident," which spookily prefigures Dylan's motorcycle crash of July 1966, which turned out to be probably the luckiest thing that could have happened to him at the time.

Visions of Johanna

Although most of the songs on *Blonde On Blonde* were written as the album was being recorded, 'Visions Of Johanna' had been with Dylan several months by the time it was recorded in Nashville for the album. Indeed two earlier versions had been cut at New York sessions in late November 1965 and January 1966 with The Band, as he tried to discover the song's ideal setting. Along the way, a few changes were made in the lyrics, mostly minor alterations—"like silk" becomes "she's delicate," little boy lost goes from being "so useless and so small" to being just "so useless and all"— but with a couple of more substantial revisions to the final verse involving the deletion of the line "He examines the nightingale's code" and the switching of the positions of the fiddler and the peddler.

◀

DAVE VAN RONK, ONE OF DYLAN'S OLDEST NEW YORK FRIENDS, KNEW HE WAS NO JUNKIE.

Given the lyrical malleability indicated by these changes, it's perhaps best not to try and ascribe too literal an interpretation to 'Visions Of Johanna', which is more of an impressionistic mood piece anyway. If it doesn't really matter to the writer whether it's the peddler or the fiddler who speaks to the countess, why should it matter to us? The song remains one of the high points of Dylan's

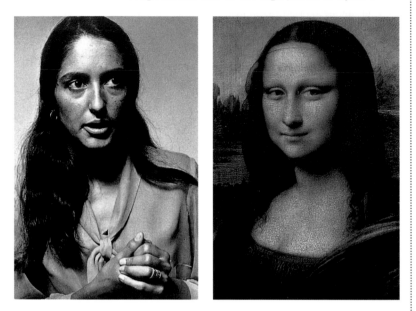

"I had the feeling the two of them were in cahoots to make sure I never thought the song was anything to do with me" **JOAN BAEZ**

canon, particularly favored among hardcore Dylanophiles, possibly because it so perfectly sustains its position on the cusp of poetic semantics, forever teetering on the brink of lucidity, yet remaining impervious to strict decipherment.

For a long time, the song went under the working title of 'Seems Like A Freeze-Out' (a term meaning "to stand-off"), which evokes something of the air of nocturnal suspension in which the verse tableaux are sketched. They're full of whispering and muttering, low-volume radio, echoes and ghosts, a misty, crepuscular netherworld inhabited by the increasingly familiar denizens of Dylan's imagination, a parade of low-lifes, functionaries, all-night girls and slumming snobs.

Here and there, images and lines accrete into possible wisps of meaning: the line in verse four

about "the one with the mustache," for instance, may refer to the Mona Lisa, also mentioned in the same verse—or, more specifically, to Marcel Duchamp's "revision" of the Mona Lisa by the addition of a graffiti mustache to a print of the portrait. (It has also been noted that the picture in question is a three-quarter length portrait, which may account for why its subject may be unable to find her knees.) And Joan Baez apparently felt suspicious that certain images in the song referred to her, particularly after Allen Ginsberg, possibly primed by Dylan, tried to pump her for her opinions on the song. "I had the feeling the two of them were sort of in cahoots to make sure I never thought the song had anything to do with me," she told Anthony Scaduto.

Certainly, on the most basic level the song is simply a delineation of the narrator's differing feelings towards a purely carnal lover—the always available Louise—and the more spiritual, but unattainable, Madonna-figure Johanna, whose most likely model would be Sara, whom Dylan had recently married (and whom he described to Robert Shelton as "Madonna-like"). On a deeper level, however, 'Visions Of Johanna' would seem to be about the artist's search for transcendence, the constant attempt to locate inspiration outside of the physical world, in some more spiritual aesthetic realm, fully cognizant of the desiccation that ultimately awaits all art through the "salvation" of curators and museums. In the final analysis, Dylan appears to be saying, the artist is doomed to pursue these visions of perfection, whatever the cost and whatever the outcome, since they are what gives meaning to his/her life—they are, effectively, all that remain.

The song's journey to its final form echoes this process of aesthetic discovery. In the earliest of the three versions, it begins as a loose, medium-tempo rocker, which alters subtly until, by the final verse, it's clear that everyone except the drummer (the rather limited Bobby Gregg, who continues to whack along regardless) has located something rather more haunting and transcendent in the song. The second version builds upon this insight, but it is not until the final Nashville version that it all comes together, with Al Kooper's eerie organ casting dusky shadows across the verses and, from the second verse through to the conclusion, Robbie Robertson's tiny, bent-note stitches of lead guitar complementing one of Dylan's most accomplished vocal performances.

"If you listen to it very critically, it's very important what Joe South's bass is doing in that," says Al Kooper. "He's playing this throbbing thing which rhythmically is an amazing bass part, and it really makes the track. Charlie McCoy couldn't have done that, he doesn't think like that. On my part, I was responding to the lyrics—like when he says, 'The ghost of electricity howls in the bones of her face,' it was very challenging to play something after that line!" It says much that the track retains that challenge for the listener over three decades later. It remains one of Dylan's finest achievements.

One Of Us Must Know

(Sooner Or Later)

The first track recorded for *Blonde On Blonde*—at New York sessions in late January 1966—'One Of Us Must Know (Sooner Or Later)' was originally released as a single in February 1966, failing to chart in America (although on its UK release in April, it narrowly missed the Top 30).

Schematically, the song is at the opposite end of the romantic trajectory from its predecessor 'Can You Please Crawl Out Your Window?': having succeeded in persuading the object of his affections to elope with him, the relationship has now run its course, foundered, and the singer has moved on to the autopsy stage, trying to divine exactly what went wrong, when, and where. The air of feverish inquest is sustained by the intense, melodramatic interplay between Paul Griffin's piano and Al Kooper's organ, while Robbie Robertson stitches the chorus together with a beautifully-judged series of tingling grace notes.

"I wasn't booked for the session," admits Al Kooper, "but I visited the session and ended up playing on it. The piano playing on 'One Of Us Must Know' is quite magnificent, it influenced me enormously as a pianist. It's probably Paul Griffin's

finest moment. He was an amazing player, but he felt badly done by when Valerie Simpson, the woman he loved, and to whom he had taught his piano style, left him and went off to achieve fame and fortune with Nick Ashford. He felt she had stolen his piano style."

The song grew out of 'She's Your Lover Now' (AKA 'Just A Little Glass Of Water'), another romantic autopsy which Dylan worked on intermittently around the same time but which was never officially released until it appeared on *The Bootleg Series, Vols 1-3*. The line "you were just there, that's all" appears in both songs. The subject of the song, which is about as close as Dylan gets to an apology, might be Joan Baez: the line "I didn't know that you were sayin' goodbye for good" could refer to her final departure from the hotel room in *Don't Look Back*, after which the pair didn't speak for several years.

Baez undoubtedly felt deeply hurt by his behavior—she couldn't bring herself to listen to his new records for quite some time, and it was only after urgings from her editor E. L Doctorow (subsequently the author of *Ragtime*) that she could be persuaded to mention Dylan in her autobiography *Daybreak*, and then only briefly, as "The Dada King." For his part, Dylan bore her no malice. To Robert Shelton, he admitted she had helped establish his name, but claimed that he didn't feel any debt to her. "I feel bad for her because she has nobody to turn to that's going to be straight with her," he explained, adding cryptically, "She hasn't got that much in common with the street vagabonds who play insane instruments."

I Want You

The third single taken from the album, 'I Want You' was a Top 20 hit on both sides of the Atlantic when it was released in Summer 1966. Musically the straightest pop track he ever recorded, the song's lyrics occupy a curious position, balanced as they are between the most direct of address and the most obfuscatory of images. It's perhaps for this reason that the song is sometimes taken to be

◀

JOAN BAEZ (LEFT) AND THE MONA LISA: UNCANNY VISIONS?

about heroin—the ecstatic profusion of imagery prompting a recurrent plea for more.

Through the verses, we encounter a typical parade of Dylan characters, too numerous to inhabit the song's three minutes comfortably: a guilty undertaker, a lonesome organ grinder, weeping mothers, fathers, daughters, sleeping saviors, the Queen of Spades, a chambermaid and a "dancing child with his Chinese suit"—the last rumored to refer to Brian Jones, to whom Dylan was on occasion not very cute, allegedly. From this confusing tangle of characters and interrogations, Dylan emerges to repeat his simplest, most straightforward of choruses, the most basic of testaments to his affection. It's as if the simple, secure love expressed so directly in the choruses offers him a refuge from the confusion and demands of his everyday life: it's the fixed point to which he can return after battling the demons of his imagination and the duties of his career.

"When we were running the stuff down in his hotel room, I went fucking mental over that track" **AL KOOPER**

It was also the last song cut for the album. "When we were running the stuff down in his hotel room, I went fucking mental over that track," recalls Al Kooper. "I kept saying, 'Let's do 'I Want You',' and Bob just kept putting it off, just to piss me off. He knew he was going to do it, but I kept pressing, because I had all these arrangement ideas, and I was afraid it wouldn't get cut, but he kept saying, 'No,' until finally, on the last night, I taught it to the band before he came in. "When he came in, I said, 'I took the liberty of teaching them 'I Want You',' and he just smiled at me and said, 'Well, yeah, we could do that.' I said, 'It's all set, just come on in and plug into this.' I had the basic arrangement in my head, but then Wayne Moss played that sixteenth-note guitar run, and I wasn't ready for that! It was a wonderful addition to what I had in mind! That was one I wrote out parts for, which the musicians embellished in their wonderful Nashville way, and it became even bigger than what I had heard in that track."

▶

LEOPARD-SKIN WAS THAT SEASON'S PREFERRED MILLINERY FABRIC...

Stuck Inside Of Mobile With The Memphis Blues Again

The second of the album's three epics crams nine complex verses into seven short minutes, each retailing an absurd little vignette illustrating contemporary alienation. In the first, the disquieting effect of an itinerant mute fails to be dispelled by the kindly attentions of ladies, leaving the narrator with a vague feeling of unease.

In the second, the unease persists through a foppish Shakespeare's conversation with a French girl. (Dylan enthused about Shakespeare to Robert Shelton, describing the playwright and poet as "A raving queen and a cosmic amphetamine brain," though in this context, the playwright's attire of bells and pointy shoes may be a reference to the stylish British pop stars Dylan had been mixing with.) The sense of disjunction is reinforced by the first of a series of Spoonerized image-confusions— involving the stolen post-office and the locked mailbox—which vividly convey the sense of synaesthetic swapping of the senses reported by many LSD takers, in which sights can be smelt, sounds viewed, smells heard, and so on.

The third verse finds a girl called Mona (perhaps the same one hymned so satirically by Bo Diddley) offering the song's narrator some advice about railroad men drinking up your blood like wine, a dubious claim which originally derives from 'I Wish I Was A Mole In The Ground', a weird traditional folk song included on Harry Smith's *Anthology Of American Folk Music* in a version by the 1920s' singing lawyer, Bascom Lamar Lunsford, who learned the song from a North Carolina neighbor, Fred Moody. Clearly relishing the extension of an earlier absurdity, Dylan trumps the image with his own deliciously absurd image of one such railwayman smoking his eyelids and punching his cigarette.

And so the madness mounts up: the narrator's grandfather goes mad and dies after building a fire in the road and shooting it; a preacher has weighty headlines stapled to his chest; further confusion—perhaps the cause of his synaesthetic turmoil—sees Dylan mixing his medicines, blowing his mind on gin and "Texas medicine," whatever that is; and in the song's most enduring couplet, the dancer Ruthie offers earthier relief from his high-class girlfriend: "Your debutante just knows what you need/But I know what you want." At the song's conclusion the narrator is overwhelmed by the barrage of absurdity, waiting to find out how much his experiences have cost him, and how he can avoid them, as if his life had become a fairground ride upon which he was trapped, an endless cycle of confusions and allusions. Which was probably closer to the truth than most realized.

"That's Joe South playing guitar on 'Memphis Blues Again'," recalls Al Kooper. "I was in awe of his abilities, so I was excited to be in the room with him. He was fantastic, he has that sort of hammering-on style that Curtis Mayfield and Reggie Young have. I was very happy with the organ on that, too, it has a lot of spontaneity. I think there's some lovely interplay between us on this one—that's where, I think, the organ and guitar are most perfectly matched. I heard it again recently and went, 'Wow!' Usually I go 'Oww!'."

Leopard-Skin Pill-Box Hat

One of the album's jokier cuts, 'Leopard-Skin Pill-Box Hat' is a plodding 12-bar blues satirizing the superficiality of fashion—and, by extension, the emptiness of materialism in general—a cogent subject for Dylan's caustic attentions in the style-obsessed '60s. The absurd millinery in question is exactly the kind of ludicrous garment which would be in fashion one day and out the next, as the industry hurried to supplant its

previous designs. It's clearly an amazing creation, balancing on one's head "just like a mattress balances on a bottle of wine"—which is to say, precariously, albeit cleverly, with an inordinate amount of time and attention spent on such a preposterous maneuver. And it's powerfully effective, able to sway the affections even of Dylan's doctor, an increasingly frequent figure in his songs.

Dylan had recently experienced the transient attractions of materialism at first hand, when, having been greatly impressed by John Lennon's 22-room Weybridge mansion on a visit there during his 1965 UK tour, he went out and bought a 31-room place of his own upon his return to America. "I bought one just as soon as I got back from England," he told Robert Shelton. "And it turned into a *nightmare!*" Also on that trip to England, he had demonstrated a remarkably mature (though ultimately mistaken) grasp of the transience of his own position and the ephemeral, fashion-based nature of fame in general, in an interview with Maureen Cleave of the London *Evening Standard*. "I've seen all these crazes come and go," he told her, "and I don't think I'm more than a craze. In a coupla years, I shall be right back where I started—an unknown." As it turned out, his appeal proved rather more enduring than the eponymous leopard-skin pill-box hat.

The album credits specifically singled out Bob Dylan as lead guitarist on this track, but while the slightly shaky guitar introduction (center-right in the stereo mix) may be by Dylan, the piercing lines coming primarily from the left channel (with a little spillage caught on the right channel microphone), including the solo break, are undoubtedly Robbie Robertson's work—as, perhaps, was the song's Chicago-blues format.

"Bob liked blues singers, but it was a different blues background to mine," Robertson told me. "His was more folk-blues, like the Reverend Gary Davis and Blind Lemon Jefferson, and I was listening more to the Chicago blues, via the Mississippi Delta—[Howlin'] Wolf and Muddy [Waters] and [Little] Walter, those people. I wasn't as drawn to acoustic music as he was—I'd been playing electric guitar since I was quite young, so it was more attractive to me. But when Bob and I were spending so much time together on tour, a lot of the time we would get a couple of guitars and just play music together, and in the course of that,

▶

ANDY WARHOL AND EDIE SEDGWICK, NEW YORK GLITTERATI CHUMS OF DYLAN: EDIE WAS THE MOST LIKELY INSPIRATION FOR 'JUST LIKE A WOMAN'.

we were trading a lot of our musical backgrounds: he was turning me on to things, and I was turning him on to things, and this trading of ideas helped us a bit in the way we approached music, both live and on record."

In May 1967, the track became the fifth single taken from *Blonde On Blonde*, though its hardcore Chicago style proved too tough for most people's tastes, and it failed to chart on either side of the Atlantic. Perhaps it might have fared better if a later version of the song had been released instead. Al Kooper explains: "In the studio, besides the Hammond organ, there was also a Lowery organ, which has some great sound effects, including a doorbell that went "ding-dong!" There was one version of 'Leopard-Skin Pill-box Hat' where it started with "ding-dong!" and the band yelled out "Who's there?" and then it went into the song. It was great! Too bad they didn't use it..."

Just Like A Woman

T he euphonious lilt of 'Just Like A Woman', with Dylan's sly croon borne as if in a sedan chair upon the delicate triplets of acoustic guitar and piano, disguises one of his more controversial songs. In the ground swell of feminist liberation which followed the counter-cultural changes of the late 1960s, Dylan was roundly condemned by some feminist commentators for the song's unflattering portrait of its subject, and the implication in the chorus that grasping, whinging and weakness were "natural" female traits, along with a specific womanly manner of making love. This, however, seems a determinedly literal way of reading a song whose melody—the most overtly "feminine" of the album—and title—a sardonic appropriation of a classic misogynist exclamation—suggest a more ironic intention. It also ignores the fact that the song's delimitations are not between man and woman, but between woman and girl: it's a matter of maturity, rather than gender.

The song was widely believed—not least by her acquaintances among Andy Warhol's Factory retinue—to be about the Factory pin-up girl Edie Sedgwick, a '60s "ace face" and New York scene-maker with whom Dylan had a brief association in 1965. (Indeed, Robert Margoulef's biopic of Edie, *Ciao Manhattan*, includes "Just Like A Woman" on its soundtrack.) A former Boston debutante and model, Sedgwick dedicated herself to meeting beautiful, talented people, with the hope that she herself might develop artistic talent of some sort, or, failing that, serve as an artist's muse. Accordingly, she became one of Warhol's iconic superstars, before transferring her attentions to Dylan, to whom she was introduced at the Kettle Of Fish bar on MacDougal Street in Greenwich Village.

Her interest may not have been purely amicable; it was rumored that Albert Grossman was interested in developing her career—though eventually even he was forced to admit defeat as to the means by which to achieve this, when it transpired that Edie was a hopeless singer. A rumored Dylan/Edie movie, meanwhile, never got beyond the talking stage. Warhol himself was apparently annoyed at her defection, as well as paranoid about Dylan's opinion of him: for some time, he apparently believed himself to be the chrome horse-riding diplomat in 'Like A Rolling Stone' (and Edie, therefore, its subject), despite the fact that the song had been written well before Dylan had met either Edie or Andy.

Edie's growing infatuation with Bob was eventually broken early in 1966 when Warhol, who had learned that Dylan had been secretly married a month or two earlier, took great relish in breaking the news to her. She drifted away from both camps, but not before making an impression on *Blonde On Blonde* —she was included among the photographs in the original inner sleeve (removed from the CD booklet), and some (including Patti Smith, who wrote a poem about her) believe her to be the inspiration for the album title. It would certainly explain the song's most often queried line, about "her fog, her amphetamine, and her pearls," which in the mid-'60s New York drug culture would have been recognized as references to marijuana, speed and pep-pills.

She eventually died of a barbiturate overdose in 1971, while 'Just Like A Woman' became one of

Dylan's most popular songs. Ironically, at a time when his publishers were kept increasingly busy collecting his royalties from the flood of cover-versions of his material—in September 1965, there were no fewer than eight of his songs in the US Top 40, half of them covers—'Just Like A Woman' was the only track from *Blonde On Blonde* to attract significant attention from other artists. It also became the song Dylan performed most often over the subsequent two decades. It's not known for sure, however, exactly when during this period the song's second line was changed from the recorded "Tonight is lost inside the rain" to the less evocative "Tonight as I stand inside the rain," as in the collected *Lyrics 1962-1985*. In the *Biograph* annotations, Dylan half-remembers writing the song on the road, in a hotel in Kansas City "or something" the previous Thanksgiving, having declined an offer of dinner at someone's house.

Most Likely You Go Your Way And I'll Go Mine

Apart from the intrusion of a quirky, nonsensical middle-eight concerning a badly-built, stilt-walking judge, this is perhaps the most straightforward Dylan lyric from the entire 1965/66 period, crystallizing the moment when a relationship finally cracks, the narrator tiring of the effort of dragging his lover along. In the *Biograph* annotations, Dylan reckons he must have written the song following a failed relationship "where, you know, I was lucky to have escaped without a broken nose." Charlie McCoy repeated his party-trick of playing bass guitar and trumpet at the same time, though the real star is drummer Kenny Buttrey, setting a sprightly pace for the others to follow with some delightful snare-rolls.

The song continues the fascination with adverbial titles that Dylan had started with 'Queen Jane Approximately' and 'Positively Fourth Street', and which would continue through much of *Blonde On Blonde*'s third side. "He probably named all of them at the same time," reckons Al Kooper. "They were called other things until he said, 'Well, what are we gonna call this? 'Absolutely Sweet Marie', 'Obviously 5 Believers', 'Rainy Day Women # 12 & 35'…like that—they were pretty much all named at the same time, as I recall."

Temporary Like Achilles

Another slow, smoky blues, this one dominated by the beautifully evocative piano of Hargus "Pig" Robbins, who achieves a perfect balance between the song's basic chord structure and the restrained trills which, aside from a brief wheeze of harmonica, serve as its sole embellishment. The song is all mood, a straightforward lament from a would-be lover kept dangling on his lady's whims: she knows the strength of his ardor, but remains largely unmoved—though not completely inaccessible.

A couple of hallucinatory images—a crawling scorpion and a velvet door—add enigmatic color to Dylan's plaint, while in the final verse, his situation is summed up by reference to the eponymous Achilles: "How come you get someone like him to be your guard?" asks Dylan. The answer, of course, is to lead her suitor on, to keep him dangling on the vague promise of distant fulfillment. In classical mythology, Achilles was virtually impregnable, save for his heel, which eventually proved his downfall; so his presence as guard of her affections suggests that, while it may indeed be difficult for Dylan to break down her resistance, it is not completely impossible. But the task will be as difficult as catching Achilles in his one weak spot, and may take a while: for "temporary" as Achilles is, he's still likely to be around a considerable time.

The chorus and part of the tune were salvaged from 'Medicine Sunday', a dour number attempted in late 1965 whose surviving minute-long fragment concludes "I know you want my lovin'/Mama but you're so hard." With a simple inversion of the first line, Dylan located the song's true direction.

Absolutely sweet Marie

Containing one of the most oft-repeated of Dylan's little life-lessons—the claim that "to live outside the law you must be honest," which served as justification for many a bohemian existence—'Absolutely Sweet Marie' is one of the album's simpler pleasures, from the poppy Lowery organ figure with which Al Kooper opens proceedings, to the wailing harmonica solo which Dylan skates over the second middle-eight break, and the sexual jesting in the lyrics.

It was whipped up on the spot in the studio. "I can remember the ones where I had the time to show it to the band," says Kooper, "and that wasn't one of them. The real unsung hero on that track is [again] the drummer, Kenny Buttrey—the beat is amazing, and that's what makes the track work."

The lyrics are a spicy combination of sexual entendre, old folk reference and surreal intrusions by various members of Dylan's repertory company of unusual characters, in this case the river-boat captain and the Persian drunkard. The first verse is as plain an expression of sexual frustration as Dylan penned: you can all but see his eyebrow cheekily raised as he sings about "beating on my trumpet" when "it gets so hard, you see." The references to the railroad (and its gate) offer variations on the common train/sex metaphor, while the "six white horses" are a further blues image of sexual potency, appearing both in Blind Lemon Jefferson's 'See That My Grave Is Kept Clean'—recorded by Dylan on his debut album—and in 'Coming Round The Mountain', the traditional song later covered by Dylan and The Band as one of the (unreleased) Basement Tapes numbers.

4th Time Around

A strange combination of the desultory and the surreal, 'Fourth Time Around' describes a romantic encounter of symbolic emptiness, whose narrative, tossed this way and that by the quirky gusts of imagery, drifts along with as little volition as its protagonists' actions. At times, it seems as if Dylan is simply rhyming whatever slips into his mind, following the story rather than dictating its course, even as it slides between verses, courtesy of an outrageously elongated "He-errrr" whose length is further exaggerated by comparison with the clipped brevity of the ensuing "Jamaican rum."

Musically, the song stands apart from the rest of *Blonde On Blonde* by dint of its lightness and delicacy, Dylan's vocal and wistful harmonica riding the rippling Spanish arpeggios of Wayne Moss and Charlie McCoy's twin acoustic guitars. "Those guitars playing in harmony, that's pure Nashville," says Al Kooper. "People don't think like that anywhere else."

John Lennon allegedly thought the song was a parody of The Beatles' 'Norwegian Wood', which appeared in December 1965 on their *Rubber Soul* album. "I thought it was very ballsy of Dylan to do 'Fourth Time Around'," recalls Kooper. "I asked him about it—I said, it sounds so much like 'Norwegian Wood', and he said, 'Well actually, 'Norwegian Wood' sounds a lot like *this*! I'm afraid they took it from me, and I feel that I have to, y'know, record it.' Evidently, he'd played it for them, and they'd nicked it! I said, 'Aren't you worried about getting sued by The Beatles?' and he said, 'They couldn't sue me!' " And indeed, they didn't.

ACHILLES AT SCYROS, FROM A POMPEII FRESCO NOW PERMANENTLY IN NAPLES ARCHAEOLOGICAL MUSEUM.

Obviously 5 Believers

The fourth and last of *Blonde On Blonde*'s Chicago-blues workouts (after 'Pledging My Time', 'Leopard-Skin Pill-Box Hat' and 'Temporary Like Achilles'), 'Obviously 5 Believers' is the closest the album comes to an out-and-out rocker. Save for apparently arbitrary references to "fifteen jugglers" (presumably from the stock circus company with which Dylan populated his songs) and the "five believers" of the title, it's a basic love moan that steams along on Robbie Robertson's hot-rod lead guitar, with Charlie McCoy's harmonica fills serving as links between the verses.

"I think that was the track I did that got everybody to accept me," reckons Robbie Robertson. "It's a funny thing in Nashville, it was very clique-ish: the musicians that played on sessions there didn't like any outsiders coming in, and because Bob Johnston had already got these guitar players in there, when I came along it was kind of like, 'What do we need *him* for?'—nobody *said* that, but you could feel that kind of a vibe."

"When we played live," Robertson explains, "Bob would give me a lot of guitar solos—it was kind of a new experience for him, to have somebody he could just look over at, and they'd come out wailing; and when we were recording in Nashville, it was the same thing: he'd sing a couple of verses then look over at me, and I'd come out wailing! And it was at that point that the guys in Nashville accepted me, because I was doing something that none of them did, so I don't think they felt I was treading on their territory. They became quite friendly after that. I suppose the proof was in the pudding with these guys, that if you were doing something musically that they respected, then they respected you."

Sad Eyed Lady Of The Lowlands

'**S**ad Eyed Lady Of The Lowlands' took up the entire fourth side of *Blonde On Blonde*, a distinction rare even in the habitually elongated arena of improvised jazz, and unprecedented in pop music. For all that, it was only about the same length as 'Desolation Row', around the eleven-minute mark; but Dylan evidently wanted the song to stand alone, considering it at

▶

the time "the best song I've ever written."

A love song in five lengthy stanzas, it has a measured grace and stately pace that seems as much funeral procession as wedding march, with a depth of devotion absent from Dylan's work since 'Love Minus Zero/No Limit'. Though the song has more than its fair share of enigmatic imagery, there's no trace here of the jokey nihilism and existential absurdity that marked out *Highway 61 Revisited* and much of the rest of *Blonde On Blonde*. This time around, clearly, it's serious.

In 1976, Dylan finally confirmed what everyone had known all along, when he admitted "Stayin' up for days in the Chelsea Hotel/Writin' 'Sad Eyed Lady Of The Lowlands' for you" in his song 'Sara', from the *Desire* album. The late rock critic Lester Bangs poo-pooed this explanation with characteristic bravado in *Creem* magazine, claiming "I have it on pretty good authority that Dylan wrote 'Sad Eyed Lady', as well as about half of the rest of *Blonde On Blonde*, wired out of his skull in the studio, just before the songs were recorded, while the session men sat around waiting on him, smoking cigarettes and drinking beer."

There seems no reason to doubt either claim —the musicians were certainly kept hanging around while Dylan finished the song but, equally, he was known to work and re-work his more important songs for some time before recording them, and most of that work was probably done back in New York, before the Nashville sessions. But whatever the circumstances of its evolution, there is no doubting that the song's subject is Sara Lowndes, whom Dylan had married in a secret ceremony on November 22, 1965. Even relatively close friends were unaware of their marriage, and Dylan contrived to keep it under wraps for as long as possible—two days after the event, he answered an interviewer's query about the possibility of him settling down, getting married and having children with a brazenly disingenuous "I don't hope to be like anybody. Getting married, having a bunch of kids, I have no hope for it."

It's perhaps an indication of the depth of his devotion that he conspired to shield Sara from the public eye in a way which didn't apply to his other female friends. Their relationship, it appears, had been conducted along such lines right from the start: Joan Baez's sister Mimi Fariña recalled overhearing Dylan making a secret date with another woman —

whom she later realized must have been Sara—mere minutes after Baez had departed from a weekend get-together up at Woodstock shortly before the April 1965 UK Tour; and more recently, Edie Sedgwick (see entry for 'Just Like A Woman') was shocked to find out that the young pop rebel she had been courting was actually a happily married man.

Short, dark-haired and, indeed, sad-eyed, Sara had been married before, to *Playboy* chief Victor Lowndes—the "magazine husband" referred to in the final verse—but had since set about building a new life of her own. She appears to have been the perfect marital foil for Dylan, posing no threat to his ego and bearing him a string of children in quick succession. Possessed of a quiet but unimposing fortitude, she furnished him with a much-needed oasis of calm and sincerity away from the high-octane hurly-burly and habitual deceit of the entertainment industry.

There is a similar nocturnal feel to the song as there is to 'Visions Of Johanna', and Al Kooper confirms that it was recorded at around three or four in the morning, after Dylan had kept the musicians on hold through the evening while he finished off the song. Charlie McCoy, bassist on the track, recalled wondering "what in the hell this guy was trying to pull" as they all sat around in the basement recreation room, playing ping-pong and drinking coffee. Used to being paid by the hour for three-hour sessions, by eight in the evening they were registering perplexity, and by four in the morning they were half-asleep when Dylan called them upstairs to play.

They had been surprised when 'Visions Of Johanna', cut the previous day, had stretched beyond the seven-minute mark, but as 'Sad Eyed Lady Of The Lowlands' progressed, they began to wonder if the marathon song would ever finish. Dylan had given them only the sketchiest of outlines, and as each verse moved toward its chorus, they instinctively wound up the power, anticipating a conclusion, only to have to rein it all back in again as he began yet another verse. "People were looking at their watches and squinting at each other as if to say, 'What is this—what the hell's going on here?' " drummer Kenny Buttrey told Bob Spitz. "I have to admit, I thought the guy had blown a gasket, and we were basically humoring him." Fatigued, they tried to concentrate

"*People were looking at their watches and squinting at each other as if to say 'What is this—what the hell's going on here?'* " **KENNY BUTTREY**

on their playing, desperate not to make a mistake and have to go through the whole song again.

Extraordinarily, the song was cut in one perfect take, glowing testament to the abilities of these Nashville cats. With Kooper's organ adding wistful flourishes to Hargus Robbins' rhapsodic, rolling piano, and Buttrey's hi-hat keeping discreet time through the quiet passages, it remains a masterful piece of work, suffused with a weary resignation which seemed to signal the conclusion not just to *Blonde On Blonde*, but to a whole era. Nobody, however, could foresee the form that conclusion would take.

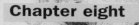

The Basement Tapes

ODDS AND ENDS

ORANGE JUICE BLUES (BLUES FOR
BREAKFAST) (RICHARD MANUEL)

MILLION DOLLAR BASH

YAZOO STREET SCANDAL
(ROBBIE ROBERTSON)

GOIN' TO ACAPULCO

KATIE'S BEEN GONE
(ROBERTSON/MANUEL)

LO AND BEHOLD!

BESSIE SMITH (DANKO/ROBERTSO

CLOTHES LINE SAGA

APPLE SUCKLING TREE

PLEASE, MRS. HENRY

TEARS OF RAGE (DYLAN/MANUEL)

TOO MUCH OF NOTHING

YEA! HEAVY AND A BOTTLE OF BRE

AIN'T NO MORE CANE (TRAD.)

CRASH ON THE LEVEE
(DOWN IN THE FLOOD)

RUBEN REMUS (ROBERTSON/MANU

TINY MONTGOMERY

YOU AIN'T GOIN' NOWHERE

DON'T YA TELL HENRY

NOTHING WAS DELIVERED

OPEN THE DOOR, HOMER

LONG DISTANCE OPERATOR

THIS WHEEL'S ON FIRE
(DYLAN/DANKO)

By summer 1966, something had to snap; Dylan had simply been working too hard for too long on too many fronts. His tour with the Hawks seemed to go on forever, and despite the extraordinary music they were making (as evidenced by the widely-distributed live bootleg purporting to come from the Royal Albert Hall concert in London, but actually recorded at the Manchester Free Trade Hall), in country after country they encountered the same mix of hysteria and hostility. Things got so bad that at the Paris Olympia concert, when sections of the crowd started whistling during a break between songs, Dylan responded, "I'm just as anxious to go home as you are. Don't you have a paper to read?"

Even his more supportive fans posed a threat, as he realized when a girl lunged at his head with scissors as he was leaving the stage at one concert, snipping off a lock of his hair. Things were getting dangerous out there, strapped to the accelerating projectile of fame at exactly the moment that celebrity became a global concept. Few others—the Beatles and the Stones, perhaps—had experienced such hysterical adulation before, and there had been more of them to share it around: for though he had his band alongside him, they went largely unrecognized; Dylan was the complete focus of attention.

The debilitating effects of the tour were exacerbated by his increasingly out-of-control offstage lifestyle, which involved lots of drugs and little sleep. Donn Pennebaker, who was filming the tour for another cinema-verité film, remembered Dylan being physically sick in the back of the limousine in which he and John Lennon were traveling. But Bob refused to slow down, snatching every opportunity to work on songs. Pennebaker recalled watching Dylan and Robbie Robertson dashing off dozens of songs in a row one night, never even letting up enough to write them down; the next day, nobody could remember them. "I did it enough to know that there must be something else to do," he said later of this period of constant touring. "It wasn't my own choice; I was more or less being pushed into it—pushed in, and carried out..."

He was not best pleased, then, when upon his return to America, he discovered that Albert Grossman had lined up another 60 concerts. Besides that, there was the usual round of interviews and promotional duties to be carried out in support of the just-released *Blonde On Blonde*, and there were broadcasters and publishers pushing for completion of the new tour film, *Eat The Document*, which Dylan was intent on editing himself, and his book *Tarantula*, which had seemed a good idea a year before when he had signed up to write it, but which had since become more of a chore. Everybody, it seemed, wanted a

"It wasn't my own choice; I was more or less being pushed into it—pushed in, and carried out..." **BOB DYLAN**

part of him. "Everybody is always taught to be thankful for their food and clothes and things like that," he told Nat Hentoff, "but not to be thankful for their obscurity." His values were changing.

The atmosphere was changing, too, as the downside of the fast life began to take its toll. Old friends like Richard Fariña, Geno Foreman and Paul Clayton had died—Fariña in a motorcycle accident, the others through drugs—and many of his own inner circle of friends, like David Blue and Bob Neuwirth, had slipped into drug addiction or alcoholism. Dylan had exhibited a fascination with death since his first album, and had recently admitted to Robert Shelton, "You know, I can think about death openly. It's nothing to fear. It's nothing sacred. I've seen so many people die." All around Dylan, darkness seemed to be drawing in.

It seemed almost inevitable, then, when on July 29, 1966, Dylan was badly injured in an accident while out riding his Triumph 500cc on Striebel Road, near his home in Woodstock. Dylan had been an avid rider ever since buying his first bike, a Harley 45, as a teenage tearaway back in Hibbing. He was, however, a terrible driver, by all accounts. "He used to hang on that thing like a sack of flour," recalled Joan Baez of her times out riding with Bob. "I always had the feeling it was driving him, and if we were lucky we'd lean the right way and the motorcycle would turn the corner. If not, it would be the end of both of us." It was not the first accident he had been in: back in

◄

DYLAN IN LONDON, 1966.

Hibbing in 1958, he had been badly shaken after hitting a three-year-old boy who had run out between parked cars, chasing an orange. Luckily, the child wasn't badly injured. All he could remember, he told his girlfriend Echo Helstrom, was the orange rolling across the street.

After the motorbike crash in Woodstock, it was reported that Dylan had broken his neck, and rumors swiftly spread that he was either dead or in a persistent vegetative state, the next worst thing to dead. As it happened, he had merely cracked a

"I always had the feeling that it was driving him, and if we were lucky we'd lean the right way and the motorcycle would turn the corner." **JOAN BAEZ**

vertebra, but he grabbed gratefully at the opportunity to take time out from his schedule to recuperate. All of a sudden, the biggest rock star in the world became its most reclusive, as Dylan followed the examples of his friends Marlon Brando and Phil Spector, and shut himself away from the world in Byrdcliffe, his Woodstock home. For the next few years, he shunned public contact, settling down to raise a family, paint, and maybe make a little music when the fancy took him.

As luck would have it, the Hawks had moved into a large pink house nearby, where, after more than a decade spent on the road, they were coming to terms with life as a group, trying to find their own sound in their own time. With equipment borrowed from Peter, Paul & Mary, they set up a makeshift rehearsal studio in their basement, and set about working on some new material.

"The tape machine was set up behind Garth," recalls Robbie Robertson, "and he would just turn it on and turn it off, mostly. It was just a stereo input, so I think we used four mikes mixed down to a stereo pair—it could have been more—but some of the sound was leakage on to another mike: a lot of things didn't even have a microphone on them, it would just leak on to another microphone. "It was just getting an idea down on tape, most of

▶

DYLAN RECUPERATES IN WOODSTOCK, 1968.

those things, so there was no care taken whatsoever with the quality of the recordings and the balances. They were done exactly the opposite to everything that you learn in how-to-make-a-record school: the worst thing you can have is cement walls, all studios have sound stuff all over the walls; and then there was a big furnace right in the middle of all this, which is bad for the sound—but

nobody was thinking about what was right for the sound, it was just a case of getting an idea down on tape as a little blueprint or something like that. It was a discovery process, which was quite different from what we had done on our own in the past, and quite different from what we had done with Bob."

Before long, Dylan was driving on over to hang out with them and play. The results, never intended for consumption, would take on legendary status when they were bootlegged as *Great White Wonder*, and were eventually officially released eight years later as *The Basement Tapes*.

"For the most part, we did them in the afternoons," recalls Robbie Robertson. "The idea was just for the Band to have our little clubhouse, where everybody could go every day, hang around, play a little music, work on some songs, without disturbing anybody. We said, 'God, this place is really starting to feel good,' and so Bob would come over and hang around just like the rest of the guys. Up in the living room, there were a couple of typewriters, and every once in a while, somebody would sit down and hammer something out, just fooling around, having some fun. Somebody would say, 'I have an idea for this,' and go down in the basement, and pretty soon everybody else would lumber down, and we'd start fooling around on things. And it started to take on a character, almost. We'd record these things and

"I've never written anything hard to understand, not in my head anyway, and nothing as far out as some of the old songs. They were out of sight..." **BOB DYLAN**

listen back to them, and it would be so funny to us, it would just crack us up! It was such a good-spirited situation, so non-pressured, that it just felt good to be there."

The sound of the recordings made in the basement was warm and intimate, markedly different from the big, powerful rock sound that Dylan had pumped out in concert with the Hawks. This was partly by design and partly through necessity. "One of the things is that if you played loud in the basement, it was really annoying, because it was a cement-walled room," explained Robertson. "So we played in a little huddle: if you couldn't hear the singing, you were playing too loud. It just became a completely different approach to that we had been using before."

The results drew heavily on the folk music that Dylan had studied in his early years in New York—not the self-righteous social protest songs he had mastered and then discarded, but the traditional music from the early decades of the century that he had encountered on compilations like Harry Smith's celebrated six-LP *Anthology Of American Folk Music*. This was a strange, dark kind of music, full of bizarre stories and weird imagery,

and riddled with death—and worse. The previous summer, in his interview with Nora Ephron and Susan Edmiston, Dylan had criticized the folk music "authorities" who wanted him to "keep things simple."

"Folk music is the only music where it *isn't* simple," he contended. "It's never been simple. It's weird, man, full of legend, myth, Bible and ghosts. I've never written anything hard to understand, not in my head anyway, and nothing as far out as some of the old songs. They were out of sight... 'Nottamun Town', that's like a herd of ghosts passing through on the way to Tangiers."

He expanded upon the same theme to Nat Hentoff: "Traditional music is based on hexagrams. It comes about from legends, Bibles, plagues, and it revolves around vegetables and death. There's nobody that's going to kill traditional music. All these songs about roses growing out of people's brains and lovers who are really geese and swans that turn into angels—they're not going to die...traditional music is too unreal to die. It doesn't need to be protected... I think its meaninglessness is holy."

Listening to the songs which make up *The Basement Tapes*, one begins to grasp what he means. These are songs of departure, but rarely arrival; of the search for salvation; and of nonsense as the coin of hidden meaning. They're populated by a typically wide, typically odd range of characters, who seem to inhabit a parallel world to the one we live in. And in the main, the lyrics sound as off-the-cuff and extemporized as those on Dylan's recent albums had been meticulously polished; in several cases, the words sound as if they've been made up on the spot, simply to fill in the spaces between the choruses. And some sound as if they're just attempts to make the other musicians laugh.

"I remember a couple of things that we thought, 'Well, nobody should hear *these*,' just because of the subject matter, or because they were filthy, y'know?" says Robertson. "It was like, We'd better put these in the furnace! But someday somebody will go in the furnace probably, and they'll be out too, just a little burnt."

Musically, the songs were completely at odds with what was going on in the rest of the pop world, which during the long hot summer of 1967 was celebrating the birth of the hippie movement with a gaudy explosion of "psychedelic" music—mostly facile paeans to universal love draped in interminable guitar solos of dubious quality. Drawing on a palette that included traditional instruments such as accordion and mandolin alongside the various drums, guitars and keyboards at their disposal, Dylan and the Band (as they would become known, by default) conjured up a raw and rootsy, joyful, juicy sound in which fear and frolic co-existed in the same notes, a raggedy blanket spun from strands of country, blues and gospel music.

"It wasn't that way necessarily on purpose," explains Robertson, "it was just that there was such a tremendous freedom in thinking, 'Nobody's ever going to hear this, we can try anything.' " But of course, people did get to hear them. Dylan was still the most sought-after songwriter in the pop business, and so an acetate of some of the songs was circulated by his publisher among artists keen to cover Dylan material. After an album of songs which—'Just Like A Woman' aside—few had dared to cover, the sketchy and approachable style of *The Basement Tapes'* songs made this one of his most productive periods, as far as cover versions went: Manfred Mann hit big with 'The Mighty Quinn' (which was unaccountably left off the official album); Julie Driscoll made a successful cover of 'This Wheel's On Fire'; The Byrds continued their association with Dylan by recording both 'Nothing Was Delivered' and 'This Wheel's On Fire'; Fairport Convention did 'Million Dollar Bash'; Peter, Paul & Mary had a minor hit with 'Too Much Of Nothing', reasonable recompense for their loan of the recording equipment; and the Band included versions of 'I Shall Be Released', 'Tears Of Rage' and 'This Wheel's On Fire'—the last two of which they had co-written—on their debut album *Music From Big Pink* the following year.

The original *Basement Tapes*, however, remained officially unreleased until, dusted-down and smartened up, they were issued as a double-album in 1975, in a sleeve featuring Dylan, the Band and a motley crew of characters from the songs posing around a furnace in a basement (actually the basement of the Los Angeles YMCA). Despite its tardiness, it reached the Top 10 on both sides of the Atlantic.

Odds And Ends

The album opens in friendly, welcoming fashion with one of its simpler pleasures, a ramshackle rocker that clocks in at under two minutes, just enough time for three short verse/chorus combinations and the briefest of breaks from Robbie Robertson prior to the final verse. Yet another complaint of amorous betrayal that could pass as an allegorical reflection on his own position *vis-a-vis* the media and former fans, the song opens with the singer's careful plan undermined by treachery, continues with him dogged by the treacherous, and concludes with him abdicating his position and advising his tormentor(s) to "get on someone else." The chorus—"Odds and ends, odds and ends/Lost time is not found again"—effectively functions as a kind of editorial comment upon the entire *Basement Tapes* recordings themselves, noting their fragmentary form and fleeting pleasure. Richard Manuel takes the drum seat on this one.

Million Dollar Bash

Of all the *Basement Tapes* songs, 'Million Dollar Bash' most gracefully pivots on the urban/rural divide which marks Dylan's shift in attitude following his bike crash. In its ludicrous lyrical style, it's clearly in a straight line of descent from such earlier absurdist narratives as 'Tombstone Blues' and 'Stuck Inside Of Mobile With The Memphis Blues Again', but this time Dylan's left the city for the country: instead of the cast of urbanites and outcasts that peopled previous songs, the populace of 'Million Dollar Bash' consists of hicks like Silly Nelly and Turtle, and instead of the streetwise scenarios of the preceding three albums, the action here has a rustic, barnyard setting.

The pace of the action, too, is much slower—indeed, if life got much slower than this, it would be in reverse gear. In place of Dylan's previous

113

drug-laced flights of paranoid fancy, the mood here is more laid back, as of old geezers sitting around, chewing the fat and putting off doing any work until the last possible moment. Dylan's delivery has a draggy, world-weary, weather-beaten quality, as if he can barely be bothered to relate the song. Which is hardly surprising, since virtually nothing happens: someone spins a yarn, the garbage man empties the trash, and the narrator delivers his potatoes, possibly to a moonshine still. That's what passes for action around these parts, which may be why all the conversation and excitement in the neighborhood centers on the prospect of the fantastically glamorous and ridiculously expensive party of the title, an event akin to a World's Fair (or, indeed, a Millennium Dome Experience) which might redefine these humdrum lives.

It won't, of course: part of the overall "message" of *The Basement Tapes* is that, whatever their tribulations, the roots of such rural lives run far too deep for them to be easily uprooted by flashy superficialities like the 'Million Dollar Bash', which was doubtless thought up by a cabal of accountants and advertising executives, and designed by men with ponytails. After all, what could such people have to interest a man who, like Turtle, has "his cheeks in a chunk" and "his cheese in the cash"? Not much, one suspects. But that, of course, doesn't stop Turtle and his chums dreaming: in such communities, anticipation is probably always that much sweeter, whatever the ultimate disillusion. In its own way, 'Million Dollar Bash' has as much to say about the decline of rural America—and in far less melodramatic terms—than a youthful finger-wagging exercise like 'The Ballad Of Hollis Brown'.

> ◀
> **VICE-PRESIDENT HUBERT H. HUMPHREY: WENT MAD LAST NIGHT DOWNTOWN, IT'S CLAIMED. "HMM, SAY, THAT'S TOO BAD."**

Goin' To Acapulco

As with 'Just Like Tom Thumb's Blues', in 'Goin' To Acapulco' Mexico holds out the promise of loose morals and good times. Yet this must be the most mournful of good-time songs, sung as if the prospect of "Goin' to have some fun" contained its own karmic downside, incurring a moral debt to be repaid in full at some unspecified later date. "It's a wicked life, but what the hell," the narrator muses in the first verse, as he ponders a trip down south to see Rose Marie, a golden-hearted hooker whose favors can be bought with a song.

Given his apparent desolation, it's hardly surprising he keeps being drawn back to her arms; the alternative, as the last verse makes plain in a cheeky masturbation metaphor which likens his flagging libido to a broken-down well, is just to take himself in hand and "go pump on it some." The intervening verse is all anticipation, concluding with a beautiful couplet that both echoes the weather-sensitivity of 'Crash On The Levee' and establishes the first of the album's prevailing train images. Like several of the *Basement Tapes* songs, however, there are numerous differences between the song's lyrics as recorded for this album, and the printed version included in Dylan's official *Lyrics 1962–1985*, so it's probably inadvisable to place too specific a meaning on it.

Lo And Behold!

'Lo And Behold!' continues the theme of movement, with a train journey into the abiding mystery of the American heartland that becomes a search for his own identity. It's a fruitless pursuit of revelation, the narrator seeking some place—or some event—that might elicit the exclamation of the title, but always winding up in dreary places like Pittsburgh. He, however, gets more extraordinary as the song goes on: the first verse opens in relatively straightforward fashion, with him setting off for San Antonio—presumably, judging by his shame at revealing his identity to the ticket-collector, to escape some unspecified hometown infamy.

Entering Pittsburgh in the second verse, he overhears a testy, disquietingly absurd exchange between two fellow passengers, Moby Dick and Molly, about the latter's "mound"; then suddenly, by verse three, he's buying a herd of moose—the flying variety, of course!—and pondering a trip to Tennessee. His madness seems complete: "Gonna save my money and rip it up!" he exults, establishing himself finally as an outlaw from American greed and materialism. Is this the "crime" for which he felt such shame a couple of verses earlier? Whatever, by the final verse, he seems much more secure in his identity, slick and powerful and full of tricks, having regained enough of his earlier ebullience to ride into town, he claims, "on a Ferris wheel."

The whole song reads like a tall tale told by a self-aggrandizing barfly, and Dylan sings it with a wry blend of swagger and nonchalance, as if daring any man in here to deny his story, while mocking them for even giving it the time of day. The rousing chorus harmonies—which prefigure the famous harmonies which would become one of the hallmarks of the Band's music—join in like drinking pals saluting him with foaming beakers, urging the narrator on to ever more ridiculous flights of fancy, rising at the end to leave him no place to go but further into fantasy, the true source of American identity.

Clothes Line Saga

'C lothes Line Saga' was originally recorded as 'Answer To Ode', the ode in question being Bobbie Gentry's 'Ode To Billie Joe', one of Summer 1967's most evocative hits, in which a family dispassionately discusses the suicide of Billie Joe MacAllister over dinner. Parodying Gentry's downbeat, offhand narrative style, this is a back-porch gossip over the garden fence, occurring literally while taking in the washing—a reminder of how such basic forms of human contact cement a society together, however empty and pointless they may seem.

Nobody commits suicide in the 'Clothes Line Saga', although, we learn, the Vice-President did apparently go mad the previous night downtown, a minor interruption to the status quo greeted with all the excitement it deserves—"Hmm, say, that's too bad", sung as if Bob's attention was already wandering—before folk get back to the important business of checking whether the clothes are dry yet. At the time, the Vice-President was Hubert Humphrey, who incited such paroxysms of apathy in the American people that when he stood as the Democratic presidential candidate at the next election, they preferred to vote for Richard Nixon instead.

The song's essence is contained in its second line, "Nobody said very much"; indeed, 'Clothes Line Saga' could be read as Dylan celebrating his release from significance, enjoying the opportunity just to write songs without having to have them mean something. A few months earlier at the Royal Albert Hall concert, he had revealed how tired he was of having to explain his work when he lectured the audience from the stage. "What you're hearing is just songs," he fretted tetchily. "You're not hearing anything else but words and sounds. You can take it or leave it. If there is something you disagree with, that's great. I'm sick of people asking: 'What does it mean?' It means nothing!"

115

Apple Suckling Tree

uilt on the melody of 'Froggy Went A-Courting', the nursery rhyme Dylan would cover on his 1992 *Good As I Been To You* album, 'Apple Suckling Tree' opens with the composer's tentative piano figure, feeling its way into the song, before the bass, drums and organ join in, with tambourine lending a touch of gospel revival-tent syncopation. The song's galumphing feel is due to Robbie Robertson's inexpert hand at the drum kit, one of the frequent occasions on which the musicians switched instruments.

"Everybody would play different instruments," confirms Robertson. "I'd come down and somebody else would be playing guitar, so I'd pick up the bass or play the drums, something like that—somebody would pick up a horn or a fiddle or a mandolin, whatever, and just try their best to handle it! It wasn't like anybody had a real idea for something, they would just look around, see an instrument sitting there, and start doodling around on it until something started to happen." Since Levon Helm had not yet rejoined after quitting the Hawks before the 1966 World Tour, the drum seat was the one most in need of filling—usually by pianist Richard Manuel, since with both Garth Hudson and Dylan on hand, there was not such a shortage of keyboard operators as there was of drummers.

► **ROBBIE ROBERTSON OF THE BAND, RESTING BETWEEN ENGAGEMENTS.**

Another song whose recorded version bears scant relation to the lyrics as printed in Dylan's *Lyrics 1962–1985*, 'Apple Suckling Tree' would seem to be a quickly extemporized, oddly light-hearted meditation upon mortality, the singer anticipating that time when it will be "just you and me" buried beneath the tree in question. "A lot of them were made up as we went along," agrees Robertson, "a lot were made up a few minutes before laying them down, just writing down an idea and trying it out to see if it's going anywhere. Once you'd got it down, you'd say, 'Okay, that's an idea,' and move on to something else. It was a very un-precious attitude." The result here is one of the album's most un-precious songs, poised in the shadows between celebration and admonition like a good-time ghost.

Please, Mrs. Henry

 drinking song of authentic tipsiness, 'Please, Mrs. Henry' features a drunkard's confused invocations to a barmaid, moving with intemperate randomness through an alcoholic fog of desires. First he thinks he's had enough to drink and wants to be taken to his room; then as he wavers in the hallway, lustfulness overtakes him and he propositions her with a fanciful string of animal metaphors; rejected, he becomes sullen and truculent, waving her away; finally, poised for a piss, he's trying to catch her eye again for another round of drinks, his penniless state notwithstanding. Rolling along on the back of bar-room piano and tiddly organ, it's one of the more simple and good-natured songs in Dylan's entire canon, buoyed with a light-heartedness that finds the singer corpsing into a chuckle as the final chorus begins.

Tears Of Rage
(Dylan/Manuel)

One of the three or four most complete—and intriguing—*Basement Tapes* songs, 'Tears Of Rage' is Dylan's equivalent of the blind king's wasteland soliloquy in *King Lear*, applied to his own nation. Wracked with bitterness and regret, its narrator reflects upon promises broken and truths ignored, on how greed has poisoned the well of best intentions, and how even daughters can deny their father's wishes.

In its narrowest and most contemporaneous interpretation, the song could be the first to register the pain of betrayal felt by many of America's Vietnam War veterans, who found their patriotic efforts, carried out with neither question nor compromise, squandered by a country that simply got fed up with caring about the conflict. As the national mood shifted, these men found their dead friends had effectively laid down their lives for nothing, denied even the dignity of dying for a

righteous cause, so tainted had the war in question become. In trying to commemorate their comrades, they were routinely treated as if they were asking for something they didn't deserve; the nation's embarrassment over the matter made them unworthy claimants upon its compassion, always made to feel like thieves.

Certainly, from no other song of that era does one glean the sense of a nation split against itself. In a wider interpretation of 'Tears Of Rage', this song harks back to what anti-war protesters and critics of American materialism in general felt was a more fundamental betrayal of the spirit of the American Declaration Of Independence and the Bill Of Rights. Having, as one of its founding fathers, helped define the country, the song's narrator watches sadly as his ideals are diluted and cast aside by succeeding generations, who treat them as "nothing more/Than a place for you to stand." In place of idealism is rampant materialism, with a

price placed upon even one's emotions by a society that has come to know the cost of everything, but the value of nothing.

With Dylan's weeping delivery matched by the high, keening harmonies of Rick Danko and Richard Manuel and shaded by the stately tread of Garth Hudson's wistful organ, 'Tears Of Rage' is the most affecting of the *Basement Tapes* performances. Richard Manuel wrote the music for it, having been handed a typewritten sheet of the lyrics by Dylan one day in the basement. Though he later admitted not fully understanding the song, Manuel instinctively settled upon the highly evocative melody which provides the perfect atmosphere of enduring, irrevocable lamentation. The next year, he would sing lead on the Band's own version of the song—included on their *Music From Big Pink* debut—a reading made even more harrowingly funereal by the addition of Garth Hudson's mournful horns.

Too Much Of Nothing

Ponderous and declamatory in the verses, frail and haunting in the choruses, this offers the earliest indication, with its references to "the day of confession" and everything having "been written in the book," of the biblical slant which was creeping into Dylan's songs, and which would cast a great shadow over his next album, *John Wesley Harding*.

During his retreat up in Woodstock, Dylan was reported to keep a Bible open at a lectern in his study. Its grim parables and sense of moral absolutism deeply inform 'Too Much Of Nothing', which serves as both lamentation of spiritual emptiness and warning of its dire consequences. As the melody rises through the latter half of each verse, one can visualize an evangelist berating his congregation, with the high chorus harmonies of Rick Danko and Richard Manuel representing the angelic salvation which the preacher extends as the alternative to a life of sinful pleasure. Deriding the modern world as spiritually bereft, Dylan warns of the societal breakdown and ruthlessness that are bound to follow (which became a familiar theme through his recordings of subsequent decades), and advises seeking redemption through giving away one's money (which, oddly, did not).

Yea! Heavy And A Bottle Of Bread

Perhaps the most bizarrely inconsequential of the *Basement Tapes* recordings, "Yea! Heavy And A Bottle Of Bread" is pure nonsense, its lines knocked together from offhand, random phrases with an instinct for the enigmatic that rescues the song from being forgettable. Dylan's delivery is deceptively conversational, adding to the illusion of common sense, and though there's something tentative and spontaneous about the recurrent little piano phrase that adds a soupçon of character to the song, the other musicians join in lustily enough on the choruses to dispel suspicions about its ultimate destination (though not, perhaps, in the case of the baritone harmony on the final "bread," which fluctuates drunkenly before settling on its proper note). Ticking along blithely, as if it knows exactly where it's going, 'Yea! Heavy And A Bottle Of Bread' winds up as one of the most engaging of the album's songs, its appeal accentuated, if anything, by the fact that its meaning is unfathomable.

◀

PROTESTORS AGAINST THE WAR IN VIETNAM, 1968.

Crash On The Levee
(Down In The Flood)

Initially called 'Crash On The Levee', but retitled 'Down In The Flood' in Dylan's official *Lyrics 1962–1985*, this, of all the *Basement Tapes* songs, is the one which best carries the authentic spark of real history: a cohesive meld of mood, theme and delivery, it could easily have been written by some wary inhabitant of the Mississippi flood-plain, warning of the impending disaster in apocalyptic terms reminiscent of that earlier biblical flood survived by Noah.

This is due in part to the air of familiarity lent by specific geographical reference (to Williams Point), and in part to the antique mystery of lines like "Well it's sugar for sugar/And salt for salt," which in this case is indeed authentically antique, the line being adapted from Richard "Rabbit" Brown's 1927 song 'James Alley Blues', a warning about one of New Orleans' more dangerous thoroughfares, in which he sings "I'll match you sugar for sugar, I'll match you salt for salt." (The song would be familiar to Dylan through its inclusion in Harry Smith's *Anthology Of American Folk Music*.)

119

Tiny Montgomery

 nother trifle with more character than meaning, 'Tiny Montgomery' has an engaging boozy bonhomie, its eponymous subject sending out greetings to an impressive cast of characters that includes Skinny Moo, Half-track Frank, Lester, Lou, some monks and the entire CIO union organization. Tricked out in short, imponderable phrases—"Honk that stink/Take it on down/And watch it grow"—chosen more for sound than sense, it has the weird, hermetic logic of a private language, the kind of thing that members of cults or secret organizations use to communicate with each other.

Given the shady nature of the characters whom Montgomery hails, and the fact that he refers to San Francisco as "ol' Frisco," a term nobody—certainly not the town's residents—has used for many a year, I suspect that Tiny has languished long in one of America's jails, and is bidding farewell to a cellmate about to be released, asking him to send regards to his chums back in his old stamping ground.

► THE BAND ON STAGE, 1969.

You Ain't Goin' Nowhere

When The Byrds included 'You Ain't Goin' Nowhere' on their pioneering country-rock album *Sweetheart Of The Rodeo* in the summer of 1968, it provided confirmation of sorts that the country sound revealed at the end of Dylan's *John Wesley Harding* earlier that year was more than just a passing phase, that there was more to his new rural outlook than just 'I'll Be Your Baby Tonight'. With 'You Ain't Goin' Nowhere', it seemed that following his years as the quintessential urban hipster, Dylan had followed his own instruction and strapped himself to a tree with roots.

On Dylan's original version, however, the country flavor is somewhat less pronounced, present more as an undercurrent, though there's an irresistible pull in that direction via the lilting chorus melody. Judging by an earlier, unreleased version—a bootleg version, as it were—whose verses are filled up with off-the-cuff nonsense about having to feed the cat, it seems likely that the chorus was the first part of the song devised, with the verses being filled in later.

Mind you, the completed song as it stands makes little more sense than its feline predecessor: while the brisk meteorological details—the frozen railings, rain and clouds—lend the first verse a stark rural cohesion, subsequent stanzas drift further away from logic until the final verse twists off into a *non sequitur* concerning Genghis Khan's inability to keep his kings supplied with sleep. Not for the first time in the basement, the chorus is what gives drives the song forward, regardless of what's happening in the verses. Robbie Robertson is the drummer.

Don't Ya Tell Henry

More rustic shenanigans, with a lady love and a whole barnyard menagerie keen on keeping some secret from the eponymous Henry. Their recurrent rejoinder "Apple's got your fly" sounds like nothing so much as a line from a children's skip-rope rhyme, but the song as a whole plays as cowboy farce.

With Levon Helm taking lead vocals with characteristic Southern *brio*, 'Don't Ya Tell Henry' could be a prototype for the sound the Band would reveal shortly after on their own albums. Like the other tracks done solely by the Hawks without Dylan, it's more polished than most of the *Basement Tapes* performances, with an arrangement that plays Robbie Robertson's guitar off against Helm's mandolin, while Garth Hudson plays rippling bar-room piano over a rhythm punched along by the dry snap of Richard Manuel's drums.

By the time Levon Helm joined the rest of the group up in Big Pink, he was shocked—and a little worried—to find out how good a drummer Manuel had become. "Richard was an *incredible* drummer," Helm acknowledged in his autobiography *This Wheel's On Fire*. "He played loosey-goosey, a little behind the beat, and it really swung... Without any training, he'd do these hard left-handed moves and piano-wise licks, priceless shit—very unusual... I just realized that my mandolin playing was going to have to improve if I was to have anything to do onstage while Richard played drums."

◄

DYLAN (FRONT) WITH THE BYRDS, WHO COVERED MANY OF HIS SONGS, INCLUDING 'YOU AIN'T GOIN' NOWHERE'.

Nothing Was Delivered

oughly based on Fats Domino's 'Blueberry Hill', this is a pedestrian, mournful blues pushed along by Richard Manuel's piano triplets (there are no drums on the track). Dylan's vocal and Robbie Robertson's guitar are of a piece, dramatic but intimate, as if sharing confidences about the flunked deal covered in the song. It's one of the most direct stories on the entire *Basement Tapes* album, with somebody being held to account for non-delivery; but it's flexible enough to accommodate a number of interpretations, from a simple drug-deal gone wrong to more serious political deceit. Whichever it is, the tone is more sad than angry, as if the betrayal hurts the singer's sense of honor more than his pocket. "Take care of yourself and get plenty of rest," he advises the reneger, an ambivalent salutation that's part threat and part solicitous farewell.

Open The Door, Homer

hough the title and the version of the song included in *Lyrics 1962–1985* address the instruction to Homer, the song as sung refers to Richard. It makes a little more sense when you learn that Richard Manuel's

nickname among the group was "Homer," and that the invocation "Open the door, Richard" was a staple routine used by comics at the Apollo Theater in Harlem in the 1940s and 1950s as a kind of weekly running joke–the various confusions between the characters stuck on opposite sides of the door never being resolved by the door being opened, of course. In 1947, Jack McVea and Dan Howell wrote music to accompany burlesque duo "Dusty" Fletcher and John Mason's comedy routine, the quartet enjoying a postwar novelty hit with the result.

Poised between irony and self-assurance, the song lopes along jauntily, tendering obscure bits of baffling advice, some commonsense, others with the cryptic power of folk remedies: value your memories properly, they won't come again; flush out your house if you don't want to be housing flushes; swim a certain way if you want to live off the fat of the land; and forgive the sick before you try to heal them. The sensible ones lend a sort of bogus credence to the less sensible, while the sheer conviction of the chorus vouches for the advisor's *bona fides*: it's good advice he's offering, and not before time too, because, as the singer acknowledges, "I ain't gonna hear it said no more"—so impenetrable are such folk remedies, old wives' tales and rural wisdoms becoming, we're losing the ability to even understand them, let alone question their efficacy.

Long Distance Operator

A funky blues extension (no pun intended) of Chuck Berry's 'Memphis Tennessee' in the Chicago blues style, with Robbie Robertson's strangulated guitar fills piercing the song's fabric like arrows through the heart. Richard Manuel takes lead vocals, yearning to hear his baby's voice down the wire, and wailing awhile on harmonica. Simple and strident, it's half an idea fleshed out to a riff, but none the worse for that.

This Wheel's On Fire
(Dylan/Danko)

C losing the album at a peak of sinister mystery, 'This Wheel's On Fire' finds Dylan straining to hit the highest notes, as if emotionally wracked by his experience. Given suitably enigmatic melody by Rick Danko, Dylan's lyric draws again on Shakespeare's *King Lear* ("Thou art a soul in bliss/But I am bound/Upon a wheel of fire")—itself inspired by the biblical visions of Ezekiel, possibly the Old Testament's nuttiest prophet—to offer what seems like a *mea culpa* for past transgressions, a moment of self-revelation in which the singer realizes that in order to get to *this*, it was necessary for him to go through *that*. The road down which the flaming wheel rolls is, of course, the road of excess which, Rimbaud claimed, leads to the palace of wisdom.

In his *Lyrics 1962–1985*, Dylan illustrates 'This Wheel's On Fire' with a badly-drawn cartoon depicting three people exclaiming "Look out!", "Yikes!" and "Holy cow!" as they leap out of the way of a (non-blazing) runaway cartwheel, but this seems a cavalier deprecation of a serious work. The mood of the song itself is far more portentous, capturing a soul suspended on the cusp of torment and deliverance, unable to arrest its headlong drive toward destruction, yet aware of the tasks which have yet to be completed. It is virtually impossible not to see the locked wheel of Dylan's Triumph 500 in the title, the very wheel upon which his own accelerating pursuit of disaster was borne so swiftly, and then arrested so abruptly. The verses brim with unfinished business, anchored by the certainty that "we shall meet again."

In the UK, Julie Driscoll had an April 1968 Top 5 hit with the song, backed by Brian Auger & The Trinity; it was also covered by the Byrds, and re-recorded for the Band's *Music From Big Pink*. A quarter of a century later, it provided the perfect theme music for the 1990s British TV sitcom *Absolutely Fabulous*, where it brilliantly evoked the high-octane burn-out of the show's hippie-hangover characters.

◀

CHUCK BERRY,
INSPIRATION FOR 'LONG
DISTANCE OPERATOR'.

JOHN WESLEY HARDING

AS I WENT OUT ONE MORNING

I DREAMED I SAW
ST. AUGUSTINE

ALL ALONG THE WATCHTOWER

THE BALLAD OF FRANKIE LEE
AND JUDAS PRIEST

DRIFTER'S ESCAPE

DEAR LANDLORD

I AM A LONESOME HOBO

I PITY THE POOR IMMIGRANT

THE WICKED MESSENGER

DOWN ALONG THE COVE

I'LL BE YOUR BABY TONIGHT

John Wesley Harding

Between his accident in summer 1966 and his appearance at the Woody Guthrie Memorial Concert in January 1968, little was seen or heard of Bob Dylan. In the period immediately following the accident, he spent much of his time editing the TV special that had been commissioned by ABC and which, despite the network's dismissal of it as "totally unsatisfactory," would eventually appear as *Eat The Document*.

"He wore a neck-brace for a long time," recalls Robbie Robertson. "That was mostly during the editing of *Eat The Document*, when I was living at his house, and the film editor Howard Alk was there. Bob and I would go in another room and fool around, play a little music, then come out and do a bit of editing, until the process wore him down and Howard and I would go ahead and work on it a while. That film was very much in the spirit of *The Basement Tapes* as well—there was no structure, it was very experimental; there was something going on at those times that let you feel like you didn't have to be doing this for anybody in particular, so you did it for yourself."

Having dispensed with one obligation, Dylan used his time to recuperate, kick back and raise a family. Ignoring the rumors that inevitably grew as his isolation lengthened, Dylan spurned any attempts by reporters to investigate his situation until, in May 1967, he told the *New York Daily News*' Michael Iachetta that he had been "...porin' over books by people you never heard of, thinkin' about where I'm goin' and why am I runnin' and am I mixed up too much, and what am I knowin' and what am I givin' and what am I takin'. And mainly what I've been doin' is workin' on gettin' better and makin' better music, which is what my life is all about."

Working on getting better was primarily the job of Dylan's physician in nearby Middletown. Dr. Ed Thaler, a long-time leftist and civil-rights activist, had been recommended to Bob by his friend, the folk-singer Odetta. All the other facets of Dylan's life were, however, more informed by the birth of Jesse, his and Sara's first child together. The effect on his life was transformative. Bernard Paturel, the former Woodstock cafe owner who took on the job of handyman-cum-security guard at the Dylans' around this time, admitted that until Bob had met Sara, he thought it was simply a matter of time before the singer died. "But later," he admitted, "I had never met such a dedicated family man. There's so many sides to Bob Dylan, he's round." Another acquaintance of this period, neighbor and musician Happy Traum, claimed that Dylan "turned into such an ordinary guy that he was actually a little boring to be around."

After loosening up through the summer of 1967 in the Band's basement, Dylan felt ready to record the follow-up to *Blonde On Blonde*. In October and November he made three trips down to Nashville to record what would be released as *John Wesley Harding*, using just the *Blonde* rhythm section of bassist Charlie McCoy and drummer Kenny Buttrey in an attempt to emulate the sound that Canadian folk-singer Gordon Lightfoot had got using the same crew. Pedal steel guitarist Pete Drake was added on a couple of cuts.

The recording of the album was in sharp contrast to the protracted hanging-around of the *Blonde On Blonde* sessions, however. Preparing themselves for another marathon bout of ping-pong and occasional playing, McCoy and Buttrey were shocked to find the material written and Dylan ready to record; the album was finished in three swift sessions—a total of six hours recording, according to Buttrey. The original intention had been for some of the songs to have overdubs added later but, after some thought, Dylan decided to release it as it stood.

"I remember Bob going and recording that when we were working on the *Big Pink* stuff," recalls Robbie Robertson, "and when he came back, I remember he was referring to it as unfinished, and actually talking about me and Garth doing some overdubs on it. When I heard it, I said, 'You know what, maybe it is what it is, and it doesn't need to be embellished, doesn't need to be hot-rodded at all; there's a certain honesty in the music just the way it is.' And pretty soon you get used to something—you listen to it a while and it starts to sound more finished than maybe it did in the beginning—and so he ended up using it the way he had recorded it."

"I didn't know what to make of it," Dylan himself later admitted. "I asked Columbia to release it with no publicity and no hype because this was the season of hype... People have made a lot out of it, as if it was some sort of ink-blot

◀

DYLAN WITH HIS SON JESSE BYRON, 1968.

test or something. But it was never intended to be anything else but just a bunch of songs, really."

At a time when everything was getting louder and more flamboyant and colorful, *John Wesley Harding* had an emphatic diffidence. It is one of the most quietly-recorded albums ever. It sort of shuffles in modestly with the title-track, and never bothers straining for the listener's attention: the tales are here to hear, it suggests, but you'll have to pay attention.

When it appeared in February 1968, psychedelia was at its floral peak, with sleeve designs like those for *Sgt. Pepper's Lonely Hearts Club Band*, the Incredible String Band's *5000 Spirits*

"The song has to be of a certain quality for me to sing ... One aspect it would have to have is that it didn't repeat itself" **BOB DYLAN**

and, most recently, Hendrix's *Axis: Bold As Love* illustrating the era's rococo tendencies. In the face of this cosmic maelstrom, *John Wesley Harding* offered a design of quite striking understatement: accompanied by a motley trio of characters, a hunched, thinly-bearded Dylan peers shyly out of a plain black and white snapshot set into a beige-gray frame. No bright colors. No fancy curlicues. Some funny hats, but no cosmic intentions. It was as if Dylan was deliberately distancing himself from the generational imperatives of an era he himself had done so much to define.

Fans searching for significance soon found it in the sleeve photo: turned upside down, it was possible to discern the faces of the Beatles and, some claimed, the hand of God emerging from the bark at the top of the tree. Photographer John Berg, when informed about the faces, checked his original and found them there, a purely serendipitous presence. He had taken the photo in the garden of Sally Grossman, Dylan's manager's wife (and the woman accompanying Dylan on the cover of *Bringing It All Back Home*), when the temperature was 20° below zero. Hence Dylan's hunched pose: he and the others—Lakhsman and Purna Das Baul, of the Bauls Of Bengal musical group,

and Charlie Joy, a local carpenter/stonemason who happened to be working at the Grossman's—would pose for a few frames, dash back inside for a few warming slugs of brandy, then go back out for another frame or two. Snatched between slugs, the sleeve would come to represent a turning-point in pop, the precise moment at which psychedelia, having reached its furthest extent, retreated to the more comforting confines of country-rock.

The sleeve photo summed up the woolly western atmosphere of the album, which is populated with drifters, immigrants, hobos and outlaws. Here, Charlie Joy looks like an old Union infantryman and Dylan a shy gunslinger captured for posterity in a journalist's camera; the Bauls, meanwhile, with their raggedy mix of eastern and occidental vestments, resemble nothing quite so much as the Indian guides who would be used to lead pioneer wagon trains and cavalry troops through dangerous, uncharted territory. This, Dylan seemed to be saying, would be a dry and dusty journey into Indian country. Though he seemed to be wearing the same brown suede jacket as on the *Blonde On Blonde* sleeve, there was none of that album's air of stifling urban decadence; instead, a rural breeze whispered through its lonely margins.

Not that anyone realized it at the time, but following the jovial singalongs recorded in the Band's basement, which sometimes seemed to be just hearty choruses separated by verses of whatever popped into Dylan's head at any given moment, *John Wesley Harding* contained no choruses at all, as if such whimsical, user-friendly business had been ruthlessly swept aside in pursuit of a simpler, more ascetic notion of songwriting truth. And with the sole exception of the lengthy 'Ballad Of Frankie Lee And Judas Priest', all the songs were condensed, three-verse miniatures. In a conversation with John Cohen published in *Sing Out!* magazine in 1968, Dylan revealed that he had originally wanted to record an album of other people's songs, but had struggled to find enough songs that could fulfill his stringent criteria for inclusion. "The song has to be of a certain quality for me to sing and put on a record," he explained. "One aspect it would have to have is that it didn't repeat itself. I shy away from those songs which repeat phrases, bars and verses, bridges..."

Consequently, in sharp contrast to the prolix surrealism and lyrical pyrotechnics of his "electric trilogy," Dylan's new album offered a series of brief, cryptic parables which both in form and, in some cases, content, reflected the time he had spent studying the Bible during his recuperation—indeed, he later referred to it as "the first biblical rock album." And despite his subsequent scornful dismissal of those who saw the album as some kind of psychologically revealing "ink-blot test," *John Wesley Harding* did seem to contain various allegorical musings upon the singer's own situation, transmuted through a style that married Western myth to religious allegory.

As if to tease would-be interpreters, the album featured a rear-sleeve short-story which drew on the three kings of the nativity, here searching for the "key" to the new Dylan album. Lampooning the more ludicrous excesses of fervent Dylanologists, a character called Frank puts on a frenzied performance, waving his shirt around, stamping on a light bulb and punching out a plate glass window, which seems to satisfy the three kings that there is, indeed, deep meaning in the album. And indeed, there is: in various guises, from horseman to hobo, drifter to messenger, Dylan confronted his own fears and temptations through these songs, using the album as a means of mapping out his new ethical convictions in relation to his past life. As he said ten years later, *"John Wesley Harding* was a fearful album—just dealing with fear, but dealing with the Devil in a fearful way, almost."

John Wesley Harding

Contrary to Dylan's claim in the song, John Wesley Hardin—the real Texan outlaw's name has no "g"—was no great friend to the poor. He did, however, maintain that he never killed anyone who did not deserve it, which is not quite the same thing. He carried a gun in each hand, which he used to dispatch his more than 30 victims with efficient ruthlessness.

Born the son of a Methodist preacher on the 26 May 1853, Hardin lived a life of gambling, roaming and killing, with several notches on his gun-handles before he reached the age of 21, largely as a result of the hair-trigger temper for which he was famed. Again contrary to Dylan's interpretation, he was not immune to the occasional foolish move, the most serious being when he attracted the attentions of the Texas Rangers by killing a deputy sheriff of Brown County, Texas. Hardin was tracked down and captured in Pensacola, Florida in July 1877, and sentenced to 25 years in jail the following year. He was released with a full pardon in 1894, having spent his time in prison learning law. Upon his release he became a lawyer, and it was while prosecuting a case in El Paso, Texas, that, on August 19, 1895, he himself was finally killed, shot in the back of the head by one John Selman, a local constable, in an echo of the death of Jesse James mentioned by Dylan in 'Outlaw Blues'.

Such are the facts about the real-life outlaw. There are several possible reasons for Dylan's altering his name here, the most obvious being that, as he later claimed, it was simply a mistake—though this seems unlikely, especially given that the gunslinger was apparently an ancestor of the singer-songwriter Tim Hardin, one of Dylan's more talented contemporaries. There is the remote possibility of a fear of libel, although under American law, it is impossible to libel the dead. The most likely reason, then, is that the name-change, along with the alterations to Hardin's true life story, indicate that Dylan was not writing about this one outlaw specifically, but about the outlaw myth which runs so deeply through American folklore, and which even today encourages militant right-wing Americans in a bogus claim on pioneer individualism.

In the late Sixties, however, after decades in which the Hays Code and the domineering presence of John Wayne had ensured that the Western was the most conservative of movie genres, the outlaw-outsider myth was being re-assessed, with counter-culture overtones being re-introduced through such movies as Arthur Penn's *Bonnie And Clyde* and *Little Big Man*, George Roy Hill's *Butch Cassidy And The Sundance Kid*, and even Sam Peckinpah's *The Wild Bunch*. Thus does Dylan's outlaw embody the popular Robin Hood traits of selfless courage, evasive cunning, dislike of authority and generosity toward the poor. All outlaws, Dylan is perhaps suggesting, should be this way.

Taken as an allegorical reflection upon his own career, the song could be a succinct assessment of how the young singing sharpshooter roved across the nation's airwaves, helping emancipate the disenfranchised, and smiting with his pen only those who most deserved it, before evading the attentions of fame and the futile attempts to pin him down to a specific stance or message. And as for that fortuitous bike accident, well, given his circumstances—the final lines seem to wink—how foolish a move did that turn out to be?

In 1969, Dylan admitted to *Rolling Stone*'s Jann Wenner that there was no such hidden meaning in the song, that he had simply intended to write a long cowboy ballad but had run out of steam in the second verse. Rather than discard a nice tune, he quickly added a third verse and recorded it, then put it at the start of the album to lend it a significance it perhaps didn't deserve, and head off criticisms about its slightness. In the event, the song plays as concentrated western epic, a précis of outlaw legend in which the truth rattles hollowly about inside the myth.

► THE MARCH ON WASHINGTON, AUGUST 28, 1963. DYLAN EVENTUALLY TIRED OF BEING THE 'SINGING SPOKESMAN' FOR POLITICAL GROUPS.

As I Went Out One Morning

With 'As I Went Out One Morning', Dylan used the conventions of the traditional ballad—the archaic form of the title, and the presence of a fair damsel—to criticize the ingrained, autocratic attitude he had encountered in his dealings with the civil rights movement a few years earlier.

In this case, however, the fair damsel proves to be a siren spider-woman. While out taking the air "around Tom Paine's" (a reference to the revolutionary libertarian writer who was a touchstone for the civil rights movement of the Sixties), he offers help to the imprisoned damsel, who then

attempts to ensnare the singer more deeply in her cause—just as Dylan had been required to fend off a constant stream of requests from political organizations following his initial, unprompted contributions: after acting purely from personal conviction, he discovered that there were forces who claimed those convictions their own property, along with his songs and, they presumed, his time. "I've found out some things," Dylan told Toronto journalist Margaret Steen around the end of 1965. "The groups promoting these things, the movement, would try to get me involved with them, be their singing spokesman—and inside these groups, with all their president/vice-president/secretary stuff, it's politics. Inside their own pettinesses they're as bad as the hate groups. I won't even have a fan club because it'd have to have a president, it'd be a group. They think the more people you have behind something, the more influence it has. Maybe so, but the more it gets watered down, too. I'm not a believer in doing things by numbers. I believe that the best things get done by individuals..."

The presence of Tom Paine in the song is doubly significant. In the first place, it links directly to the Emergency Civil Liberties Committee, the acceptance of whose Tom Paine Award proved such a drunken debacle for Dylan in 1963. In the second place, it draws attention to the precarious balance between liberty and equality that has dogged left-wing organizations throughout the century—specifically as to how greater equality might be achieved without making catastrophic incursions into personal liberties. Paine was a free-thinker whose individualism eschewed ideological dogma, and it's appropriate that in the final verse, it's he who in turn rescues the singer from the damsel and apologizes for her presumption.

I Dreamed I Saw St. Augustine

Just as Dylan's John Wesley Harding character bears only slight resemblance to the historical figure upon whom he is based, so too does his St. Augustine differ from its historical precursor—not least in being put to death by a mob.

The real Augustine was in fact an eminent bishop of the Catholic Church's North African ministry, rather than a martyr. A philosopher-cleric,

he is most well-known for his *Confessions* and *City Of God*, works in which he described his youthful life of debauchery and subsequent conversion to Christianity, and for his unusual, pioneering attitude toward the theological problem of evil, as formulated in his *Encheiridion*: "Since God is supremely good he would not allow any evil in his works unless he were sufficiently omnipotent and good to make good come even out of evil."

It's this position, poised on the cusp of good and evil, which seems most relevant to Dylan's song, in which the ghostly figure of the cleric stands for the singer himself, left weeping against a mirror in the final verse, contemplating his own failings and desire for salvation. He is, perhaps, regretting his own earlier criticisms of religion, in which he may have unjustly condemned individuals of Augustine's nobility and holiness along with the organized church they represented. Alternatively, it may be that he suddenly realizes his own part in luring the righteous from their path through his own brand of the Devil's music.

Augustine is depicted in Dylan's dream as wearing a golden coat and carrying a blanket, signifiers respectively of the worldly excesses of mankind in general and the Catholic Church in particular, and the more ascetic leanings of the

"Watchman, what of the night? The watchman said, The morning cometh, and also the night..." **ISAIAH 21: 11-12**

prophet. He seeks the "...souls/Whom already have been sold," the first of several references on the album to the commercialization of man's inner being, notably in 'Dear Landlord' and 'The Ballad Of Frankie Lee And Judas Priest'. There are, he claims, no modern martyrs among humanity's most gifted individuals to lead mankind toward the light, and man is accordingly condemned to seek his own transcendence—though he should be assured that he is not alone in his search.

The inference is clear: Dylan, who had narrowly avoided becoming a martyr of sorts when he survived his motorbike accident, has realized that his youthful attempts to "save" society from itself have come too late—most of American society had already sold its soul to a variety of temptations, the like of which not even Augustine could have imagined (including the pop scene in which Dylan acknowledged his own complicity), and any salvation could henceforth only come through the individual's determined efforts. Ironically, the song's opening couplet directly paraphrases 'Joe Hill', the tribute to the eponymous union martyr who, as a leading light of the American syndicalist organization The Wobblies (The American Industrial Workers Of The World) would doubtless have disputed such a denial of the efficacy of collective action.

All Along The Watchtower

In 'All Along The Watchtower', the contrasting spirits in Dylan's character, dramatized so evocatively in 'I Dreamed I Saw St. Augustine', are here characterized as the joker and the thief, both trapped in the here and now with little prospect of transcendence.

The joker rues the way that philistine businessmen make free with the profits of his creative work, without according it due respect. This was clearly a heartfelt complaint from Dylan, who had recently been embroiled in contract negotiations with both his record company CBS and his manager, Albert Grossman, both of whom he considered were treating him with less respect than he deserved. His record royalties from CBS were nothing special, and Grossman seemed to consider him simply a cash cow to be milked as quickly and as deeply as possible, piling tour date upon tour date with little regard for his client's physical and emotional well-being or for his creative needs.

And that was just the tip of what appeared to be a particularly venal iceberg. "If it's not the promoter cheating you, it's the box office cheating you," he complained to Robert Shelton. "Somebody is always giving you a hard time... Even the record company figures won't be right. Do you know that up to a certain point I made more money on a song I wrote if it were on an album by Carolyn Hester, or anybody, than if I did it myself. That's the contract they gave me. Horrible! Horrible!" Ultimately, after scaring CBS by signing to MGM when his contract was up for renewal (the MGM deal was subsequently nixed by Allan Klein, one of the industry's sharpest money-men), Dylan re-signed with them at double his previous royalty rate.

The thief sympathizes with the joker, adding that he's not the only one who considers the situation absurd, but warns against letting such worldly matters prey upon his mind too heavily, since there are far more pressing matters to be addressed. What these matters are is made clear in the brief outline sketched in the final verse, which draws upon the prophet Isaiah's prediction of the fall of Babylon, in Isaiah 21, 6–9: "For thus hath the Lord said unto me, Go, set a watchman, let him declare what he seeth. And he saw a chariot with a couple of horsemen, a chariot of asses, and a chariot of camels; and he hearkened diligently with much heed; And he cried, A lion; My Lord, I stand continually upon the watchtower in the daytime, and I am set in my ward whole nights; And behold, here cometh a chariot of men, with a couple of horsemen. And he answered and said, Babylon is fallen, is fallen; and all the graven images of her gods he hath broken unto the ground." And subsequently (Isaiah 21, 11–12): "Watchman, what of the night? The watchman said, The morning cometh, and also the night; if ye will inquire, inquire ye: return, come."

In the face of the howling, apocalyptic wind

approaching, it is far more important, the thief suggests, to seek remedy for the soul rather than for worldly injustices. Then again, of course, the thief *would* say that, having been responsible, by dint of his underhand trade, for some worldly injustices of his own. In Dylan's version of the song, it's the barrenness of the scenario which grips, the high, haunting harmonica and simple forward motion of the riff carrying understated intimations of impending cataclysm; as subsequently recorded by Jimi Hendrix in an arrangement so definitive as to be adopted by Dylan himself in later years, that cataclysm is rendered all the more scarily palpable through the virtuoso's dervish whirls of guitar.

The Ballad Of Frankie Lee And Judas Priest

Another misbegotten pair of symbolic characters inhabits this, the album's longest (and dullest) track, representing respectively the straight-talking, candid and simple soul (Frankie Lee: "frankly") and the forked-tongue betrayer (Judas Priest). For all its length, the song is basically a simple parable comparable to the Devil's tempting of Jesus in the wilderness, except that in this case, Frankie Lee—presumably the character with whom Dylan most identifies—eventually gives in to the temptations of the flesh, after procrastinating half-heartedly over the temptations of materialism. Dylan, like Frankie, had never placed that much importance on money and material things, but had always demonstrated a keen appreciation of the more experiential benefits of his position, the various dalliances and indulgences available to the Sixties rock demi-god.

The early verses, in which Frankie agonizes over Judas's offer of money, presumably echo Dylan's recent contractual negotiations, or those earlier in his career: certainly, Judas's attempt to rush Frankie into a hasty decision "before [the dollar bills] all disappear" closely reflects standard negotiating practice in the music business. As, indeed, does Judas's dangling of carnal carrots to help sway Frankie's mind, in the form of the

◀

JIMI HENDRIX, THE MOST DYNAMIC OF DYLAN'S MANY MUSICAL INTERPRETERS.

brothel in which he eventually exhausts himself. To Frankie, such worldly delights are represented as "Paradise," though the devilish Judas recognizes their true price is "Eternity"—Frankie's mortal soul.

Possessing little self-control, Frankie takes the bait, and as a result loses control over his destiny,

> *"I made more money on a song I wrote if it were on an album by Carolyn Hester, or anybody, than if I did it myself. That's the contract they gave me. Horrible!"* **BOB DYLAN**

not to mention "everything which he had made" in his more considered moments. After 16 nights of sustained indulgence—analogous to the high life Dylan had been encouraged to lead over the last few years—Frankie dies of thirst in Judas's arms, an indication of the insatiable, addictive nature of such behavior. It's hard to view the Judas Priest character as anyone but Dylan's manager Albert Grossman, just as the "little neighbor boy" whose guilt is "so well concealed" (and who has a vested interest in hoping that "Nothing is revealed" of his complicity in Frankie's downfall) surely stands for the various cheerleading cronies who encouraged Dylan in his dangerous excesses. The final verse, with its bland moral, serves warning that, in future, he would be exerting more control over his life and career; and indeed, when his manager's contract came up for renewal a few years later, Dylan chose to sever his association with Grossman.

► HOBOS SCAVENGE FOR JUNK AROUND NEW YORK'S SEEDY BOWERY DISTRICT.

Drifter's Escape

Built around a single suspended guitar chord, with Dylan's anguished vocal entreaties furnishing most of its melodic shape, 'Drifter's Escape' is a simple parable of the singer's release from his previous life, with the apostolic intervention of the bolt of lightning enabling his escape.

As the song opens, the drifter is trapped in a Kafkaesque inquisition, his crime a mystery to him—just as Dylan had been baffled by the constant criticism that had dogged his path as he drifted from folk-singer to rock star, all the way around the world. The judge seems sympathetic to the drifter's plight, suggesting that his confusion may be more successfully relieved by not actively seeking "understanding" of his situation in a strict, rational sense. The jury, however, has scented blood, and bays for more—just as, regardless of the criticisms voiced by older folkies, Dylan's fan-base had grown all the more oppressively obsessive following his transformation into rock'n'roll idol. But God intervenes to save the drifter by hurling a bolt of lightning at the courthouse, an obvious metaphor for the motorcycle accident that helped free Dylan from his previous nihilistic lifestyle.

Ironically, the drifter makes good his escape by slipping away while everybody else resorts to prayer—an indication that, while Dylan may have undergone some kind of Damascene religious conversion around the time of the accident—he did, for instance, keep a Bible handy on a lectern in his artist's studio during his recuperation—his relationship with his god remains a personal, one-to-one affair, untainted by the interference of the organized churches.

Dear Landlord

A weary, maundering piano blues, 'Dear Landlord' has been interpreted by some as Dylan addressing his god, and even—by biographer Anthony Scaduto—as Dylan's mind addressing his body (which would certainly fit in with the album's other dualistic texts, 'I Dreamed I Saw St. Augustine' and 'All Along The Watchtower'). It's more readily viewed, however, as a direct entreaty to Dylan's manager Albert Grossman—whose Woodstock house and Gramercy Park apartment the singer often used as homes, and who subsequently leased a Woodstock cottage to his client—to reduce the burden of work constantly thrust upon his shoulders. Compared to the contemptuous, dismissive tone of put-downs like 'Ballad Of A Thin Man' and 'Positively 4th Street', or the bitterness of 'Masters Of War', this finds Dylan eschewing rancor in favor of a more resolute, persuasive approach toward his opponent, as if serving notice to quit.

Again, Dylan is concerned about the price placed on his soul by the purely commercial attitude taken toward his work—such creative matters, he insists, are "beyond control," and when the time is right, he will make records again. Dylan's contract with CBS had run its course, and it seems likely that in order to help in his negotiations with Mortimer Nasatir of MGM Records, Grossman had been pestering the singer for new material, if only to demonstrate to Nasatir that the rumors about Dylan's decline—some suspected that he had suffered irreversible brain damage in the motorcycle accident—were unfounded.

At that time, nobody realized how enduring rock'n'roll careers might be, and it must have annoyed Grossman to observe his client squandering his talent and his time on a bunch of throwaway nursery-rhyme singalongs like *The Basement Tapes*, at exactly the time he most needed to reassert his public profile. In his first post-accident interview, with Michael Iachetta in May 1967, Dylan made what appeared to be thinly-veiled threats toward his management and record company, by revealing that he did in fact have songs buzzing round his head as per usual, but that "…they're not goin' to get written down until some things are evened up. Not until some people come forth and make up for some of the things that have happened. Somethin' has got to be evened up, is all I'm going to say."

Accordingly, in the second verse Dylan advises that his landlord should cool his jets awhile: there's no point in working so hard for too much, too soon, he contends; and anyway, materialism is just a bottomless addiction—there's always something else that you don't have, always another glittering temptation leading you on, right through to the end of your life. The final verse finds the singer stubbornly sticking to his guns, refusing to discuss the matter or adopt a more conciliatory position. I know you're good at making money, he assures his landlord, but we'll get along better if you try not to ignore the more intrinsic qualities of my work—it's not *just* product, after all.

I Am A Lonesome Hobo

he album's most straightforward moral parable, 'I Am A Lonesome Hobo' finds the eponymous vagrant offering free advice to those who might think themselves his betters. Despite having tried a variety of criminal pursuits to get by, including bribery, blackmail and deceit, he still retains enough self-respect to eschew begging, the ground zero of human activity. Or at least, he's never been caught begging, which is a different matter entirely…

Once wealthy and well-fed, the circumstances of his downfall are sketchily presented, in a manner typical of the album as a whole; but the crux of the matter is faithlessness, a lack of trust in his brother. It's left him an outsider, someone whose life is so apart from the normal realm of societal experience that he might as well be an alien. But in his solitariness, the hobo has found a certain philosophical stability, which leaves him standing in the garb of prophet rather than beggar, a salutary lesson for those who drift away from righteousness.

I Pity The Poor Immigrant

Set to the traditional folk melody 'Come All Ye Tramps And Hawkers'—which Dylan had earlier borrowed for 'The Ballad Of Donald White', one of his earliest (unreleased) compositions—'I Pity The Poor Immigrant' is one of the album's most confusing songs, balanced precariously between compassion and condemnation. Is Dylan singing about a real immigrant, or just about someone who lives their life *as if* an immigrant, a displaced visitor in an alien society? Following hard on the heels of 'I Am A Lonesome Hobo' and 'Drifter's Escape', it's an outsider parable of a sterner cast, Dylan's judgment flinty and unstinting, though his gentle and piteous delivery belies his tough attitude.

Through the three verses, Dylan builds up an itinerary of the immigrant's unprepossessing

▶
HAPPY FAMILIES: BOB AND SARA AND THE KIDS, 1969.

characteristics, which starts off with a propensity to strive for evil, and carries on through a damning catalogue of lying, cheating, greed, self-loathing, uncharitableness and ruthlessness—a fairly accurate portrait of everyday business practice, in other words.

The American experience of immigration is different from that of most European countries: while ostensibly more welcoming of foreign immigrants, America has traditionally offered them little reliable access to justice. The result has been that each successive immigrant community has been forced to throw up its own "strong men" to guard its interests, and in time these localized guardians have grown into powerful crime figures, most famously with the Mafia, though the process doubtless holds true for all subsequent waves of immigrants, through to the Jamaican Yardies and Russian Mafiosi of today.

It may be that Dylan is satirizing this process, criticizing the prospect of great bounty with which America lures other races and nations to its doorstep. In a country founded on greed and theft, who can blame those who fancy a slice of the pie for themselves? In a sense, all immigrants to the United States have fallen "in love with wealth itself" simply by wishing to become Americans. The final line, in which Dylan contemplates the moment at which the immigrant's "gladness comes to pass," is a beautifully double-edged conclusion, the singer both pitying the immigrant who achieves his or her selfish dream, and savoring the point at which such dreams finally curdle in a horrifying flash of self-realization.

"...A wicked messenger falleth into mischief; but a faithful ambassador is health" **PROVERBS 13:16-17**

The Wicked Messenger

The eponymous messenger is, of course, Dylan himself, the bringer of harsh home truths, and certainly a man possessed of the kind of mind "that multiplied the smallest matter." Like the messenger, Dylan had spent much of his recent life touring assembly halls, until he too found his feet burning up from the hectic pace of his schedule.

Again, the song is riddled with biblical allusion: the title itself derives from Proverbs 13:16–17: "Every prudent man dealeth with knowledge; but a fool layeth open his folly. A wicked messenger falleth into mischief; but a faithful ambassador is health." The high priest Eli, from whom the song's messenger came, was one of the more knowledgeable and intellectual characters of the Old Testament. To have been sent by him would imply a heavy reliance on intellect rather than instinct, suggesting that Dylan perhaps felt he had valued rationality too highly over spirituality.

The revelatory, heart-opening message the messenger himself is given, "If ye cannot bring good news, then don't bring any," pivots on the notion of *good news*, which in the gospel sense refers strictly to the Christ story. If Dylan had not, in fact, already undergone conversion to Christianity, he was certainly doing his best to make it appear that way.

Down Along The Cove

The album's final two songs prefigure Dylan's full-blooded move into country music on his next album. With Pete Drake's pedal steel guitar sidling around Dylan's gently syncopated piano figures, 'Down Along The Cove' is an understated, catchy little thing of no import whatsoever beyond offering Bob an opportunity to express his guileless, open affection for his "little bundle of joy," most likely Sara, but possibly one of their two children that had been born in 1967, Jesse Byron and Anna. Where before he had denied his marriage, and even, on one occasion recounted by the journalist Jules Siegel, suggested that Sara hide from a reporter in a hotel closet, here he wants to shout his love from the rooftops, pleased as punch that any passers-by watching the two of them walking along hand-in-hand will recognize their love.

I'll Be Your Baby Tonight

The simplest song Dylan had probably written since high school, 'I'll Be Your Baby Tonight' has the self-contained perfection of a natural classic, achieved through a sly manipulation of the songwriter's standard romantic clichés. At one point, it's almost as if he started out rhyming "moon" with "June," only to relent and have the moon instead shine "like a spoon." In the context of the album as a whole, its relaxed, acquiescent tone comes as a soothing balm after such a parade of austere parables, while in the context of Dylan's career, it serves notice of his next career shift, which would see him embracing not just the musical talents of Nashville, but its sound and style as well.

◄

FRESH IMMIGRANTS TO AMERICA TAKE THE PLEDGE OF ALLEGIANCE.

135

GIRL FROM THE NORTH
COUNTRY

NASHVILLE SKYLINE RAG

TO BE ALONE WITH YOU

I THREW IT ALL AWAY

PEGGY DAY

LAY LADY LAY

ONE MORE NIGHT

TELL ME THAT IT ISN'T TRUE

COUNTRY PIE

TONIGHT I'LL BE STAYING HERE
WITH YOU

Nashville skyline

here would be another protracted delay, of some 16 months, before Dylan's next album, and if *John Wesley Harding* had seemed light years away from *Blonde On Blonde*, *Nashville Skyline* was off the map of what fans had previously considered to be Dylan territory. Even the reflective *John Wesley Harding*, for all its musical diffidence, had contained plenty of lyrical food for thought, but *Nashville Skyline* found pop's greatest poet apparently abandoning allusion, allegory and anything approaching deep meaning or mystery in favor of trite blandishments like "Love is all there is, it makes the world go round." The music, too, was at best efficient, and mostly perfunctory; a series of routine country arrangements that wouldn't have sounded out of place on a Merle Haggard or Charley Pride record. What on earth had happened to Bob Dylan?

Following the release of *John Wesley Harding*, Dylan made a public appearance in January 1968—his first public performance since his accident. He and the Band appeared at two memorial concerts held at Carnegie Hall in honor of Woody Guthrie, who had finally succumbed to the ravages of Parkinson's disease the previous October. In the good-spirited, boisterous manner of *The Basement Tapes*, Dylan and the Band celebrated Guthrie's life with rousing rock versions of Woody's 'Grand Coulee Dam' and 'I Ain't Got No Home', and a more somber run through 'Dear Mrs. Roosevelt'.

With his surrogate father-figure gone, Dylan was further hit by the death of his real father, Abraham, in June 1968. Shortly after, Sara gave birth to another son, who was named Seth Abraham Isaac Dylan, after Bob's late father.

The rest of the year passed in an uneventful fashion, with Dylan spending time with his family and writing a few songs for his next album. In February 1969, he flew to Nashville once again to record with a slightly larger pool of musicians than before, the core rhythm section of Charlie McCoy and Kenny Buttrey was joined by pianist Bob Wilson and guitarists Charlie Daniels and Norman Blake; Pete Drake again took the pedal steel seat.

The new material was straight country-pop, quite unlike any of his previous work apart from 'I'll Be Your Baby Tonight'. This came as a shock to fans, although Dylan's interest in country music actually dated back to his teen years in Hibbing,

when he had pored over Echo Helstrom's mother's collection of old country 78s from the Forties and Fifties, painstakingly teaching himself the songs as he sat on the Helstroms' front steps. Visitors to the convalescent Dylan's Woodstock home in 1967/8 had also noted that, as well as the Bible

"This man can rhyme the tick of time
The edge of pain, the what of sane" **JOHNNY CASH**

which furnished much of the inspiration for *John Wesley Harding*, his study also contained a volume of Hank Williams songs, which were clearly a strong influence on his new direction. Indeed, in 1967, as a bargaining chip in his attempt to sign Dylan to his label, MGM chief Mortimer Nasatir had dangled the prospect of Bob's being able to add music to a sheaf of recently discovered Hank Williams lyrics, in a kind of posthumous collaboration. Dylan was, by all accounts, very interested, having been a Williams fan since his youth, and it's not inconceivable that it was this which prompted the notion of doing a country album.

It was, nevertheless, a strange time to be going country. If a generation ever needed a spokesman, they needed one in 1968. The social and political unrest that had been building throughout the Sixties reached critical mass that year, with the assassinations of Robert Kennedy and Martin Luther King, and widespread protests against American involvement in Vietnam sparking violent demonstrations in Paris, London and Chicago. The civilized world appeared to be falling apart at the seams, just as Dylan had "predicted" in songs like 'Desolation Row' and 'Gates Of Eden', yet Dylan was nowhere to be seen—and on the strength of *John Wesley Harding* was retreating into religious moralism, not exactly the kind of thing needed to rally the troops at that juncture.

Released in May 1969, *Nashville Skyline* suggested that his time spent in rustic seclusion had alienated him from the world outside the gates of his own personal Eden. In an interview with *Rolling Stone* Dylan claimed, "These are the types of songs that I always felt like writing when I've been alone to do so. [They] reflect more of the

◀

DYLAN ONSTAGE AT THE ISLE OF WIGHT FESTIVAL, 1969.

inner me than the songs of the past." Which, considering there was scant evidence of any inner life in the songs, offered serious pause for thought.

The reviews were "mixed," with some critics admiring the craft and polish, while others damned the craven lack of ambition. Making matters worse, at a mere 27 minutes, *Nashville Skyline* was little more than half the length of albums like *Bringing It All Back Home* and *Highway 61 Revisited*—it was rubbish, and there wasn't enough of it!

Not that this affected sales much: after 'Lay Lady Lay' became a hit single, *Nashville Skyline* topped the album charts on both sides of the Atlantic, going on to become the biggest-selling album of Dylan's career. However, it's probably remembered less for its music than its uncanny prescience: for in its wake came a flood of crossover country-rock albums by rock artists, starting with the Byrds' *Sweetheart Of The Rodeo* a few months later to the point where the Eagles could become the most commercially successful act of the Seventies. Just as he had done many times before, Dylan had instinctively tapped into a widespread disaffection with the direction of popular music, and suggested the way forward.

With hindsight, Dylan recognized the album's limitations. In a 1978 interview, he admitted it was necessary to read between the lines. "I was trying to grasp something that would lead me on to where I thought I should be," he explained, "and it didn't go nowhere – it just went down, down, down. I couldn't be anybody but myself, and at that point I didn't know it or want to know it."

Girl From The North Country

The album's opener was actually the last track cut, at a session specifically arranged for Dylan and Johnny Cash to lay down a few impromptu duets.

While Cash's appearance surprised some fans, he had actually been one of Bob's earliest supporters, championing Dylan in the uncertain days following his first album, when Dylan was known as "Hammond's Folly." "I thought he was one of the best country singers I had ever heard," claimed Cash, who developed a correspondence with Dylan and, when the songwriter was taking flak for his apparent abandonment of protest songs, demanded in the pages of *Broadside* magazine that his critics should "Shut Up! ... and let him sing!". "We just became friends," he explained later, "like any two songwriters might, you know?"

Their friendship was revived when Dylan made a trip from Woodstock to see Cash's Carnegie Hall show in September 1968, and cemented with the *Nashville Skyline* sessions; Cash even gave his seal of approval to Bob's work by contributing a sleeve-note poem which compared Dylan's songs to "strong, quick flashes of light," claiming "This man can rhyme the tick of time/The edge of pain, the what of sane." Later, in June 1969, Dylan reciprocated by appearing on a Cash ABC-TV special.

Here, the song functions as the first of two overtures or false starts to the album proper, putting off the moment when his new material has to be heard—as if Dylan is, if not embarrassed, then apprehensive about his new songs. It's a strange, stilted performance, with both men struggling to accommodate each other's inflections, and trading absurdly off-key phrases at its conclusion. Yet for all of its imperfections, there's something genuinely moving about the way their incongruent voices suggest the distance in time and place between the singers and the song's subject.

Nashville Skyline Rag

The second of the album's two overtures is another first for Dylan, being his debut recorded instrumental. It's a pukka piece of work in sprightly bluegrass style, with a succession of neat solos on pedal steel guitar, dobro guitar, acoustic guitar and piano; but for fans encountering it for the first time, it served mainly to postpone the resolution of those questions about Dylan's new voice which had been raised by the opening Dylan/Cash duet.

To Be Alone With You

T hose questions were answered as soon as Dylan asked producer Bob Johnston, "Is it rolling, Bob?" over the intro vamp of this, the album's first new song proper. Dylan had indeed "grown" a new voice—but while the acid sneer of the electric albums could be traced back to his more bitter protest anthems, there was little precedent for this new, syrupy croon, which encapsulated all that was anodyne and bourgeois about country music.

In *Rolling Stone* Dylan explained the change in his voice, as entirely down to his having given up smoking. Others heard echoes of the young, pre-New York Dylan, when as a student in Minneapolis he had sung in a sweet, smooth tenor, only altering his style to the harsher inflections of his first album when he became obsessed with Woody Guthrie.

While many of *Nashville Skyline*'s songs sound as though they were written for Elvis Presley to perform, "To Be Alone With You" was composed specifically with Jerry Lee Lewis in mind. There's a suggestive slant to some of the lines which, with the final verse's drawing-together of the carnal and the religious, would suit Lewis down to the ground, while both the arrangement and Dylan's delivery self-consciously ape Lewis's rolling country style.

I Threw It All Away

D ylan later admitted that when he went down to Nashville to record *Nashville Skyline*, he only had four complete songs ready, of which the earliest was "I Threw It All Away", which he had played for George Harrison on the latter's visit to Bob's Woodstock home the previous November. It's one of the album's few undisputed classics, a tender lament for lost love

▲

DYLAN ARRIVES AT LONDON AIRPORT FOR HIS CONCERT AT THE ISLE OF WIGHT, 1969.

"...It didn't go nowhere—it just went down, down, down..." **BOB DYLAN**

which showcases Dylan's new croon to its best advantage. It's also a demonstration of how audacious he had become in his songwriting, following a beautifully-sustained image of ultimate satisfaction ("Once I had mountains in the palm of my hand/ And rivers that ran through every day") with one of the most ingenuous, faux-naif cliches he ever wrote ("Love is all there is, it makes the world go round").

Underpinned by the gentle tinting of the organ and finely-picked acoustic guitar, this is a delicate performance whose sentiment finds Dylan, for the first time in his career, taking the blame for a broken relationship. Previously, in songs ranging from "Don't Think Twice, It's Alright" to "One Of Us Must Know (Sooner Or Later)", he had shifted the blame or equivocated over where fault lay, picking apart his relationships in emotional autopsies; but here he does not just accept the blame for the breakup, he makes it a rod for his own back, by punishing himself with his loss. However, since Bob had by then settled into the loviest and doviest of contentment with his wife Sara and their burgeoning brood, it seems unlikely that the lyrics of "I Threw It All Away" were ripped from the pages of his own life, as such earlier songs had been.

Peggy Day

If "I Threw It All Away" features Dylan's lyricism at its most audacious, "Peggy Day" finds it at its most inconsequential, lending weight to the suggestion that he only had four finished songs ready. He could easily have knocked this one out the previous evening at the Ramada Inn, and still had enough time left over to eat a hearty dinner, watch a four-hour movie, and sue for world peace. Dylan later claimed, possibly in jest, that he had written the song with The Mills Brothers in mind, though it's hard to imagine their warm harmonies being wasted on a trifle like this.

Little more than a spoonerised joke in which his desire to spend the night with the eponymous Peggy Day is succeeded by his desire to spend the day with, er, Peggy night (the Lyrics 1962-1985 specifies the lower-case "n", confusingly rendering "Peggy" an adjective), it demonstrates how even the most trivial material can be buffed to an adequate—if not exactly respectable—lustre by the attentions of skilled session musicians, particularly Pete Drake's lazy curlicues of pedal steel guitar in the break before the final verse. But even

allowing for the musicians' combined experience playing on a host of coutry sessions, it's hard to believe they could have come up against anything quite as trite as "Peggy Day". It sounds like it too —there's a throwaway casualness about the whole performance which exactly matches the material.

Lay Lady Lay

Originally commissioned as the theme for the film of *Midnight Cowboy*, but finished too late for inclusion (the producers went with Harry Nilsson's version of Fred Neil's "Everybody's Talkin'" instead), "Lay Lady Lay" became Dylan's first chart single since "Rainy Day Women #12 & 35", despite his initial opposition to its release. It eventually went on to become the biggest-selling single of his career, and was accorded the honour of being the opening track on his retrospective Biograph box set.

At the time he was writing the material for *Nashville Skyline*, Dylan told friends and interviewers that though he had previously placed great store on the lyrics in his songs, now he felt that the music was more important. "Lay Lady Lay" illustrates the attendant change in his writing

▶ **THE MAN IN THE WHITE SUIT: DYLAN PLAYS AT THE ISLE OF WIGHT FESTIVAL, 1969.**

technique: where once he would write a poem first, then set it to music later, in the Biograph liner-notes, Dylan recalls coming up with the tune's four-chord progression and then filling it up with "la-la-las", which quickly transformed into the song's title. "It's the same thing with the tongue, that's all it is really," he admitted.

Whatever the song's genesis, it's the music, and Dylan's delivery of the lyric (rather than the lyric itself), which makes "Lay Lady Lay" a success. Despite the bluntness of its sexual demand, Dylan manages to evoke deep warmth and tender yearning through his delivery of lines as poetically sterile as "And you're the best thing that he's ever seen". Musically, the song's appeal lies in the tension between the flowing pedal-steel guitar and the staccato cowbell percussion, a combination which surprised even drummer Kenny Buttrey.

Finding it difficult to figure out a drum part for the song as it was being rehearsed in the studio, Buttrey asked Dylan and producer Bob Johnston in turn for ideas, and was given what he considered jive suggestions, Johnston recommending bongoes and Dylan cowbells. Right, thought Buttrey, I'll show you how bad that will sound—and so he got studio janitor Kris Kristofferson to hold the cowbell and bongoes as he played them through the next take. Nobody was as surprised as the drummer when the percussion fit the song like a glove. "I'll be damned!" he exclaimed. "This is the tastiest drum part I ever played!"

One more night

The easy-going "One More Night" sounds more like a songwriting exercise than anything born out of the fires of inspiration. Certainly, it's the closest Dylan's entire oeuvre comes to the classical country perfection of Hank Williams, both in its confident wielding of simple phrases like "I'm as lonesome as can be" and "the moon is shinin' bright", and in the way its jocular surface disguises the undertow of roiling emotion, glimpsed in the "dark and rolling sky" that accompanies the singer's misery.

The song is also notable as another example of Dylan's changing attitude towards women: although the reason for the breakdown of his relationship—the singer's inability to be what his lover wants him to be—echoes that of earlier songs like "It Ain't Me, Babe", here he acknowledges that it's not just a lover he has lost, but his best pal. Which, in the context of the permissive but still patriarchal late Sixties, was quite an admission.

Tell me that it isn't true

Of all of the album's songs, "Tell Me That It Isn't True" most sounds like it was written expressly for Elvis Presley. Dylan's delivery even seems suspiciously like a Presley pastiche and the lyric's resolute reliance on the corniest of romantic clichés could have been designed not to frighten off a singer who frequently voiced his mistrust of the younger generation's involvement in more complex political issues.

With organ phrases adding urgency to the song's concern, it's as close as the album gets to being emotionally overwrought—"I Threw It All Away" may be sadder, but compared with its air of abject resignation, "Tell Me That It Isn't True" still holds out hope that the situation may be rescued, a hope which brings a different kind of fretfulness. Dylan admitted to Jann Wenner that the song was one of his favorites on the album, even though it had turned out completely different to the way he had imagined it. " It came out real slow and mellow," he explained,"I had written it as a sort of jerky, kind of polka-type thing." The mind boggles.

> "It came out real slow and mellow. I had written it as a sort of jerky, kind of polka-type thing." **BOB DYLAN ON 'TELL ME THAT IT ISN'T TRUE'**

Country Pie

nother light-hearted filler, "Country Pie" does at least have the authentic ring of redneck comedy. Beneath the gastronomic surface, the song is basically a statement of Dylan's love for country music. Bizarrely, however, some of his more imaginative commentators chose this moment of the greatest extension of Dylan's conservatism to claim that the line about saddling up a "big white goose" was a veiled reference to heroin—perhaps the most extraordinary interpretation ever placed on one of his songs.

For most fans, however, the truly revealing lines came in the second middle-eight section, where Dylan claimed he wasn't "runnin' any race" —as clear an admission as any that he had ceased to be concerned about the things which used to exercise his imagination, and was now settled into a simpler lifestyle. As if in corroboration, the tricky syntactical gift which had once served to machine-gun elaborate, evocative phrases into cramped spaces in songs like "Subterranean Homesick Blues" was now being used simply to list pie-fillings: "Blueberry, apple, cherry, pumpkin and plum". To many, this seemed a poor exchange—particularly since, at the end of the song, listeners were none the wiser as to Dylan's preferred flavours.

Tonight I'll Be Staying Here With You

nother of Dylan's personal favourites from the album, "Tonight I'll Be Staying Here With You" has a grace and apparent sincerity which is largely denied to the rest of *Nashville Skyline*. It is one of the few tracks on the album on which he sounds completely at ease with the country-music mode, and where it doesn't sound like he's just running through genre exercises or pastiches.

Riding a groove whose rolling piano and flowing pedal steel guitar were punctuated by some terse country picking (probably by Charlie Daniels), Dylan's lyric found him—after years of songs in which trains offered the enticing prospect of freedom or a ticket to the future—turning his back on departure and deliberately missing his train in order to stay with his beloved. For Dylan, such a denial of his instinctive wanderlust is surely the greatest possible tribute that he can pay to the woman whose love keeps him here.

In the penultimate verse, a random act of kindness—offering his seat if there's "a poor boy on the street" who might want it—drew an analogy

"These are the types of songs that always felt like writing... [They] reflect more of the inner me than the songs of the past." **BOB DYLAN**

with Dylan's own situation. After almost a decade as the involuntary spokesman for a generation, he has decided he doesn't want to travel that line any more, and if there's any young singer who wants to take up that mantle, well, they are more than welcome to all the hassle that goes with it.

A succession of putative "new Dylans" appeared over the next few years, the best of whom—Loudon Wainwright, Jackson Browne, Bruce Springsteen—eventually developed personalities of their own. But as the scene which he had revolutionized several times over in the Sixties continued, through the rise of country-rock, to respond to his pioneering work, Dylan remained an elusive, enigmatic figure, perennially out of step with changing musical fashions, a soul alone.

Dylan would go on to record worse albums than *Nashville Skyline*, and a handful which could rank alongside the best of his Sixties work, but he would never again define the zeitgeist the way he did in that decade. Nor, for that matter, would anybody else.

Bob Dylan 1960s Discography

All compositions by Bob Dylan, except where noted in *italics*.

Albums

BOB DYLAN

RECORDED: NOVEMBER 1961

RELEASED: MARCH 1962

You're No Good (*Jesse Fuller*)/Talkin' New York/In My Time Of Dyin' (*trad. arr. Dylan*)/Man Of Constant Sorrow (*trad. arr. Dylan*)/Fixin' To Die (*Bukka White*)/Pretty Peggy-O (*trad. arr. Dylan*)/Highway 51 (*Curtis Jones*)/Gospel Plow (*trad. arr. Dylan*)/Baby, Let Me Follow You Down (*Rev. Gary Davis*)/House Of The Risin' Sun (*trad. arr. Van Ronk*)/Freight Train Blues(*Roy Acuff*)/Song To Woody/See That My Grave Is Kept Clean (*Blind Lemon Jefferson*)

THE FREEWHEELIN' BOB DYLAN

RECORDED: JULY 1962–APRIL 1963

RELEASED: MAY 1963

Blowin' In The Wind/Girl From The North Country/Masters Of War/Down The Highway/Bob Dylan's Blues/A Hard Rain's A-Gonna Fall/Don't Think Twice, It's All Right/Bob Dylan's Dream/Oxford Town/Talking World War III Blues/Corrina, Corrina (*trad. arr. Dylan*)/Honey, Just Allow Me One More Chance (*Henry Thomas*)/I Shall Be Free

THE TIMES THEY ARE A-CHANGIN'

RECORDED: AUGUST–OCTOBER 1963

RELEASED: JANUARY 1964

The Times They Are A-Changin'/Ballad Of Hollis Brown/With God On Our Side/One Too Many Mornings/North Country Blues/Only A Pawn In Their Game/Boots Of Spanish Leather/When The Ship Comes In/The Lonesome Death Of Hattie Carroll/Restless Farewell

ANOTHER SIDE OF BOB DYLAN

RECORDED: JUNE 1964

RELEASED: AUGUST 1964

All I Really Want To Do/Black Crow Blues/Spanish Harlem Incident/Chimes Of Freedom/ I Shall Be Free No.10/To Ramona/Motorpsycho Nitemare/My Back Pages/I Don't Believe You/ Ballad In Plain D/It Ain't Me Babe

BRINGING IT ALL BACK HOME

RECORDED: JANUARY 1965

RELEASED: MARCH 1965

Subterranean Homesick Blues/She Belongs To Me/Maggie's Farm/Love Minus Zero—No Limit/Outlaw Blues/On The Road Again/Bob Dylan's 115th Dream/Mr Tambourine Man/Gates Of Eden/It's Alright, Ma (I'm Only Bleeding)/It's All Over Now, Baby Blue

HIGHWAY 61 REVISITED

RECORDED: JUNE–AUGUST 1965

RELEASED: SEPTEMBER 1965

Like A Rolling Stone/Tombstone Blues/It Takes A Lot To Laugh, It Takes A Train To Cry/From A Buick 6/Ballad Of A Thin Man/Queen Jane Approximately/Highway 61 Revisited/Just Like Tom Thumb's Blues/Desolation Row

BLONDE ON BLONDE

RECORDED: JANUARY–MARCH 1966

RELEASED: MAY 1966

Rainy Day Women #12 & 35/Pledging My Time/Visions Of Johanna/One Of Us Must Know (Sooner Or Later)/I Want You/Stuck Inside Of Mobile With The Memphis Blues Again/Leopard-Skin Pill-Box Hat/Just Like A Woman/Most Likely You Go Your Way And I'll Go Mine/Temporary Like Achilles/Absolutely Sweet Marie/4th Time Around/Obviously 5 Believers/Sad Eyed Lady Of The Lowlands

THE BASEMENT TAPES

RECORDED: JUNE–OCTOBER 1967

RELEASED: JULY 1975

Odds And Ends/Orange Juice Blues (Blues For Breakfast) (*Richard Manuel*)/Million Dollar Bash/Yazoo Street Scandal (*Robbie Robertson*)/ Goin' To Acapulco/Katie's Been Gone (*Robbie Robertson/Richard Manuel*)/Lo And Behold!/Bessie Smith (*Rick Danko/Robbie Robertson*)/Clothes Line Saga/ Apple Suckling Tree/Please, Mrs. Henry/Tears Of Rage (*Bob Dylan/Richard Manuel*)/Too Much Of Nothing/Yea! Heavy And A Bottle Of Bread/Ain't No More Cane (*trad. arr. the Band*)/Crash On The Levee (Down In The Flood)/Ruben Remus (*Robbie Robertson/Richard Manuel*)/Tiny Montgomery/You Ain't Goin' Nowhere/Don't Ya Tell Henry/ Nothing Was Delivered/Open The Door, Homer/Long Distance Operator/This Wheel's On Fire (*Bob Dylan/Rick Danko*)

JOHN WESLEY HARDING

RECORDED: OCTOBER–NOVEMBER 1967

RELEASED: JANUARY 1968

John Wesley Harding/As I Went Out One Morning/I Dreamed I Saw St. Augustine/All Along The Watchtower/The Ballad Of Frankie Lee And Judas Priest/Drifter's Escape/Dear Landlord/I Am A Lonesome Hobo/I Pity The Poor Immigrant/The Wicked Messenger/Down Along The Cove/I'll Be Your Baby Tonight

NASHVILLE SKYLINE

RECORDED: FEBRUARY 1969;

RELEASED: MAY 1969

Girl From The North Country/Nashville Skyline Rag/To Be Alone With You/I Threw It All Away/Peggy Day/Lay Lady Lay/One More Night/Tell Me That It Isn't True/Country Pie/Tonight I'll Be Staying Here With You

Singles

Mixed Up Confusion/Corrina, Corrina (March 1962)

The Times They Are A-Changin'/Honey, Just Allow Me One More Chance (March 1965)

Subterranean Homesick Blues/She Belongs To Me (April 1965)

Maggie's Farm/On The Road Again (June 1965)

Like A Rolling Stone/Gates Of Eden (August 1965)

Positively 4th Street/From A Buick 6 (October 1965)

Can You Please Crawl Out Your Window?/Highway 61 Revisited (January 1966)

One Of Us Must Know (Sooner Or Later)/Queen Jane Approximately (April 1966)

Rainy Day Women #12 & 35/Pledging My Time (April 1966)

I Want You/Just Like Tom Thumb's Blues (live) (July 1966)

Just Like A Woman/Obviously 5 Believers (September 1966)

Leopard-Skin Pill-Box Hat/Most Likely You Go Your Way And I'll Go Mine (May 1967)

If You Gotta Go, Go Now/To Ramona (July 1967, Benelux only)

I Threw It All Away/Drifter's Escape (May 1969)

Lay Lady Lay/Peggy Day (August 1969)

Tonight I'll Be Staying Here With You/Country Pie (December 1969)

Italic page references refer to photographs.

4th Time Around 105
Absolutely Sweet Marie 105
All Along The Watchtower 130–1
All I Really Want To Do 56
Another Side of Bob Dylan 52–63
Apple Suckling Tree 116–17
As I Went Out One Morning 128

Baez, Joan 9, 21, 31, 37, *39*, 45, 68–9, 70–1, *70*, 77, 79, 82, *98*, 99
The Ballad of Frankie Lee And Judas Priest 131–2
Ballad of Hollis Brown 43
Ballad In Plain D 62–3
Ballad Of A Thin Man 86–7
The Band 93, 113, *121*
The Basement Tapes 108–23
The Beatles *65*, 105
Biograph 23, 84
Black Crow Blues 56
Blonde on Blonde 92–103
Bloomfield, Mike 83, 85
Blowin' In The Wind 23–25
The Blues Project 66
Bob Dylan 8–17
Bob Dylan's 115th Dream 73
Bob Dylan's Blues 28
Bob Dylan's Dream 31–2
Boots Of Spanish Leather 48–9
Bringing It All Back Home 64–77
Broadside (magazine) 20, 24, 26, 35, 38
Buttrey, Kenny 104, 105, 125, 137, 141

Can You Please Crawl Out Your Window? 91
Carnegie Hall 10, 50–1, 137
CBS 11, 19, 21, 130–1, 133
children 125, 135, *135*, 137
Chimes Of Freedom 58
Clayton, Paul 31, 53, 54, 77
Clothes Line Saga 115
Columbia *see* CBS
Corrina, Corrina 34–5
Country Pie 142
Crash On The Levee 119

Danko, Rick 91, *91*, 118, 123
Dear Landlord 132–3
Desolation Row 89

Don't Look Back 69, *69*, 70–1, 77, 79
Don't Think Twice, It's All Right 30–1
Don't Ya Tell Henry 121
Down Along The Cove 135
Down In The Flood 119
Down The Highway 26–7
Drake, Pete 125, 135, 137, 140
Drifter's Escape 132
drugs 53, 54, 68, 74, 96–7

Eat The Document 109, 125
Elliott, Ramblin' Jack 54, 58, 74

The Freewheelin' Bob Dylan 18–35
From A Buick 6 86

Gaslight Cafe, Greenwich Village *24*
Gates of Eden 75–6
Ginsberg, Allen *66*, 72, 79
Girl From the North Country 25–6, 138
Goin' To Acapulco 114
Greenwich Village 9, 11, 23, *24*, 27, 65, 90
Gregg, Bobby 67, 86, 98
Griffin, Paul 67, 88, 91, 99
Grossman, Albert 20, 21, 22, 79, 131, 132–3
Guthrie, Woody 13, *14*, 15–16, *27*, 43, 60, 125, 137

Hammond, John 9–10, 12, 19, 20, 21, 22, *23*
A Hard Rain's A-Gonna Fall 28–30
The Hawks 93, 110–23
Helm, Levon 93, 116, 121
Hendrix, Jimi *130*, 131
Hester, Carolyn 9–10, *10*
Hibbing 25, 46–7, 110
Highway 61 Revisited 78–91
Highway 61 Revisited 87–8
Honey, Just Allow Me One More Chance 35
House Of The Rising Sun 11–12

I Am A Lonesome Hobo 133
I Don't Believe You 61
I Dreamed I Saw St. Augustine 129–30
I Pity The Poor Immigrant 134
I Shall Be Free 35
I Shall Be Free No. 10 59
I Threw It All Away 139

I Want You 99–100
I'll Be Your Baby Tonight 135
Isle Of White Festival *139, 140*
It Ain't Me Babe 63
It Takes A Lot To Laugh, It Takes A Train To Cry 85
It's All Over Now, Baby Blue 77
It's Alright, Ma 76

John Wesley Harding 124–35
John Wesley Harding 127–8
Jones, Brian 86, 100
Just Like A Woman 102–3
Just Like Tom Thumb's Blues 88

Kapralik, David 11, 12, 19
Kennedy, President John F. 26, 28–9, *29*, 32, 33, *42*, 43, 48
Kooper, Al 83, 85, 86, 88, 90, 91, 94, 98, 99, 100, 105
Kramer, Daniel 23, 65, 67

Lay Lady Lay 140–1
Leopard-Skin Pill-Box Hat 101–2
Like A Rolling Stone 82–3
Lo And Behold! 114–15
The Lonesome Death of Hattie Carroll 49–50
Long Distance Operator 123
Love Minus Zero/No Limit 71–2
Lowndes, Sara 72, 106–7, 135, *135*

McCoy, Charlie *93*, 97, 104, 106, 125, 137
Madhouse on Castle Street 25, 26, *63*
Maggie's Farm 71
Manuel, Richard 116, 118, 121, 122–3
Masters Of War 26
MGM 131, 133, 137
Million Dollar Bash 113
Mixed up Confusion 22–3
Monterey Folk Festival 21
Most Likely You Go Your Way And I'll Go Mine 104
Motorpsycho Nitemare 60
Mr Tambourine Man 54, 58, 74–5
My Back Pages 60–1

Nashville Skyline 136–42
Nashville Skyline Rag 138
Neuwirth, Bob 54, 79, 82
Newport Folk Festival 31, 37, 71, 74, 80
Newsweek (magazine) 50–1
North Country Blues 46–7
Nothing Was Delivered 122

Obviously 5 Believers 105–6
Ochs, Phil 61, 91

Odds And Ends 113
On The Road Again 73
One More Night 141
One Of Us Must Know (Sooner Or Later) 99
One Too Many Mornings 44–6
Only A Pawn In Their Game 47–8
Open The Door, Homer 122–3
Outlaw Blues 72
Oxford Town 32–3

Peggy Day 140
Pennebaker, Donn 72, 79, 109
Peter, Paul & Mary 24–5, 30–1
Please, Mrs. Henry 117
Pledging My Time 97
Positively 4th Street 90–1

Queen Jane Approximately 87

Rainy Day Women #12 & 35 95–7
Restless Farewell 50–1
Robertson, Robbie 91, *91*, 93–4, 98, 99, 102, 106, 109, 116, *116–17*, 123, 125
Rotolo, Suze 19, 20, 25–6, 27, 30, 37, 44–6, 62–3

Sad Eyed Lady Of The Lowlands 106–7
Seeger, Pete 15, 24, 71, 80
She Belongs To Me 70–1
Sing Out! (magazine) 14, 55, 81, 126
Song to Woody 15–16
Spanish Harlem Incident 56–7
Stuck Inside Of Mobile With The Memphis Blues Again 100–1
Subterranean Homesick Blues 67, 68–9

Talkin' New York 13–14
Talkin' World War III Blues 34
Tarantula 67, 109
Tears Of Rage 117–18
Tell Me That It Isn't True 141
Temporary Like Achilles 104–5
The Times They Are A Changin' 42–3
The Times They Are A Changin' 36–51
Tiny Montgomery 120
To Be Alone With You 139
To Ramona 59
Tom Paine Award 38–9, 41, 128
Tombstone Blues 84–5
Tonight I'll Be Staying Here With You 142
Too Much Of Nothing 119

Van Ronk, Dave 11–12, 24, 90, *96*

Vietnam protesters *118*
Visions Of Johanna 97–9

This Wheel's On Fire 123
When The Ship Comes In 49
The Wicked Messenger 134–5
Wilson, Tom 21, 41, 54, 55, 60, 66, 67, 84
With God On Our Side 44
Woodstock 37, 53, 110, 132, 137
Woodstock Festival *82*

Yea! Heavy And A Bottle Of Bread 119
You Ain't Goin' Nowhere 120

Zimmerman, Abe and Beatty 46, 137

Picture Credits

The publishers would like to thank the following sources for their kind permission to reproduce the pictures in this book:

AKG London 84, 89
Advertising Archives 101
BBC Photo Archives 63
The Bridgeman Art Library, London/Giraudon/ Louvre, Paris, France, *Mona Lisa*, c.1503-6, Leonardo da Vinci 98c
Camera Press Limited 36
Corbis UK Ltd. 88, 134/Bettmann 2, 14, 18, 23, 24, 34-5, 42, 47, 58, 75, 82, 91, 103/UPI 107, 128-9, Amalie R. Rothschild 136, 140
e.t. archive 104
Ronald Grant Archive 60, 69, 79
Hulton Getty 29, 65, 66, 115, 139
Dave Peabody 93, 96
Pictorial Press 12, 30, 64, 95, 98cl, 108/Combi Press 122, Globe Photos 10, 39, Stavers 17
Popperfoto 33, 45, 49, 55, 92, 133
Redferns 121/Gems 80, Elliott Landy 5tl, 110, 116, 124, 135, Michael Ochs Archives 27r, 27l, 51, 52, 57, 118, David Redfern 5br, Brian Shuel 21, Gai Terrell 3, Val Wilmer 4, 8, 74
Rex Features Ltd. 1, 22, 40, 54, 70, 77, 78, 130
Topham Picturepoint 120

Every effort has been made to acknowledge correctly and contact the source and/or copyright holder of each picture, and Carlton Books Limited apologises for any unintentional errors or omissions which will be corrected in future editions of this book.